The Plant Spirit Familiar:
Green Totems,
Teachers & Healers
On the Path of the Witch
by
Christopher Penczak

Foreword by Judika Illes

D0706316

**COPPER
CAULDRON**
PUBLISHING

Credits

Editing: Ruby Sara
Cover Art: "Temple of Netzach" by Kala Trobe
Cover Design: Jonny La Trobe-Lewis
Interior Art: Christopher Penczak
Layout & Publishing: Steve Kenson

This book and all formulas in it are not substitutes for professional medical advice. Please confer with a medical professional before using any herbs in any manner. The publisher and author are not responsible for the use of this material.

Copyright ©2011 Christopher Penczak. All Rights Reserved. The Plant Spirit Familiar is a trademark of Copper Cauldron Publishing, LLC, in the United States and/or other countries. No part of this work may be reproduced, stored in a retrieval system, or transmitted in any form or by any means, without the prior permission in writing of the Copyright Owner, nor be otherwise circulated in any form other than that in which it is published.

For more information visit:
www.christopherpenczak.com
www.coppercauldronpublishing.com

ISBN 978-0-9827743-1-1, First Printing

Printed in the U.S.A.

Special Thanks

To the many people who supported this book:

To my partners, Steve and Adam, for all their love and support in everything I do.

To my parents, Rosalie and Ronnie, for their wisdom, support, and that first garden.

To Judika Illes, for encouraging me to sit down and actually write the book.

To Laura Gamache for opening the door into deeper herbal wisdom and healing.

To Chris Giroux for our wonderful conversations and a shared love of Dame Datura.

To Raven and Stephanie Grimassi, for their friendship, support, and teachings on plant and animal familiars of the old ways. Thank you for introducing me to true mandrake.

To Mary Hurley, my sea priestess, friend, and amazing homeopath.

To Joe and Doug of Otherworld Apothecary for opening my eyes to other realms, ideas, and traditions, and for confirming a few ideas of my own.

To Ruby Sara for her help with the ritual meal and for her all around Pagani coolness.

To Alaric Albertsson, for his superb Hillbilly Mead, knowledge of the Húsel, and his loving friendship.

To Mike Dolan for inspiration on the wand anointing wax.

To Alixaendreia and Hunter for their keen proofreading.

To kitchen witches Adam Sartwell and Dawn Hunt for their help with the sabbat cake recipe.

To Kala Trobe, for the Temple of Netzach that adorns the cover.

To Christine Tolf, for all her help over the years and in particular for the donation of many banes for crafting the Green Devil fetish.

To David Dalton for his teachings on the essence of flowers.

To Wendy Fogg for being both mentor and friend in the Green World.

To Laurie Cabot for teaching me how to make my first potion.

Praise for *The Plant Spirit Familiar*

"*The Plant Spirit Familiar,* is a fascinating journey down the shadowy green path of the occultist. Serious herbalists and magicians will find this book to be both thought provoking and provocative."

— Ellen Dugan, author of *Garden Witch's Herbal, Practical Protection Magick,* and *Natural Witchery*

"*The Plant Spirit Familiar* is a must read for all Green Witches and even for those not on the Wiccan path. This book is chock-full of green wisdom that will inspire anyone who recognizes plants as teachers, guides, and friends. Penczak fills its pages with potions, rituals, and engaging exercises guiding you to respond to what he refers to as 'the call of the green.' When you finish this book you will feel as if you've been initiated into the ancient order of the green nation."

— Pam Montgomery, author of *Plant Spirit Healing* and *Partner Earth: A Spiritual Ecology*

"Those who we nowadays refer to as 'witches' were the wise men and women who other cultures call 'shamans' and who had a detailed knowledge of plants, healing, and 'magic'. Penczak's work is a wide-ranging introduction to plant magic and will be a useful guide for those who wish to expand their magical, healing or herbal knowledge and begin working in the tradition of the plant spirit shaman."

— Ross Heaven, author of *Plant Spirit Shamanism, The Hummingbird's Journey to God* and *The Sin Eater's Last Confessions*

Other Books by Christopher Penczak

City Magick (Samuel Weiser, 2001)
Spirit Allies (Samuel Weiser, 2002)
The Inner Temple of Witchcraft (Llewellyn, 2002)
The Inner Temple of Witchcraft CD Companion (Llewellyn, 2002)
Gay Witchcraft (Samuel Weiser, 2003)
The Outer Temple of Witchcraft (Llewellyn, 2004)
The Outer Temple of Witchcraft CD Companion (Llewellyn, 2004)
The Witch's Shield (Llewellyn, 2004)
Magick of Reiki (Llewellyn, 2004)
Sons of the Goddess (Llewellyn, 2005)
The Temple of Shamanic Witchcraft (Llewellyn, 2005)
The Temple of Shamanic Witchcraft CD Companion (Llewellyn, 2005)
Instant Magick (Llewellyn, 2005)
The Mystic Foundation (Llewellyn, 2006)
Ascension Magick (Llewellyn, 2007)
The Temple of High Witchcraft (Llewellyn, 2007)
The Temple of High Witchcraft CD Companion (Llewellyn, 2007)
The Living Temple of Witchcraft Vol. I (Llewellyn, 2008)
The Living Temple of Witchcraft Vol. I CD Companion (Llewellyn, 2008)
The Living Temple of Witchcraft Vol. II (Llewellyn, 2009)
The Living Temple of Witchcraft Vol. II CD Companion (Llewellyn, 2009)
The Witch's Coin (Llewellyn, 2009)
The Three Rays of Witchcraft (Copper Cauldron Publishing, 2010)
The Witch's Heart (Llewellyn, 2011)

Table of Contents

List of Figures & Charts

The Call of the Green

Foreword by Judika Illes

Until I was eight, my family lived in a fifth floor apartment on Case Street in Elmhurst, Queens, one of New York City's outer boroughs. One of my mother's sisters lived in the same building one floor below, while another sister lived a few blocks away. To call the environment "urban" would be a massive understatement. We did not have a backyard. We did not have a garden. Nor did I play in anyone else's backyard or garden.

My experience with plants was limited. Every summer weekend we went to Jones Beach where I loved the petunias that lined the walkway between the parking lot and the sand. One of my aunts, famed for her 'green thumb,' maintained a jungle of potted plants on her fire escape in the summer, bringing them inside when the weather turned frosty. But really, the only "nature" I experienced on any kind of regular basis involved visits to Central Park and the Queens Botanical Garden.

I was the only child in a family of adults. Even my sister and cousins were all at least a dozen years older than me. When my mother visited her sisters and friends, I was brought along but was inevitably the only child present. Some of the adults played with me, but in general I was left to my own devices.

We frequently visited my mother's sister who lived a couple of blocks away. While the adults socialized, I was given free reign of my aunt's apartment. She possessed a lot of small objects that fascinated me and I would rearrange them, creating tableaux and playing out fantasies. Among my favorites was a small, lidded, ornamental jar. It was empty—there was nothing in it—but in my fantasy, I envisioned it filled with an herbal salve. There was nothing vague about this vision: it was very specific. This salve was fragrant, had the thick texture of an unguent or ointment, and possessed magickal healing powers. In my mind's eye, I could see the green herbs it contained.

We visited my aunt a lot and I played out this fantasy frequently. I cannot remember who I envisioned myself healing, but in my solitary game I was the healer. I was maybe three or four years old at the time and I had never actually seen a salve like this. I wouldn't until many years later. My mother was not a fan of herbal healing: no product like this was used on me nor did I witness anyone else using or concocting such a salve. Decades later, however, I create such salves, use them and handle them frequently, and I can state unequivocally that my childhood vision was totally accurate. So how did I know? It was just a pretty little jar: why would it evoke this reaction from me? Past life memory? Genetic memory? Latent psychic ability? Maybe I was just a kid with a really vivid imagination. Or maybe it was the Call of the Green.

When I first read Christopher Penczak's introduction to his brilliant book, *The Plant Spirit Familiar*, I gasped aloud in recognition. Christopher describes similar, if different, experiences. In his case, he was younger than ten when a sprig of curly parsley on the side of a plate evoked a profound and disproportionate reaction. That little herb triggered first play, and then "fantasy" that wasn't exactly fantasy, and then a life-path as a Witch, healer, author, and visionary plant seer. Christopher writes, "It was play, but it was something more, something I couldn't put into words."

Well, exactly. He could be describing my childhood experiences as well as his own. And if there are two of us, logic dictates that there must be more. I suspect I will not be the only one gasping with recognition while reading *The Plant Spirit Familiar*. The Call of the Green resonates powerfully for so many of us, especially those walking the Witch's path. As for newcomers: welcome! There is no better guide to this mysterious, magickal realm than Christopher Penczak.

Botanicals and botanical-based materials are the most prevalent components of spellcraft and yet there is comparatively little discussion of the Green World, the spiritual, sentient realm of plants. Modern Witchcraft freely discusses animal familiars and spirit guardians, yet plants are too frequently treated as objects or commodities for use, rather than as vital, living beings that consciously partner with us in magick, communicate with us and guide us.

The Plant Spirit Familiar, a revolutionary book, remedies this situation. Christopher writes evocatively and honestly about his own experiences and adventures in the Green Realm and offers us his insights and practical advice. He writes: *I call this plant-based connection the Call of the Green. It's an opportunity for spiritual development through the plant world, to have your spiritual blood run green with the living light of plants, and to grow wise in the way the plant world grows wise.*

The Plant Spirit Familiar is a book of rituals, meditations, and plant magick, but it also serves as a portal or gateway to the Green World. Enter and be prepared to be amazed. To quote Christopher:

The hedge is open but never broken.
So mote it be.

— Judika Illes

Introduction

lants have always been important to me. My father set the first example of tending and care-taking the Green World for me. Despite working a hard, stressful, corporate forty-hours-plus job during the week, from the spring to the fall he would spend much of his weekends and nights tending to a vegetable garden, growing all sorts of food. Like a typical kid, I didn't particularly care for the vegetables, but I liked the garden. My father approached the garden the way he approached his other work. It was all very neat, with the plants organized symmetrically in rows. He prepared in the winter with seedlings and grow lights. He researched the latest methods of fertilization and insect control, and tested something every year, seeking to improve his productivity. Yet it was all still green and good and growing. Our name, Penczak, reportedly translates to "grain farmer" in the old country, linking our Polish ancestors directly to an agrarian tradition. Though neither of us grew grains, we grew plants, and we used what we grew. We still do.

Rather than vegetables, I became fascinated with herbs. I was younger than ten years old when my journey began at a restaurant for dinner. I was perplexed by the garnish: a sprig of curly parsley. I remember the smell; there was something oddly familiar about the smell of parsley. I romanticize now that it was a past life memory, but I grew up with a gardener who also raised herbs, and with an Italian mother who used parsley in cooking, so it could have just been a regular memory, not a past life recall. But something was triggered in me at that moment in the restaurant. I wanted to understand why the parsley was there and what it was used for, and the quest to answer that question got me interested all sorts of herbs and flowers while still in grammar school. I started my first Book of Shadows and magickal formulary without ever hearing those terms, as this was some time before the popularization of Wicca for the teen market. I included lore on making dandelion wine and lavender tea.

Next to my dad's big garden, I started my own, growing lavender, thyme, sage, mint, lemon balm and, of course, parsley. I have vivid memories of meticulously harvesting lilac flowers as they fell, one by one. I'd go traipsing through the woods and the swamp, and I once lost a boot in the mud, hobbling home partially shoeless with skunk cabbage in hand. I wouldn't find out the magickal correspondences of these herbs until years later, including the information that parsley is an herb of the cunning man, associated both with blessings and with dark magick, and of course, with the Devil.

I collected my herbs in little bottles, playing with them as a pretend wizard, yet taking the plants seriously. It was play, but it was something more, something I could not at that time put into words. I carried my jars of herbs around with me in a large wooden cigar box like they were my best friend. None of my friends were that interested, but if I made the plants a part of a sword-and-sorcery pretend game, they would play. I'd mix my potions in my backyard and in my bedroom.

My interest in plants led me to alchemy. Alchemy, depicted as a superstition by the mainstream resources available to me at my local small town library, led me to an interest in chemistry and science, and away from the magickal aspects of plants. It was not until years later, through personal psychic experiences, that I was led back to magick via Witchcraft and to return to my love of herbs as my initial approach to 'New Age' magick led to herbal medicine and alternate healing. In the end, I think I was guided by an impetus to play with little bottles. I think most herbalists and Witches have that drive. There is simply something beautiful about colored liquid catching the light in a glass bottle. It's almost as healing as the remedy itself.

I'm not quite sure what led to the development of these teachings and the creation of this book. I wasn't taught its content by any teacher. You won't find anything quite like this in most other Witchcraft books, though you will find shadows of it throughout our history. There are Witches pursuing material in a very similar vein and I'm indebted to them and what they have shared. I wish it were a whole, unbroken tradition I am passing on to you, but it's not. It's a mix of the divine inspiration or "awen" of the Celtic traditions, that flows from the gods through us, and of lore received from both personal mentors and books. I was lucky to have herbal teachers who had a "spirited" view of the Green World, who taught me to work with each plant as an ally, an entity to be communed with, while also teaching me the science of medicine and diagnosis. Like Witchcraft, art and science were blended into my herbal skills. I was taught that we learned how the plants cured by speaking with the plants. There was no trial and error. Science would back up eventually what we learned, but if you look to any of the living indigenous herbal traditions, the healers will tell you the plant spirits told them how to use the plants. I took that lesson to heart.

Much of the lore I share here was intuitively obtained, drawn from my own visions and communications with the plants. It draws from the teachings of herbal medicine and the traditions of both Witchcraft and holistic healing through flower essences. Many of the lessons in this book are built upon the basic ideas shared by Elliot Cowan in his groundbreaking *Plant Spirit Medicine* book and the teachings he shared with the herbal community, as well as those who followed in his footsteps and reached out even further on the path. My fascination with the healers of Central and South America, and their parallels to European Witchcraft, became an influence upon my practice. The information shared by traditional Witches, including authors Raven Grimassi and Daniel A.

Schulke, inspired me greatly. Even bits of lore culled from as unlikely a source as the Bible proved useful in my exploration. When approached as a cultural book of mythology rather than theology, it can yield some interesting information. Ultimately, all of these things went into the internal athanor of my consciousness, to be alchemically transmuted and distilled into something for modern Witches, magicians and healers seeking to go deeper into the mysteries of the plant world and the wisdom of green gnosis.

   This is an intermediate book, and the basics of ritual and meditation will not be covered. It presumes a certain level of experience and working knowledge. If you are brand new to meditation, journeywork, and ceremony, I suggest you work with this book while referring to some of my previous works, particularly the Temple of Witchcraft series. You don't have to be a Witch or Pagan to work with these teachings, but they are written from that spiritual perspective. I recommend that you read the entire book to understand the theme and practice, then go back to do the exercises and rituals as you are drawn. They do build upon each other, so I suggest acquiring a greater mastery over earlier workings before moving onto the more advanced ones. May the plants share their knowledge, power, and love with you, and in turn may you then share it with the world.

Part One:
The Leaves of Tradition

Chapter One:
Familiar Spirits

I f you are going to explore the Green World of plant familiars, it's important to understand exactly what a familiar is to a Witch. And like many things in Witchcraft, you can get as many definitions as the number of Witches you ask. The term "familiar" has a long history, but not many agree as to what it means in our modern traditions.

The use of the word "familiar" in Witchcraft is found in several contexts, ranging from medieval witch trials to contemporary Chaos Magick. One of our earliest historic mentions of the familiar spirit comes not from a Pagan source, but from the Bible. The Old Testament story of the Witch of Endor references familiar spirits:

Now Samuel was dead, and all Israel had lamented him, and buried him in Ramah, even in his own city. And Saul had put away those that had familiar spirits, and the wizards, out of the land. And the

Philistines gathered themselves together, and came and pitched in Shunem: and Saul gathered all Israel together, and they pitched in Gilboa. And when Saul saw the host of the Philistines, he was afraid, and his heart greatly trembled. And when Saul enquired of the LORD, the LORD answered him not, neither by dreams, nor by Urim, nor by prophets. Then said Saul unto his servants, Seek me a woman that hath a familiar spirit, that I may go to her, and enquire of her. And his servants said to him, Behold, there is a woman that hath a familiar spirit at Endor. And Saul disguised himself, and put on other raiment, and he went, and two men with him, and they came to the woman by night: and he said, I pray thee, divine unto me by the familiar spirit, and bring me him up, whom I shall name unto thee. And the woman said unto him, Behold, thou knowest what Saul hath done, how he hath cut off those that have familiar spirits, and the wizards, out of the land: wherefore then layest thou a snare for my life, to cause me to die? And Saul sware to her by the LORD, saying, As the LORD liveth, there shall no punishment happen to thee for this thing. Then said the woman, Whom shall I bring up unto thee? And he said, Bring me up Samuel. And when the woman saw Samuel, she cried with a loud voice: and the woman spake to Saul, saying, Why hast thou deceived me? for thou art Saul. And the king said unto her, Be not afraid: for what sawest thou? And the woman said unto Saul, I saw gods ascending out of the earth. And he said unto her, What form is he of? And she said, An old man cometh up; and he is covered with a mantle. And Saul perceived that it was Samuel, and he stooped with his face to the ground, and bowed himself. And Samuel said to Saul, Why hast thou disquieted me, to bring me up? And Saul answered, I am sore distressed; for the Philistines make war against me, and God is departed from me, and answereth me no more, neither by prophets, nor by dreams: therefore I have called thee, that thou mayest make known unto me what I shall do.

– 1 Samuel 28, 3-15 (King James version)

Basically, the Witch, as depicted in this story, is more akin to a medium or spiritualist in our modern context. She is someone who has the ability to summon and speak with the dead, conjuring the spirit of the departed Samuel for King Saul so that Saul can ask for his advice. In the ancient world, such a practitioner would be classified as a necromancer. Though that word brings up a lot of fear in people today, conjuring images of grave robbing, skulls and zombies, it simply means anyone who works with the dead, particularly to receive information about the future. All ancestral magick could technically be considered necromancy, so our TV psychics who connect individuals to the dead are actually continuing the illustrious tradition of the Witch of Endor and could therefore be considered necromancers. What sets this woman apart from others in the land is that she "hath a familiar spirit." Basically, her familiar spirit is an intermediary spirit, a go-between connecting the human Witch to the spirit world. The familiar is not defined or described, so we don't know what kind of spirit it is, but it acts as a guide, helping her navigate the realm of the dead and call up the specific spirit she seeks. In this case, her familiar allows the Witch to contact, summon and communicate with Samuel for Saul.

So in its most simple form, the familiar spirit is a spirit that is quite literally *familiar* with a Witch, and the Witch is familiar with it. They have created a partnership, forming a bridge between the physical and the spiritual world. We might assume that the relationship is mutually beneficial; though the benefit to the spirit is not clearly articulated in the story, it seems clear that the Witch would not be able to perform her services without the familiar spirit.

The Medieval European Familiar

Another popular context for the term familiar again comes from non-Pagan sources, and specifically relates to the medieval witchcraft trials from a time period modern Pagans call the Burning Times. During the Christian persecutions of those they suspected as witches, the concept of the familiar spirit is raised again. While most of the Inquisitors' images of witchcraft are considered fictitious by modern Witches today, giving more insight into the sexually and spiritually repressed minds of the prosecuting Christians rather than the true practice of Witchcraft, there are a few strands of possible truth that emerge from the tortured confessions. One concept that repeats itself is that of the "Devil," as a part of his pact with the witches and in exchange for their allegiance and their soul, granting the witch the power to do magick and cast curses. But the Devil also gives the witch a "familiar" in the form of an animal traditionally associated with witchcraft. Someone who has a connection with a strange and unusual animal, such as the classic black cat, might be identified as a witch because of that animal relationship. Other animals include weasels, hares, mice, crows, ravens, toads, lambs, chickens, wrens, cows, owls, foxes, spiders and snakes. The witch hunters believed normal people didn't have such pets, even though quite obviously they did have many of these animals domesticated on their farms. The ownership of one of these animals was often employed as an excuse to accuse someone of witchcraft. It seems to be the unusual relationship with the animal that is the real basis of fear, stemming from the belief that "normal" people couldn't commune with or tame animals in the wild. These animals grew to have a somewhat malevolent presence in the eyes of ordinary folk, who then concluded that people who communed with these animals must therefore have been in league with the Christian Devil and had received the animal as a familiar to finalize their unholy pact. That was the only explanation according to Inquisitors. The familiar served as a connection to the Devil and the infernal powers of Hell, fueling the magick and in some ways acting as a go-between for the witch and the Devil. Sometimes it was the animal itself, believed to be a demon or devil, that gave the witch power, and there was little mention of the Devil directly. The familiar instructed the witch in the ways of enchantment and was the "vehicle" for the enchantment, carrying out the witch's wishes, usually involving baneful magick. They would seemingly "carry" the curse, physically or spiritually.

The following example, from "The Trial of the Lancaster Witches" (reprinted in *The Wonderful Discoverie of Witches in the Countie of Lancaster* by Thomas Potts), shows a black dog familiar instructing the witch in the classic technique of clay poppets:

> *[a black dog] bad this Examinate [James Device] make a Picture of Clay, like unto the said Mistress Towneley: and that this Examinate with the helpe of his Spirit (who then euer after bidde this Examinate call it Dandy) would kill or destroy the said Mistris Towneley.*

Isobel Gowdie, famous and unusual confessor to witchcraft in Scotland said, "Each one of us has a spirit to wait upon us when we please to call upon him." She is also known for claiming to shapeshift into the form of a hare as well as for stating that covens are made up of thirteen members. Isobel was unusual in the fact that she gave such a clear and detailed confession.

In these and similar instances, the familiar is described as a devil, demon or imp in animal form, yet could take on other forms a well, including other animals and people, or it could take no form at all and be invisible to the eye. It could appear or disappear at will. It could appear in the form of normal animals of unusual size, such as cows the size of rats, or take on a chimera-like combination of several different animals. It could speak to the witch, and the trials recorded their reconstructed conversations, although they were usually collected under threat or torture. Familiars could even be shared with or passed on to other witches, or inherited from a family member.

The familiar's relationship with the witch was not one of subservience, but partnership. There was a sense of "give and take"– bargaining and negotiation between the witch and familiar for power or occult lore. One theory is that they were not animals at all, but other witches who could disguise themselves through magick to appear as animals, and then seduce innocents to their evil ways through promises of power.

Though the witchcraft trial transcripts are far from cohesive and show a wide variety of thoughts and ideas, most of which are suspect, there are some ideas within these descriptions that are not so different from ideas involving spirits in other tribal traditions. Perhaps the original teaching had something to do with an animal totem, given to the individual by a horned father or animal lord.

The writings of Matthew Hopkins, self-professed Witchfinder General who led his reign of terror in the 1600s through the English countryside, contain information on the Witch's familiar. His quite colorful depiction of familiar spirits is presumably based upon his experience with accused witches. One such woman, Elizabeth Clarke, whose mother was also accused of Witchcraft, confessed under torture to keeping five familiars. Hopkins' account can be found in *The Discovery of Witchcraft and Witches* by Matthew Hopkins and John Stearne:

The Discoverer never travelled far for it, but in March 1644 he had some seven or eight of that horrible sect of Witches living in the Towne where he lived, a Towne in Essex called Maningtree , with divers other adjacent Witches of other towns, who every six weeks in the night (being always on the Friday night) had their meeting close by his house and had their severall solemne sacrifices there offered to the Devill, one of which this discoverer heard speaking to her Imps one night, and bid them goe to another Witch, who was thereupon apprehended, and searched, by women who had for many yeares knowne the Devills marks, and found to have three teats about her, which honest women have not: so upon command from the Justice they were to keep her from sleep two or three nights, expecting in that time to see her familiars, which the fourth night she called in by their severall names, and told them what shapes, a quarter of an houre before they came in, there being ten of us in the roome, the first she called was:

1. Holt, who came in like a white kitling.

2. Jarmara, who came in like a fat Spaniel without any legs at all, she said she kept him fat, for she clapt her hand on her belly and said he suckt good blood from her body.

3. Vinegar Tom, who was like a long-legg'd Greyhound, with an head like an Oxe, with a taile and broad eyes, who when this discoverer spoke to, and bade him goe to the place provided for him and his Angels, immediately transformed himselfe into the shape of a child of foure yeeres old without a head, and gave halfe a dozen turnes about the house, and vanished at the doore.

4. Sack and Sugar, like a black Rabbet.

5. Newes, like a Polcat.

All these vanished away in a little time. Immediately after this Witch confessed severall other Witches, from whom she had her Imps, and named to divers women where their marks were, then number of their Marks, and Imps, and Imps names, as Elemanzer, Pyewacket, Peckin the Crown, Grizzel, Greedigut, n&nc. which no mortall could invent; and upon their searches the same Markes were found, the same number, and in the same place, and the like confessions from them of thesame Imps, (though they knew not that we were told before) and so peached one another thereabouts that joyned together in the like damnable practise ....

Fig. 1: Art from **The Discovery of Witchcraft and Witches**

Though Witches today don't accept this Christian concept of "imps", I find it interesting that the Biblical idea of a familiar spirit in regards to the Witch of Endor has now taken on animalistic tones, perhaps pointing the way towards the true nature-based and shamanic practices of the European Witches. Many modern practitioners of magick today have a strong and unusual relationship with the animal world. Some rare practitioners can seemingly charm the birds from the trees or quite literally "soothe the savage beast," enabling them to have close and intimate encounters with creatures in the forest with no harm to themselves.

Medieval Christians simply used the term that was known to them from the Bible, "familiar," to describe that unusual relationship they saw between certain people and animals. Perhaps if European shamanic practices did survive in some form, these healers and magical practitioners, now living in at least a nominally Christian society, adopted the term *familiar* to describe their totem relationships, as the original Pagan context was disappearing.

Different from the Witch of Endor, these folk magic practitioners were charged to care for their animal familiar, often accused by the witch hunters of either feeding it from their breast, or from an abnormal "Witch's mark" or "Witch's teat" such as a mole, wart or birthmark, and the animal would feed on their blood. The spirit in animal form would gain sustenance from the Witch, and in turn, do her bidding, aiding in magick and acting as her eyes, ears and hands in the world. The reciprocal nature of the relationship was more apparent than with the Witch of Endor, and is more similar to the reciprocal relationship a tribal shaman would have with a spirit ally.

In more mystical texts, such as *The Lesser Key of Solomon*, various "demons," known as Goetic spirits, are catalogued and their powers listed. Many of these spirits are said to "give good familiars." Both the familiars and the Goetic spirits themselves are described in terms of tutelary spirits, spirit tutors or teachers, who instruct the magician in secret knowledge, such as the virtue of stones, herbs or reading omens. This is similar to the shamanic traditions of having a spirit teacher and/or an animal spirit who acts as guide and guardian during travels to the other world. In many ways, European grimoires attempted to codify universal magickal experiences of the spirit world in the context of Judeo-Christian magick and theology, yet when the veneer is peeled back, the common threads of more primal and tribal magick become apparent.

In the later traditions of village healers and cunning folk, who typically did not identify as Witches or Pagans, familiars were often equated with faeries or ancestor spirits. In some European lore, the line between the dead and the fey was rather blurry, as the faery races were not seen so much as plant and nature spirits, but rather spirits "beneath the ground," where the dead dwell. Cunning folk viewed the familiar spirit, no matter its outward animal form, as the return of an ancestor to aid in healing and "white witchcraft." In the Christian context within which most cunning folk worked, it was believed that if the ancestor did return to help, then of course the work was sanctioned by God, as God would not allow the spirit to return for evil purposes, and a heavenly ancestor would not jeopardize the soul of the descendant.

Such practitioners of this mix of rural folk belief and Christian magick were sometimes known as "white witches" in particular parts of England, as well as unwitchers, blessers and finders, depending on their particular specialty and skill. Some cunning folk were even called on to find or stop "evil" witches! The connections to both the faery races and to the dead is an interesting thread found among both those convicted as "evil" witches and those cunning folk sanctioned, or at least mostly left alone, by mainstream authorities. In reality, whatever magick was being practiced at its core was not that different; just the outer form changed.

Animal Totems

In shamanic traditions, the animal familiar takes on a different view, and perhaps leads us to deeper truths regarding earlier forms of European Witchcraft. Today the concept has been popularized with the terms *totem* or *power animals*. Shamanic practitioners of many different cultures believe that everyone has a spirit ally, often in the form of an animal. That animal is our primary ally and embodies either our basic animalistic nature, or the lessons we are learning in this lifetime. This animal spirit is not corporeal, though we, and others, can have strong visions of its presence to the point where we believe it is physically present. Some may have unusual encounters with a living representative from their totem's species. The totem's job is to protect us from unwanted spirits of illness and misfortune, guide us on the path of our life in tune with our nature and, if we are open and willing, to teach us its animal wisdom.

Those who are seriously ill or in spiritual jeopardy have lost their animal spirit or damaged their connection to it. Shamans in the South American traditions outlined by modern shamanic pioneer Michael Harner in his book *The Way of the Shaman*, would first correct this problem in any patient by either retrieving the lost animal spirit and reconnecting it with the human client, or finding another animal spirit and convince it to act as guide and totem for the patient.

Deeper healing can involve working with the wisdom of other animals as necessary to create change within an individual. Each animal's wisdom is considered by many Native tribes to be its "medicine." Magick is referred to as medicine in these traditions because it is the power to heal and to bring harmony and balance. Each animal, based on its habitat, life cycle, and lore, has a different medicine, and when we are lacking in that quality, the spirit medicine of that animal can help heal us.

An easy example is the dog. Both in its behavior and in folklore, the dog is best known for the characteristics of loyalty and friendship. Someone who does not feel like they have friends, or cannot be loyal, can benefit from a shamanic practitioner retrieving the spirit of dog medicine, and through ritual, transfer that energy to the client. The energy may then express itself in the client's life in the form of opportunities to be loyal, make friends and attract loyal friends in return.

Each animal has its own medicine. While "normal" people each have at least one totem spirit, and sometimes tribes or communities have a collective totem, shamanic practitioners can have many animal allies. The more work they do in communion with the spirit world, the more opportunities they have to make allies with animal spirits. These spirits become "familiar" to them, and act as intermediaries with the non-physical, much like the Witch of Endor's familiar spirit. And while the popular image of the shaman is one who works with animal spirits, an experienced shamanic practitioner will work with a variety of spiritual entities, including the spirits of animals, plants, stones, the stars, the land, deities and ancestors. The following journey will help you connect to your own animal ally.

Animal Ally Journey

Prepare yourself for a spiritual journey. If you like, play some drumming music (the music should have a fast tempo), or arrange for a friend to drum for you. Drumming a strong, fast beat, at least 120 beats per minute, can facilitate the trance state necessary to journey. You can alternatively use simple relaxation music, or best yet, go outside someplace and let the sounds of nature guide you.

Create a sacred space by whatever method you choose, such as casting a circle. A simple honoring of the seven directions (north, south, east, west, above, below and center) can work well for the less experienced practitioner. Center yourself and breathe deeply. Say this prayer to the Earth Mother and the Horned God, Master of the Animals:

I call to you, Mother of the Earth,
Goddess of all that is Green and Good,
Whose flesh and blood, greed and red, support me in all things.
And I in turn will eventually feed those of the green and red blood.
I ask for your support now.
I ask that you hold this Sacred Space with me,
Here and now as well as in a time beyond time, and a place beyond place.
I ask to rejoin the family of the living,
of the wild creatures of the forest and mountain,
Fields and valleys,
waters and deserts,
hills and plains,
Depths and skies.
Blessed be.

I call to you, Lord of the Wild.
I call to you, Dark God of the Land.
I call to you, Hunter and Hunted.
Born of Flesh and Blood,
Breath and Bone.
I am one of yours, one of your pack, your herd,
For I too am flesh and blood.
I seek the mysteries of the creatures.
By Hoof and Horn,
By fang and fur, feather, fin and claw,
By all Fauna seen and unseen,
Known and Unknown,
I call to you.
Grant me knowledge and conversation with my animal familiar.
Grant me wisdom and healing with my animal familiar.
Grant me the magick and medicine of my animal familiar.
For the highest good,
Harming none.
So mote it be.

Envision a great tree before you, with only the thinnest of veils separating you from it. Pass through the veil and stand before the great tree. Look into its roots for a passage that seems to open for you and only you. Follow this root tunnel into the otherworld. It may climb up, down or deeper within the tree. Follow the tunnel to its end, and at the light at the end of the tunnel, you will find a land within the otherworld. Seek out your animal totem. The Earth Mother or Horned God might immediately introduce you to an animal spirit, or you might have to journey to find the spirit or the gods yourself. Tradition says any animal you see, even if only in glimpses, three or more times and that is friendly to you, could be a totemic ally.

Speak with the ally. It might speak back, or answer you by showing you images, giving you feelings, or simply returning a "knowing." Communicate as you would with a new friend, asking questions and answering questions in turn. You are building a relationship. Make sure you ask, "What is our work together?"

Return the way you came, and know that you can always go back, repeating this journey to visit with your ally. Those spirits that appear only in flashes will grow stronger in your vision the more you practice making contact. Ground yourself upon returning by imagining strong roots anchoring you to the world and releasing excess energy to the land. Thank the Earth Mother and Horned God. Release your sacred space. If you honored the directions, simply honor them again to release your sacred space and return to normal awareness.

Artificial Familiars

Not all familiars are seen as naturally occurring spirits. Some are considered to be "artificial" in the sense they are constructed by the Witch or magician, with no existence prior to their first summoning, and no long-term independent existence from the magician with a few rare and notable exceptions. Modern ceremonial magick and its rebellious child, Chaos Magick, have popularized the notion of the artificial familiar with terms such as "artificial elemental," "servitor spirit," "thoughtform," and "construct." In Tibetan magickal lore, a similar concept is found in the teaching of the tulpa. Translated by western researchers as "thoughtform," a tulpa usually relates to a complex entity created by willpower that can reach a level of power where it becomes semi-visible to others and can even take on an existence independent of its creator.

Traditions of Witchcraft that are influenced by ceremonial magick, particularly those prior to anything akin to the modern shamanic revival, such as the Alexandrian line of British Traditional Wicca, use this terminology. In the biography of Alex Sanders entitled *King of the Witches* by June Johns, the term familiar is used not to refer to an animal spirit, ghost, or guide, but to a spirit constructed and conjured by the Witch to go forth and perform acts of magick or gather information. June Johns defines the familiar as "A mass of energy or power raised by the Witches and sent to work their will." In some ways, its creation is implied in the sending of the Cone of Power, though the familiar seems to exhibit some manner of independence in Sander's biography. Sander's familiars may be likened to the Medieval Inquisitor's view of the familiar as a spirit that goes forth carrying the Witch's spell.

The simple thoughtform construct of every spell can be considered to be an artificial familiar, an energy form to set in motion and manifest a spell intention, timed to be expire upon the completion of the spell. People are always working with such thoughtforms, or energy constructs. Most are unconscious and work against us as unwanted patterns, or psychological "tapes" or programs that replay within us. Witches, magicians and those advocates of self-help manuals, affirmations, and creative visualization techniques work to clear unwanted thoughtforms and use helpful thoughtforms to their personal benefit.

Such familiars are generated either for short-term or long-term use through ritual, usually involving a ceremony of naming, the construction of a "home" such as a talisman, bottle, box, or statue, and the giving of specific instructions. This is much like our image of the genie, or djinn, in the bottle. The home is made in alignment with occult principles that correspond with the nature and purpose of the construct. A crafted familiar for love magick will have a home constructed of Venusian items – copper, rose quartz, Venusian herbs and sigils. A familiar for protection will have Mars and/or Saturn correspondences. The spirit will go there to rest and regenerate after tasks. The instructions will be clear and specific, and often with a self-destruct sequence, in terms of a command or an end date. Typically the more powerful of these familiars will need to be "fed" with either psychic energy and intent, or physical objects and offerings that are in alignment with the construct's nature. The spirit's home can either feed the spirit, or be the medium through which the offerings are made, with offerings being placed in the bowl, bottle or box of the spirit. It is important to make sure the spirit has an energy source, lest it feed off of the creator's own energy and cause imbalance and illness. Most practitioners believe it is important to end the "life" of the familiar and create new familiars when needed rather than have them linger.

The magickal theory on such constructed beings differs among practitioners. Those with more of a psychological slant see such constructs as akin to psychological "complexes" working with the magician, rather than against them. It's like splintering off a portion of awareness and energy, then setting it towards a specific task; the ritual accoutrements are just a focus for the magick. The origin of the spirit is within the awareness of the magician, and ultimately must return to it.

Those with a more mechanical view think of the artificial elemental like a magickal machine, built from the raw materials of the universe, i.e. the basic energies of the elements (hence the name *elemental*), and/or planetary energies. Like any machine, the magician sets it forth to perform its function, and it does so until either the magician no longer needs it or it breaks down.

Lastly, there are those who believe the construction of such creatures is akin to creating life and while that which is created may not necessarily be *human* life, it is life nonetheless. Rituals of sex magic—and even the Great Rite in token—are said to conceive a "Magickal Childe", which can refer to the effects of the ritual, or the creation of an artificial elemental. It is similar to the legends of alchemists crafting the *homunculus*, a small, artificial human. Such practitioners have a hard time dismissing, deconstructing, or destroying the spirit, and dislike the names "artificial" or "servitor." In a few rare cases, such entities have been said to go beyond the lifespan of a typical construct, but more often than not, such attempts at freeing such a spirit end up only harming the creator by setting forth a spirit with no clear purpose, will, or source of energy.

Practitioners without a belief in the supernal nature of polytheism believe all gods and goddesses, spirits, angels, demons, saints and totems are simply artificial constructs, masses of psychic energy created and programmed by humans to respond in such a way. The practice of "god making" doesn't invalidate the experience of the gods, but simply points to a human, not a divine origin. The venerations of wells, rivers, mounds, ancestors and heroes "create" the gods. Then these powers take a life of their own, beyond their cultural and geographic boundaries.

I personally think divinities have an origin that is both supernal and human. The ultimate consciousness is divine, just as our own is, but the "interface" through which we experience these entities, their "dress" and mannerisms might originate in human awareness. Yet it shows how powerful the process of constructing such artificial familiars can ultimately be.

The Fetch

Research in the shamanic traditions, comparatively untouched by modernization and Christianization, at least compared to the native European traditions, has caused us to look at European lore with a different eye. Both occultists of the Western Mysteries and historical reconstructionists with spiritual leanings seek to tease out the hidden mysteries in poetry, folklore and myth. This has led to the teaching of the *Fetch* in modern neo-Pagan groups.

The Fetch comes from the term *Flygia* or *Flygja* and is usually construed as a part of the soul complex in the Teutonic traditions. Unlike our fairly modern concept of one soul within the body, ancient people of many traditions believed in a *soul complex*, an anatomy of the soul that lists many different parts, or to some, many different souls, that serve different functions just as the organs of the body do. Even esoteric Christians differentiated soul from spirit and body, and in alchemy these three basic "parts" were known by the principles of Sulfur, Mercury and Salt. In the Norse traditions, the Flygia is one of these "souls" in our consciousness. The Flygia is the part of our consciousness that "fares forth" into the spirit worlds, the nine worlds, to seek information and experience.

To the occultist, the Flygia is akin to the astral body, sent forth into the spirit realms. In forms of Traditional Craft, systems of witchcraft said to predate the modern Wicca revival, this part of the soul is considered the "double" – the spiritual twin that can be separated from the body. The double here is equated with the Fetch. Traditions differ as to origin of the Fetch double. For some, it is a part of the individual. While many think everybody has a double or Fetch, others believe it is unique to those who are blessed with the Witchblood, and therefore not all humans have a Fetch double. For many it is not a matter of fate, but a matter of spiritual work. One must develop or construct the Fetch through intention or the ordeal of initiation.

Others define the double as a separate spirit bonded with the Witch, what is known as a *co-walker* in the Faery traditions. The co-walker spirit walks this world with the Witch or seer, almost like a shadow, experiencing the world with their human partner, and lending their power and sight to them. This represents the bond between human and spirit; a permanent alliance bridging between the worlds.

While in ceremonial forms of magick and British Traditional Wicca initiation is measured in ranks and degrees, in many Traditional Craft groups it is the evolution of the Fetch relationship that marks progression and development. At first it manifests as an animalistic double, like the shamanic totem discussed above. Known as the Fetch beast, the Witch aligns with these primal animal instincts and unlocks the power of the animal world and its wisdom into their path. While many people see their totem animal as the creature they like or admire most, the Fetch is the beast that represents who you are animalistically at your core, and may not be the flattering and popular wolf, raven and eagle. The discovery of the Fetch beast self is one of the great mysteries, not easily discovered, and the development of this relationship helps to truly unlock the mystery.

At a second stage, the Fetch can also appear as the Fetch-mate, lover or husband/bride. Psychologists may discuss it in terms of the anima/animus, yet this is a spiritual entity that is both a part of you and independent of you. Alchemists would refer to this as the Divine Marriage, of the inner solar king and lunar queen. The faery co-walker relationship is similar to this development, as human traits are balanced and new powers are discovered with this union. The lover turns to spirit-spouse, and there is typically an aspect of royalty or nobility to the entity, and this relationship confers upon the individual sovereignty and a relationship with the land, the ancestors and the spirit world.

Lastly the Fetch develops into something beyond comprehension and words. Human nature becomes balanced, and that balanced human nature, in full consciousness, is then merged with divine nature. Though the Fetch might still manifest as animal or mate, it is the living conduit of this divine merging, and soon has no distinction between the Witch and itself. They go on beyond life and death to join the Mighty Dead of the Witchcraft traditions, "free from fate" and reborn again. Some magicians describe the appearance of the Fetch at this stage as an abstract symbol, a geometric form that can never be fully understood or comprehended. The magician's self image might even become that form, like a faceted gem or spotless sphere reflecting all of creation and thereby remaining invisible, for it is the one thing not reflected in the light. In the Toltec sorcery of Carlos Castaneda, this would be "breaking the human mold" where one becomes empty and reflects all of infinity.

In many ways, the concept of the Fetch can include any and all of the previous images of the familiar spirit – animal, human, construct and something trans-human beyond our comprehension. It ties neatly within our modern Craft, drawing from the cauldron of spiritual inspiration that is bound by the British Isles, including Pagan lore from the Saxons, Romans, Celts and pre-Celtic Stone Age tribes, as well as European Christianity's views on Witchcraft, and contemporary Pagan reactions to Christian traditions.

In modern Witchcraft today, encompassing a wide variety of traditions and influences, the familiar is all of these things and more. Most popularly, modern Witches refer to special animals within their life as familiars; those who are not simply pets, but appear to possess an advanced consciousness. Such creatures aid in magick some way. Sometimes their presence at ritual lends power to the magick performed. Others guard the door of the temple, or appear in shamanic visions as otherworldly allies while also being physical companions. Witches might refer to their totem or Fetch as their familiar, though very few refer to their spirit guide as a familiar spirit, even though that's arguably the root usage of the term.

Understanding the mysteries of the animalistic familiars, those of both flesh and blood and those solely of spirit, can give us insight into the nature of those familiars that hail from the Green World.

Chapter Two:
Plant Spirits

he seeds for the spiritual tradition of the Witch's plant familiar are found in the same fertile ground as the medieval witches with their imps and animal familiars, flying ointments and midnight sabbats. Yet the seeds have lain dormant, untouched and never spoken of until some recent stirring in the modern Craft movement. Now they are growing roots and spreading leaves, making sense of the more unusual lore left to us by our spiritual ancestors and recorded by our persecutors and destroyers. Tendrils of the traditions that survived in hidden groves of secret traditionalists are now coming to light as well.

Among the woodcuts depicting medieval witches are images of a root that walks like a man. Known as mandrake, this intoxicating and toxic plant is associated with powerful magick. Its root grows into a human shape, and it is shown walking like an imp, like a witch's familiar given by the "Devil." Though a seemingly innocent plant from the natural realm, it has a sinister reputation, associated with death, sex, the hanged man and the crossroads. When dug up, it is said to emit a scream so deadly to kill anyone who heard it, or so the legend says. Those who sought its power would tie a dog to the root and place meat just outside the dog's reach. The animal's tugging would uproot the mandrake and either kill the dog, or, being an animal also associated with Witchcraft, the dog would be somehow immune to its deadly shriek. The mandrake, also known as a manakin, was believed to be able to move on its own and do the bidding of the witch who owned it, protecting the home, gaining secrets and healing. All together, it sounds quite similar to the witch's animal familiar from these dark times.

Fig. 2: Mandrake Woodcut
Based on a depiction from Jacob Meydenbach's *Hortus Sanitatis,* 1491

Chapter Two: Plant Spirits

The mandrake was not the only plant attributed with spiritual powers. Many such plants were associated with the witch. Interestingly enough, there is a list of familiars with plant names from the sixteenth and seventeenth century witchcraft trials depicted in Jacob Grimm's *Teutonic Mythology*. They include: Wohlgemut (Oregano), Schöne (Daisy), Peterlein (Parsley), Rautensrauch (Rue) and Hölderlin (Elder). Grimm makes comparisons to Shakespeare's elves and faeries named for herbs such as Peaseblossom and Mustardseed. Perhaps Shakespeare was pointing to something from tradition, or poetically struck upon a truth? Did these trial records imply a tradition of animal familiars or imps with plant names? Faery allies with plant names? Plant spirits alone? Was there a difference between these three in the minds of the inquisitors or the witches themselves?

Perhaps this is all fleeting evidence to point us in a new direction and understanding of our spiritual ancestors. Perhaps plants were not only important for ointments, spells and herbal cures, but also played a spiritual role, as an intermediary with the otherworlds, like the imps, ancestors and animal familiars in medieval lore. Perhaps the concept of familiars was not limited to the animal world, or to the world of the ancestors, but included spirits with a green origin.

The key concept to the plant familiar lies with the plant spirit. Plants are not unconscious objects, but vital living creatures who exist both in their life and in their "death," retaining both power and consciousness when harvested, dried and ingested. While many would believe magickal spells and formulas to be akin to chemistry, mixing the "right" ingredients together to create a result, most magicians understand there is a subtle force behind the magick. A Witch or magician must tap into that force, catalyzing it with their will.

Herbal Folk Magick

In Wicca there is talk of "charging" an herb or stone to make magick. While some think of this as a battery metaphor, i.e. filling the object with a magickal charge of energy, it is really more akin to giving the essence of the stone or herb a mandate, a charge, or an order to carry out. Most Witches do not think of the implication behind this act, and simply look at herbs, stones, oils and other natural items as objects, as tools that have the proper energy to perform a spell. Yet if we are giving something an order to be fulfilled, it implies there is a consciousness behind the "tool," something alive that can receive communication.

Some of my most profound spiritual experiences have happened while making potions. While in trance, I would "charge" each of my ingredients before stirring them into the brew. I learned that to charge an item is to mingle your energy with its energy, your consciousness with its consciousness, creating a connection. Through that connection you use your inner vision, your words and your feelings to communicate to the plant its purpose in the spell, charm or potion. Though I can't say I received any clear direct communication back in those initial experiences, the exchange of energy between me and even the dried plant between my fingers was intense, and sometimes more important than the actual potion being made.

While it might seem fairly obvious that practitioners of a nature religion would realize that all of nature is alive and conscious, this has not always been explicitly taught in terms of spellcraft. Many are taught, or self-taught from books, a very mechanical method of gathering herbs and crafting them together in spells and potions. While Wicca draws its practice from British folk magick, and herbal charms and cures are a well known part of such practices, be they Pagan or Christian, I'm not sure if such folk practitioners would use terms like "charging." They certainly didn't use the concept of "energy" or "vibration." Those apprenticed to such British folk Witches might talk about the "magic," "power" or "virtue" of a plant, but that was as esoteric as it gets. Wicca has certainly been influenced by the 19th-20th century occult movement in this way, and in turn, it has influenced those practicing Pagan-oriented folk traditions. To understand our own lore, we might have to look at surviving, established folk traditions that have had less contact with the modern occult movement.

The practitioners of Hoodoo have a deep understanding of the plant spirit. Hoodoo is an American folk magick system sometimes mistaken for Voodoo as it shares some similar influences with that African diasporic religion. Practitioners of Hoodoo and related arts are called root doctors or conjurers, as much of the work deals with the use of roots. Striking a similar chord with the European lore surrounding the mandrake, many root doctors prepare roots and herbal charm bags by speaking to the plant, telling it, like a good friend, what was needed. Plants and roots may be "wooed" like a lover, given "gifts" of perfume to smell good, alcohol to feel good, or flattered with a recitation of all their wonderful skills and powers. The plant in turn responds by magickally helping the owner of the charm manifest their desired result or experience. Roots and charms are used to protect, attract love and sex, grant success when gambling, win in legal disputes or destroy enemies. The key to this work is not in giving the plant any "energy" specifically, as such practitioners do not think in such terms, but to speak to it, to commune with its intelligence and tell it what they want in specific terms. This implies a consciousness that can respond to the spoken work and act upon it.

While I believe that in essence Wiccan and Hoodoo practitioners are performing the same practice for an end result, they each possess a different cultural aesthetic and different underlying mechanics. Each can learn from the other in order to deepen the experience with the plant and have more successful magick. Various forms of herbal folk magic found across the world use principles similar to these, though the expression will be unique to the culture and time period where the magick is practiced.

Wiccan terms today can seem more modern, and therefore speak to the modern, skeptical practitioner who feels it's silly to talk to the plant. Modern science is just now clearly articulating the effect that speaking to a plant, or playing music near a plant, has on its growth cycle starting with the controversial study *The Sound of Music and Plants* by Dorothy Retallack. People can accept communication with the living plant, but the idea that the consciousness can survive in the dried root, leaf or flower is foreign to most of the scientifically inclined. Hoodoo practitioners have a romance that brings out the flavor of old world magick and conjures a powerful personal link to the plant. Using both modern and old world techniques makes the magick even more effective. The following consecration exercise will help you connect with the spirit of a plant.

Plant Consecration

Hold the plant, fresh or dried, in your receptive hand. For most people, this is the left hand. Hold the projective hand, usually the right, over it. Inhale deeply and as you do, and imagine you are inhaling the very life force of the heavens above you, including the Sun, Moon, planets and stars down into your crown, while also inhaling through the soles of your feet the Earth's own life force. Feel these forces mingle in your heart, and when you exhale, exhale out through the palms of your hands, into the herb. Feel the herb fill not only with a part of your own life force, but also with the supercharged energies of the heavens and Earth. Feel it awaken with this influx of power. Think, feel, and imagine what the herb should be doing in your magick. What is its purpose? What will it be like when it fulfills that purpose? Feel it. Believe it. Know it. Speak to the plant like a good friend. Move your projective hand over it in clockwise circles and tell the plant what you want it to do as if you were asking a friend for a favor. For example:

Oh lovely lavender,
You bring peace to everyone around you.
You bring centeredness and calmness to all you touch.
You clear and heal those in need.
Please bring that peace and calmness to me.
When I carry you in this purple pouch,
Envelop me in your peace and love
So that none may disturb my tranquility.
So mote it be.

When done consecrating your plant, use it in your magick – adding it to potions, medicines, charms and spells as needed. With this consecration, you have the spirit of the plant in alignment with your working.

Modern Paths of Green Wisdom

Strangely, much of the regeneration of our herbal spirit knowledge seems to come from traditions outside of Witchcraft, yet from paths that are of interest to modern Witches. Modern alternative health systems, seeking to deepen their own practices and understanding, draw from both new trends that follow older wisdoms, and the indigenous lore of tribal people. While now under the purview of alternative health, the roots of this material goes back to Pagan and tribal cultures, so it is only fitting that modern Witches today look to such material as the fertilizer to inspire the regeneration of our own traditions.

Flower Essences

My first exposure to plant consciousness in the context of modern healing was through the use of flower essences. A very good friend and fellow Witch was experiencing some problems in life. Experienced in traditional forms of psychotherapy, she still felt herself stuck, even with outside facilitation from a therapist. She turned to a flower essence consultant. Through the use of both talk therapy and a regular dose of a flower essence specifically tailored to her situation, she processed her emotions, and the physical symptoms of her stress, in a very profound way, granting new insights about her self and who she wanted to be. The process was extraordinary and impressed me very much, even though I knew little about flower essences at the time.

Based on the results I saw in my friend's life, when I was experiencing a stagnant time emotionally and a new potential physical health issue in the liver, I sought out the aid from a flower essence consultant. Over the span of three short months, I brought up repressed angers that I had not dealt with that were at the root of my physical ailment in the liver and my physical functions returned to normal. The scheduled biopsy was cancelled and my doctor chalked the results of the second test up to a false reading in the first test, as such an immediate change wasn't likely from a medical point of view. Yet I knew it was the power of the essences and the process they initiated that had caused the change.

Flower essences themselves do not look that impressive, yet it is in the subtle energy where they work. Essences are often confused with essential oils, but they are entirely different. While essential oils are distilled and concentrated chemicals drawn from plant substances through a laboratory process, flower essences, also known as flower remedies or vibrational remedies, are very dilute solutions of flowers in water, preserved with some form of fixative, usually alcohol, cider vinegar or vegetable glycerin. If sent to a laboratory for chemical analysis, scientists would detect very little, if any, plant matter in the solution of a flower essence. But it is not the plant matter doing the work. According to proponents of flower essences, the vibration, the life force, of the plant, is imprinted upon the water, and it is this vibration that alters our subtle bodies – the astral, emotional, mental and psychic levels – to create a change in our health and well being.

Flower essences are made by putting clear pure water in a clear glass or crystal bowl, floating flowers on top of it and exposing the mix ideally to direct sunlight. This solution is then strained and bottled with its preservative. Various dilutions are taken orally or topically to infuse the energy of the plant into the recipient.

Though the realm of holistic health tries to dress this process in terms of clinical precision and scientific terms, in many ways it is a very ritualistic process. There is no precise measurement of water, flowers, temperature, sunlight, or preservative. Each practitioner has his own favored method. Some have a more clinical and sterilized ritual process, while others are far more intuitive, creative, and playful. Scientifically minded practitioners are hoping to get flower essences to be accepted by mainstream science and the mainstream community, but unlike herbs and vitamins, there is very little chemical reaction to study. The effects are taking place on a different realm that science has not yet learned to measure. This doesn't make flower essences any less real, but their actions are primarily in a realm that we experience subjectively, not objectively. Many interested in flower essences today are also using esoteric tools like crystals, Reiki, shamanism and creative visualization. They consider essences to be part of the tool bag of New Age metaphysical healing.

Flower essences historically come from the tradition of homeopathy. While inspired material will cite their origin in the mythic lands of Atlantis and Lemuria, our historic knowledge of flower essences begins with the English homeopath Dr. Edward Bach in 1943. His research led him to experiment with the morning dew of flowers, and his own obvious sensitivity led him to discover what flowers helped heal specific mental-emotional-spiritual conditions. He did not subscribe to the "germ theory" of illness but believed illness was the result of disharmony, from "a conflict between his soul and personality which of necessity reacts in the form of physical disorders." (*Heal Thyself* by Edward Bach). He designed a system of flower remedies that have become a staple of modern alternative healing. They are used to treat issues such as depression, anxiety, stress and insomnia. Though a doctor and ostensibly a man of science, Dr. Bach was not supported by the scientific and medical establishment of his time, and to this day has not received wide recognition in mainstream arenas. It can be argued that his research with the essences took him well into esoteric areas, such as the use of astrology with essences, as he assigned each Zodiac sign with an essence in his system of "The Twelve Healers."

Since Dr. Bach's breakthrough with these remedies, a wide variety of experimenters and professional companies have continued the research and development of new essences in the Americas, Australia, Asia and various islands, as well as more research on British and European flowers. The modern metaphysical movement has embraced the use of essences and expanded them to include the vibrations of gems and stones, sacred sites, animals and even specific times, which includes essences for particular astrological alignments.

The vernacular of flower essence therapy has absorbed many New Age terms drawn from the Theosophical movement, seeking to bring Eastern spiritual concepts to the West, particularly due to the influence of the Findhorn Community in Scotland. It's common to see terms like *channeling, ascended masters, seven rays,* and *devas,* included along with homeopathic terminology such *miasma, potency, vital life force* and *constitution* included in materials discussing flower essences. The inclusion of this kind of unverifiable metaphysical terminology makes it less likely flower essences will be recognized by mainstream science anytime soon, though the creative research and pseudo-scientific experiments of Masaru Emoto documented in his book *Messages from Water* is helping the mainstream community see the possibility of water "recording" or "remembering" energy and intent for healing or harming. Emoto believes thoughts and words directed towards water will affect the water, and this effect can be subjectively measured by freezing the water and taking a picture of the crystal formed. Healing and helpful thoughts, including prayer, create beautiful and symmetrical crystals, while harmful thoughts and words create distorted, ugly and imbalanced crystals. Drinking water that has helpful influences increases health, while water with harmful influences can adversely affect human and environmental health. Of course this is based on the underlying assumption that symmetrical and clear crystals are "better" than imbalanced asymmetrical ones, though the general consensus of those looking at the photos seems to tend toward symmetry.

Those with a less clinical view of essences believe that each plant species has a spirit, sometimes referred to as a *group soul*, *oversoul* or most popularly, a *deva*. The deva is the guiding consciousness of the plant, and is ultimately responsible for infusing the energy, the vibrational healing quality of the plant, into the water that will become a flower remedy. Rituals of flower essence creation can be stoic and clinical - with tongs, scissors and rubber gloves — playful and creative, or occult and esoteric. Often they can include a mix of all three — but their ultimate purpose, consciously or unconsciously, is communication with the plant's spiritual intelligence to imprint its power upon the water to be used for healing.

Today, flower essence enthusiasts use essences not only for healing work of both a spiritual and physical nature, but also in ceremony, prayer, meditation, affirmations and ritual. Flower essences have grown beyond the bound of their original medical intent into something much more free-form and creative.

Flower Essence Creation

While those looking to establish Flower Essence more firmly in the realm of modern medicine will give instructions that are more clinical in nature, as a magickal practitioner I've found the practice of essence creation to be much more like crafting a magickal potion, or like the instructions regarding folk medicines from Faery Faith traditions found in the British Isles. So in my mind, the instructions here are guidelines, not hard and fast scientific rules.

The materials required for essence creation are:

Clear Glass or Crystal Bowl (not lead crystal)
Pure Water
Unbleached Coffee Filter or Cheesecloth
Preservative
Larger Dark Glass Bottle (8 – 16 Oz)
2 Smaller Dropper Dark Glass Bottles (1/2 Oz)

To make an essence, choose the plant you wish to act as the basis of your essence. Ideally the plant will be in bloom at the time of essence creation, for the bloom projects the most vital life force to be encoded in the remedy and embody the highest and most sublime spiritual forces of the plant. Essences tend to work on the spiritual bodies before the physical body, and one of the reasons why is that the nature of the energy projected from the flowers is more ethereal, while the chemical constituents of a tincture or tea are more physical. Theoretically essences can be made from roots, leaves and stalks as well, but the flower carries the most energetic potency.

Commune with the plant's intelligence and ask for permission to make the essence. You can do so through simple meditative means, entering an alpha state of consciousness and seeking a clairaudient or clairsentient answer, a psychic yes/no or simple knowing, or you can use a pendulum to receive a clear yes or no answer. You can also use this method to ask when the essence should be made and how many flowers, if any, should be picked. Clinical essence makers will urge you to use sterilized scissors, tongs and an assortment of tools which I find unnecessary in an effort to prevent your energy from tainting the essence. I think part of the magick is the relationship between the plant and the human creating the essence.

Usually before noon, fill your clear glass bowl with pure water. Some prefer spring or well water, while others prefer distilled. I prefer spring water myself. Bless and clear the water energetically, using something similar to the Plant Consecration method found earlier in this chapter. Place the water beneath the plant whose essence you wish to make. If at all possible, expose the liquid to sunlight while keeping it near the living plant. With care and love, pick the appropriate number of flowers and float them on the surface of the water. Consecrate the mix again, with the intention of creating a full strength flower essence. You can draw appropriate magickal and healing symbols over the liquid to further empower it. I suggest the Magician's Infinity Loop for general empowerment and magick. Let the water sit for three hours if it's a fully sunny day, or four to six hours if partly cloudy. Use your intuition to know when it's done.

Fig. 3: Infinity Loop

Add your preservative to the larger dark glass bottle. Traditional preservatives are alcohols such as brandy, rum and vodka, or non-alcoholic preservatives such as apple cider vinegar and vegetable glycerin. High proof alcohol yields the longest shelf life and brandy is most traditional. Fill the larger bottle anywhere from one fourth to one half full of preservative. I usually use fill my bottle approximately 1/3 full of preservative and have had no problems thus far in keeping my essences free of unwanted bacteria or mold.

Fill the rest of the bottle with the water from the glass bowl. You can strain out the flower and any extra material that might have gathered within the water using an unbleached paper filter or cheesecloth. Sometimes it's easy enough to simply pick the flowers out. Date and label this first bottle with the flower name and the words "Mother Essence." You will use this to create the essences you take internally.

Using your intuition, shake the bottle and take anywhere from 3 to 10 drops of the Mother Essence and add it to smaller dropper bottle filled with a solution of 30% preservative to 70% pure water. Seal and shake this second bottle. Label it with the flower name and the words "Stock Essence." This is the level of dilution you get when you purchase an essence at a health food store or metaphysical shop. This level is best for physical symptoms and illnesses.

To be most effective with issues of a mental, emotional and spiritual nature, again use your intuition and shake the stock bottle and add anywhere from 1 to 10 drops of stock solution to another dropper bottle with a solution mix of 30% preservative to 70% pure water. This creates a dosage bottle, and you can mix more than one flower essence from stock to a single dosage bottle, to create a blend that is unique to an individual. Blended dosage bottles can treat a wide range of spiritual issues, and create a supportive synergy of plant energies to effect long lasting change.

Intuition, research, consultation with an expert, dowsing through a pendulum, or muscle testing can be used to determine which essence(s) are best for you at this time, and your personal essence blends can change over time as you change. Dosage essences are usually taken in doses of 1-5 drops, up to three times a day.

Homeopathy

While flower essence arguably came out of the traditions of homeopathy due to the influence of Dr. Bach, they are not the same as homeopathy. Homeopathic remedies are dilute preparations of substances from the plant, animal and mineral worlds that are successively diluted and shaken, potentizing the remedy to make it more effective. While they can be prepared by an individual, most homeopaths use commercially prepared remedies usually transformed into dry lactose pellets. The concept behind homeopathy is "like cures like," and a substance that causes particular symptoms in a high dose is used in a diluted homeopathic dose to cure those same symptoms. A simple example would be to use homeopathic onion as a cure for watery eyes.

Though more scientific in production and application, homeopathy too is not supported by mainstream science. Its roots, like many of the earliest sciences, come from an earlier occultism. But we must remember many of our major sciences widely accepted today have similar roots. Astronomy rose from astrology and chemistry rose from alchemy. First proposed in 1796, homeopathy was born in a time when medicine was on a cusp of change, and included herbal remedies, early medicines, and medical astrology. It even included healing charms such as the old Aramaic "Abracadabra" charm, which was used to reduce and remove illness, particularly fevers, inflammations and respiratory illness.

The Abracadabra charm would be written as an inverted cone, diminishing by one letter on each line on paper and carried close to the chest, usually folded so the letters were not showing, tied with a ribbon around the neck. The image would diminish the power an illness had upon the wearer until it was gone. Often the charm would then be thrown in a river or buried. Modern magickal practitioners still use it today.

ABRACADABRA
ABRACADABR
ABRACADAB
ABRACADA
ABRACAD
ABRACA
ABRAC
ABRA
ABR
AB
A

Fig. 4: ABRACADABRA Charm

Medicine at this time was a strange mix of folk custom, influenced by Greco-Roman and Middle Eastern healing traditions, as well as the rising new sciences. While the medical pioneer and alchemist Paracelsus first alluded to the principles of homeopathy in our modern medical establishment, it was Samuel Hahnemann who first named and outlined our practice of Homeopathy in the late 1700s. Basing his theories on diagnoses in both physical and mental-emotional constitutions, Hahnemann was really a pioneer in holistic health, as he not only advocated these particular remedies, but changes in diet and lifestyle to improve health as well. Remedies were said to boost our *vitalism*, our vital life force grounded in our overall constitution. Each person might have a different basic vital life force remedy taken for general health, as well as other remedies taken to rectify imbalances to that core vitality. According to homeopathic thought, when we have a susceptibility to an illness, we have a "need" for a particular vibration. The illness fills that need. When we take a remedy with the concept of like cures like, the remedy fills and transforms that need, dislodging or transforming the illness. Paracelsus referred to the correct remedy as the "bride" of the illness. Together they become something new, like the alchemists divine marriage. With the rise of modern medicine, homeopathy fell out of practice, but experienced a resurgence in the late twentieth century and continues to grow in popularity as the complimentary health field grows.

Though I was exposed to flower essences early on in my plant exploration and they influenced me greatly, I was much further along the green path when I got involved with homeopathy, which includes remedies made with plants as well as with animals, minerals and metals. After a new health issue arose in my life, I sought the aid of a homeopath to determine my vital life force remedy. After a very long intake session discussing my physical health, history of disease, family history, living conditions, lifestyle, diet, exercise, relationships, schooling, phobias, sleep patterns and anything else under the sun you can think of, my homeopath determined my vital life force remedy to be *Stramonium*. *Stramonium* is the Latin and homeopathic name for the Jimson Weed plant, also known as *Datura stramonium*, Thorn Apple, or Devil's Weed. *Stramonium* is strongly associated with Witchcraft and is a plant with which I already had a spiritual relationship. I was blown away, as the homeopath seemed initially ignorant of any of the Witchcraft and shamanic lore associated with the plant. Although she is a Witch, she focused solely on a remedy's history in homeopathy —at least she did then. My homeopath thought, after dreaming upon the matter, that *Stramonium* was perfect for my general issues, and I had to agree. Overall, *Stramonium* is recommended for restlessness and nightmares, but also for people who work with the dark, with the underworld forces. After taking the remedy over a few days, I did notice a major difference in my health and vitality, and it completely deepened my spiritual experiences with Datura. My lingering illness of many months cleared up within the week.

I would urge you to consult with a reputable yet spirited homeopath open to such practices, and see if your vital life force remedy is from the plant, animal or mineral realms. Remember that homeopathy, much like magick, is both a science and art, and two different homeopaths might come to two different conclusions about your core remedy.

The Findhorn Experiment

When you first hear about the Findhorn Community of Scotland and its history, it seems to be something more suited to fantasy fiction than fact. Yet according to the participants, it's all true, and their results have been recreated, to a lesser extent and success rate, in other spiritually-oriented farms, gardens and communities.

Findhorn Ecovillage is an intentional community located on the east coast of Scotland. Formed in 1962 by a small circle of spiritual explorers, teachers and channelers, the Findhorn group believed itself to be in contact with a variety of otherworldly spiritual intelligences, including the devas of nature. Through partnership with the devas and other nature spirits, the community was able to produce exceptionally large plants and vegetables, including forty-pound cabbages, despite poor soil conditions. The small group drew notable attention from the world and eventually formed a community based upon cooperation and communication with nature that continues to operate to this day. Findhorn serves as an example to many of what is possible when we work with nature's wisdom, rather than against it. Devotees of the Findhorn community believe many of the world's problems would be solved with direct contact and guidance from nature.

The lessons and teachings of Findhorn have been adopted by numerous groups and New Age traditions, particularly those involved in flower essence work. Communion with the devas to create healing remedies has become a staple practice and entire traditions have been developed out of this concept, including flower essences, muscle testing, meditation, cooperative gardening, and energy work. The term *deva* originates in Hindu teachings of India. It refers to the "bright and shining good god," as in Hindu cosmology, everything has a ruling god, from the largest cosmic forces with the more familiar Hindu deities to the tiniest blade of grass. The term *deva* is also used somewhat similarly in forms of Buddhism. In New Age lore, based upon both the Theosophical movement and Findhorn, it has come to denote an entity in nature on a specific evolutionary track different from humanity. While sometimes used to indicate any nature spirit, elemental, genus loci or faery, the Findhorn material and related branches specifically define deva as an archetypal intelligence, a form of group soul or oversoul to a specific species of plant or type of mineral that can be communed with via telepathy and intuition, or for those less sensitive, through dowsing and muscle testing. Dorothy Maclean originally referred to these spirits as angels, then changed their name to devas.

Machaelle Small Wright, founder of the Perelandra Center for Nature Research and garden, has continued the work of Findhorn, expanding the principles of contact and partnership with nature. The name "Perelandra" references a C.S. Lewis tale set on the planet Venus. The goddess Venus, or in her Greek form Aphrodite, is not only the goddess of love, but also the goddess of flowers and cultivated gardens. A term for Roman

Witches, Venifica, is derived from her name. Wright has written co-creative gardening books to help the individual to facilitate contact with the devas using these principles and a variety of self-improvement tools—including a line of flower essences for personal healing—with the concept of nature communication at their heart.

In her book *MAP: Medical Assistance Program of the Great White Brotherhood*, Wright differentiates between devas and nature spirits. To Wright, devas are the intelligences that hold the patterns of nature, like architects, while nature spirits are the workers and builders of nature. Each plant species has an overlighting deva, guiding its evolution and development, akin to its archangel, while each individual plant has its own nature spirit, corresponding to its individual spirit. Modern practitioners, influenced by both Wright and Findhorn, tend to use these definitions of devas. While devas have been equated with the faeries and elementals, occultists would differentiate between devas, nature spirits, faeries and elementals as separate types of entities sharing some similar characteristics, but ultimately different in purpose and function.

Renewed Traditions of Nature

Some traditions, while experiencing a resurgence in popular metaphysical thought, are not so much new innovations upon traditional ideas, but rather extensions of more established traditions in our New Age. They have deep roots, but have not gained widespread notice until now with our ability to share and spread information in this age of technology. While traditions like alchemy and faery healing are known in occult circles, herbal medicine has a wider appeal, having expressions in many cultures. Today modern herbalists draw on the lore and plants of many different regions. The most unknown and esoteric of these disciplines, plant spirit healing, has a history in one specific region of Mexico, but has undergone a recent revitalization due to modern herbal practitioners.

Alchemy & Faery Faith

Both flower essences and homeopathy touch upon the older traditions of European magick. The first, alchemy, imported from the Far and Middle East, fused with a variety of beliefs including Qabalah and esoteric Christianity, seems to have little to do with the second, the indigenous faery faith found mostly in European Celtic and Saxon territories. The linking principle between the two is their capacity for healing through both the use of herbs and sacred water, and the underlying spiritual principles behind their relationship with these substances. Both alchemists and faery doctors/healers see the Green World and the water that sustains it as alive, and their practices link them to the living forces of nature.

While alchemy as a whole is a tradition with global influence and a long history, the most popular notion of alchemy comes from medieval European alchemists. Such explorers, with many notable scientists among them, including Sir Isaac Newton (who personally thought his alchemical work far more important than the scientific concepts he is known for today), saw nature as Anima Mundi, Mother Nature, or the Soul of the World. She is the greatest alchemist, but works slowly perfecting plants, animals and minerals. Alchemists worked with her, using her tools but recreating them through laboratory processes to speed up both an outer transformation as well as an inner personal transformation in the seeker on the quest to enlightenment. Herbal remedies were used to heal not only the body, but also the relationship with the soul to both nature and God, helping prepare the alchemist for enlightenment, or what has been called "the Great Work."

Fig. 5: Alchemical Mandala

Faery faith healers were not so technical, and while their complex philosophy was not clearly articulated in written form, it lay beneath all of the faery workings, and it can be seen when teased out of the surviving folklore and poetry, albeit with a Christian influence. Like the alchemists, faery healers were able to hold both religious world views simultaneously without great conflict, as the Celtic forms of Christianity were quite different in flavor and spirit than their Roman and Eastern counterparts. Even when Roman Christianity was imposed in the British Isles, the druidic-influenced Celtic Christianity still lingered amongst the people through folk tradition.

The fundamental principle in faery faith is the belief in faeries – otherworldly allies intimately connected to nature and currently living beneath the land and hills. Known as the Good Folk or the People of Peace, faeries are considered an elder race that predates humanity, and that withdrew into the land with the coming of humanity, where they secretly watch and guard the land while dwelling in a mirror world below our own that they have created. The origin of the faery folk differ in each tradition, and can include reference to native Pagan gods, fallen angels, ancient deified ancestors and nature spirits. Today, modern practitioners of faery magick most often think of the faeries as nature spirits, but older lore suggests that while they are connected to nature, they are not simply the spirits of plants, trees and rocks, but something far older, guiding the evolution of nature until the rise of man.

Many faery faith practitioners believed some illnesses were causes by faery beings when trespassed upon or disrespected by a mostly unknowing human population. People and animals could be "elf-shot" for example, and faery faith healers could cure the illnesses elf-shot caused. But faeries could also reveal the virtue of healing herbs and sacred sites for other illnesses, and in general, once allied with a human faery doctor, could walk with the human, as a co-walker, and reach with or through the human into the spirit of the patient to effect change and heal. We might think of these practices as akin to a surviving remnant of a Native shamanic healing tradition, as it's not unlike the way a traditional shaman would work, but practitioners of faery healing would not necessarily see it in such terms. Many would consider themselves good Christians doing God's work through nature.

An important connection between the alchemist and those of the faery traditions is the use of morning dew collected from the field and flowers and considered sacred to both, for it is a water that is generated neither above nor below. It magickally appears "between." Liminal places and times are sacred to both traditions. Sunrise, noon, sunset, midnight, equinoxes, solstices and cross quarter fire festival days all hold a special power because they occur "between" times. Hedges, borders, seashores, streams, swamps and mountains also are sacred for they are "between" places. Dew neither rose up from the land as a spring or well nor fell down from the heavens to be collected in lakes and the sea. It appeared suspended upon plants and was therefore considered sacred, as it is a mystery. It was used as the base of remedies, potions and formulas. It was collected off standing stones and off plants. Alchemists would throw white cloth over the field, let it absorb the dew and then ring it out, collecting quantities of the dew for their potions.

These basic principles from seemingly divergent traditions also links them to the modern flower essence creation, as Dr. Bach went back to the dew of flowers to create his healing system. Was he guided by the faeries of the Old Faith? Was he influenced, as a homeopath, by the alchemical traditions that preceded him? We might never know, but in our mythic-poetic history of magick and the plant familiar, he certainly seems to be carrying on a spiritual impetus begun long ago.

Today, the practice of modern metaphysics and alternative healing has led to a renewed interest in the faery faith traditions of our ancestors and the practice of alchemy. While the initial call starts with what the serious practitioner of these traditions would see as superficial: an interest in Tinkerbell-like faery artwork, oracle cards and benign texts with little root in traditional folklore, or an interest in purely psychological alchemy, those who hunger will eventually seek out the faery faith folk lore of an older time, or begin to conduct laboratory alchemical experiments to bring one in direct contact with the forces of nature and the divine.

Herbalism

Herbalism isn't specific to any one tradition, but rather a discipline that spans many cultures and traditions. Most tribal people have a form of plant-based medicine because plants were the only medicines available to them. These treatments grew into the more complex medicinal systems that form the underpinning of Ayurveda and Traditional Chinese Medicine. European Paganism has its own form of medicine in the form of Greek and Roman traditions, including an elemental theory not unlike those of the East, but such traditions fell into disuse with the rise of the Dark Ages when much of our medicinal and spiritual lore was lost. The wisdom was retained in part by alchemical and occult traditions surviving underground in Europe and formed the nucleus of some of the contemporary scientific movement.

The modern herbal movement draws from all of these paths. In America, herbalists claim lore on indigenous plants from indigenous herbal traditions, yet such herbalists do not necessarily practice Native American forms of spirituality. This knowledge is instead combined with both European research and folklore regarding plant medicine. "Old wives' tales" and wise woman lore gets mixed and mingled with aromatherapy, Chinese element theory and Ayurvedic nutritional advice, giving us an eclectic and wholly modern but very workable system.

When I began my venture into the herbal world, I was extremely fortunate to apprentice to a teacher who held a "green spirit" view on herbalism, continuing the "wise woman" philosophy as she called it. We started right out with the concept that the Witches of Europe were part of a European herbal tradition and their lore has been incorporated into our herbal traditions, whether we realize it or not. I felt right at home. She believed in the faery races, nature spirits and genus loci, or spirit of the place, and while our focus was medicinal herbalism and its application, our studies were not disconnected from our spirits.

Nightly activities in our apprenticeship, which were optional, were more ritualistic and esoterically oriented. It was interesting to watch my classmates bond not only with each other, but also with specific plants during our apprenticeship journey. One made friends with Chickweed and another found a strong ally in Chamomile. I personally bonded with Lemon Balm and had a strange flirtation with Lady's Mantle. I never quite got a connection with Cleavers as much as I tried, though Burdock and I came to an understanding. And while Nettle in the classroom was a favorite, it eluded me in the fields and gardens, where it is normally known for getting in the way. A classmate and friend couldn't get rid of Nettle in her garden, so she decided, metaphorically, to embrace it, lest she would be stung. Each of the plants had its own personality, as distinct, if not more so, as the personalities of students in the class. My approach to the personal spirits of the plants continued long after my apprenticeship, with new relationships to Lobelia, Mugwort and Solomon's Seal.

Our harvesting practices included prayers, offerings and permission from the plant spirit before we harvested the herb, mixing old and new ways of making peace with the plant. My teacher, Wendy, taught us that it was not only right, but it also made more effective medicine, and that remedies from an herbalist who has a spiritual relationship with the particular herb being used were infinitely more effective that mass-produced remedies found in health food stores. Even if the mass-produced herb had a more consistent laboratory level of chemical constituents, there is healing magick in the process of growing, harvesting and making of medicines. Certain herbalists have even been said to coax healing properties out of their most beloved herbs that were not typical of the herb in any textbook. This accounts for why certain tribes would use one herb for a particular illness, and another tribe would use the same species for an entirely different use. Each tribe, as a whole, had a different relationship with the plant. Today, each herbalist has a different relationship with the plant, through its plant spirit, whether the herbalist subscribes to the idea of plant spirits or not. It's inherent in the work of the green healer. Those that are truly conscious of it make more effective herbal healers.

One idea that truly struck me during our lessons was that direct knowledge had been and could be communicated directly from the plant world to the human world. Though I had experienced it directly in Witchcraft and then in a different way in flower essence training, I was amazed at this simple idea. To the view of modern science, herbal lore is scientific, discovered through a process of trial and error, like all other sciences. Yet, if your friend went to the first wise woman and asked her for a cure to a cold, flu, rash or any other illness, and she, in error, gave you a deadly poison, do you think you, or anyone else in the tribe would go back to that "wise" woman for another cure? How much experimentation would she be able to do? It takes only one mistake to end the process when dealing with humans and their health. But when they ask any healer from a surviving indigenous tradition, such as those in the Brazilian rain forest, how they learned about the healing properties of plants, scientists receive an answer that bewilders them. The tribal healers tell the scientists studying them that the healer's advance herbal knowledge on plant species and their medicinal properties comes not from trial and error, but directly from the plants themselves. The plants tell the healer what they cure, how they are used, how to be prepared and what to mix them with to be most effective. And while plants do speak metaphorically through color, shape and habitat, a teaching known in the West as the Doctrine of Signatures, the Brazilian healers are mostly referring to direct telepathic communication from plant to human.

Modern herbalists are taking a cue from these traditions by attempting to establish their own psychic contact with the plant spirits and incorporate that information along with both traditional information and scientific research on the chemical constituents of the plants.

Shamanism and Shamanic Plant Spirit Healing

Indigenous shamans are well known as the keepers of herbal lore and practical medicine, as well as spirit medicine, though it was through the popular work of Carlos Castaneda and his first book, *The Teachings of Don Juan: A Yaqui Way of Knowledge*, that the concept of plants as allies and spirit teachers first reached the general public. His teacher, Don Juan, specifically teaches him about three plants in his Toltec system of sorcery: Datura, Psilocybin and Peyote. Both Datura and the Psilocybin mushrooms are referred to as allies for the sorcerer, each with specific use, benefits, drawbacks and rituals. They are only used by sorcerers to gain extra power, while Peyote, called Mescalito, is considered a teacher and protector, because anyone can approach it. Don Juan describes them in terms of entities, of spirit, and while Datura and the "Little Smoke" mixture of the mushrooms usually takes no visible form as allies, Peyote takes an anthropomorphized form in the vision of the seeker, appearing as a man, as light, or as a terror to the user. So here we have a native Mexican tradition of distinguishing plant spirits and their use, beyond herb-craft or simple charms. Each grants different knowledge and powers. Castaneda's controversial sorcery differs from what most consider shamanism, and tends to represent a "warrior's path" different from the healers and adventurers described in other popular books, such as Michael Harner's *Way of the Shaman*.

Plant spirit healing refers to the use of the plant's spirit, its consciousness, with or without the actual herbal remedy to facilitate healing. The concept is used in conjunction with a wide variety of what is now considered "core shamanic" techniques in the modern metaphysical healing world. In core shamanism, a term coined by anthropologist-turned-shaman Michael Harner, founder of the Institute of Shamanic Studies, one may journey to retrieve "animal medicine." Through the use of a repetitive sound such as a drum to facilitate a trance state of consciousness, what Harner refers to as the *shamanic state of consciousness* (SSC), one has access to the otherworld, also known as non-ordinary reality. Imbalances, illness and misfortune are shamanically described as either a disconnection from one's primary animal totem, or the need to connect to another new animal totem to teach you new ways, consciously and intuitively, of living. Each animal is said to have a wisdom known as its "medicine," an intrinsic quality or energy that address imbalances between humanity and nature. In many native traditions, the concept of magickal power is translated as *medicine*, to emphasize the healing and communal quality of that power.

Plant spirit healing is an extrapolation of this concept of animal spirit medicine. Ideally all things in nature have a healing quality. By connecting to the spirit of nature, we can connect with that healing quality, that medicine, and adjust our personal relationship with ourselves, our world and divinity. Plants are a natural choice for working with spirit medicine in a shamanic context, as they quite literally have medicine within their physical bodies, so they would have the corresponding energy medicine within their spirit. I believe the traditions of homeopathy, flower essences and modern spiritual herbalism are intuitive attempts to reconcile with this shamanic reality. Many herbalists do this work already without the need of the classic core shamanic techniques, and many homeopaths are unconsciously connected to the spirit of their remedies, even though they appear to practice in an intellectual and clinical way.

Author and healer Eliot Cowan, author of *Plant Spirit Medicine* and teacher of a tradition of healing by the same name, gets much of the credit for popularizing this concept in the modern herbal world. He leads lectures, workshops and extended trainings in the technique as he's established it. An initiated and recognized shamanic practitioner in the traditions of the Huichol, a native people in western central Mexico, Cowan has taken the plant spirit lore learned from the Huichol and added the Chinese system of the five elements, pulse diagnosis, and a single homeopathic remedy, to craft a unique system of healing.

The Huichol's teachings are the first to most clearly articulate to modern healers, via Cowan, the relationship between the plant spirit and healing. The Huichol believe that one does not need to ingest the plant, but simply "dream" or receive the spirit of the plant from a dreamer (shamanic healer). They are not the only people to hold this concept, as it's the underpinning idea behind almost all of the traditions described in this chapter, and you can find many herbalists and healers, traditional and modern, who speak with the plants and "hear" the plants respond in a variety of ways.

Since the public release of Cowan's work, a variety of new traditions and interpretations of plant spirit medicine have appeared. Some are directly influenced by Cowan's work, or have been adapted by those who apprenticed with him, while others seem to approach the work from a completely different angle, yet arrive at a very similar spiritual place. Most notable among these in the Witchcraft tradition specifically is the work of the current magister of the Cultus Sabbati, Daniel A. Shulke, author of the groundbreaking modern grimoires *Ars Philtron: Concerning the Aqueous Cunning of the Potion and its Praxis in the Green Arte Magical* and *Viridarium Umbris: The Pleasure-Garden of Shadow*. While written in the context of a branch of Traditional Witchcraft known as Sabbatic Craft, in a mythos involving Cain and Lilith, it still expresses the belief in the powerful spirits behind the plants used in European and American Witchcraft as well as emphasizes a partnership with the plants in order to attain direct gnosis. Schulke's work has been extremely influential for me and other Witches as we seek to synthesize teachings from a variety of spiritual sources into a Witchcraft context.

In the novel *Mistress of Spices* by Chitra Banerjee Divakaruni, a seemingly fictional system of Indian spice magic describes a phenomenon similar to the plant familiar, the "root spice" or *mahamul*:

"But for each person, there is one special spice... It is called mahamul, the root spice, and for each person it is different. Mahumul to enhance fortune, to bring success, or joy, to avert ill luck. When you do not know how else to help someone, you must go deep into your being and search out the mahamul."

Divakaruni describes a very plausible system of magick akin to the cunning arts of the Witch.

According to science, plants have a wide range of active chemicals that can heal animals and humans, yet generally don't seem to derive any evolutionary benefit from possessing these chemicals. Some of these chemicals are assumed to be protective, but most are not. According to healers, plants have an independent intelligence as well as their own wants and needs. And they want to be used by the animal world. They want to be eaten. They want their role as medicine. They evolve and grow in relationship to all of creation and must forge links with the animal world. They grow from the mineral world, absorbing nutrients from the land. They draw down light from the heavens, from the Sun and process it in direct way that animals are incapable of doing. Through their medicines and spiritual properties, they forge a link to us. The rest of the animal world knows what plants cure their ailments. Many herbalists discovered their lore by watching animals eat various plants in particular seasons, or watching what animals with particular illnesses ate. Through magick, direct psychic contact and spirit communication, humans are learning to regain the intuitive wisdom they lost when we evolved from the animalistic world. All of these traditions, unconscious, intuitive or fully conscious, are forging links between the human world and the Green World through partnership with plant spirits.

Chapter Three:
Totemic Plants

 he role of the plant familiar is an amalgam of three traditional roles performed by spirit allies. First, the plant familiar assumes the role of the familiar spirit, an intermediary between the Witch and the spirit world, specifically in this case the green spirit world, the realm of nature. For a Witch, spirits of this realm include not only the spirits of the living plants, but also the realm collectively known as the World of Faery, including creatures such as the Archfey or Sidhe/Sith, elves, brownies, devas, elementals, genus loci and nature spirits. The plant familiar therefore becomes a primary nature contact, and introduces us to these deeper powers.

As an intermediary, the plant familiar fulfills its second role as a tutelary spirit, a teacher to the Witch. Specifically its area of wisdom is in the work of plants. The familiar will teach the use of plant energy, as well as the crafting of charms, potions and medicines. This teaching relationship is the foundation of our true herbal wisdom. Seeking the plant knowledge directly aligns us with our spiritual ancestors who did the same thing to generate their own traditions of healing. On a deeper level, some familiars can outline a path of not just intellectual knowledge, occult secrets, and techniques, but a path of true gnosis and personal enlightenment through the green doorway leading back to eternal paradise.

And finally, the plant familiar fills the role of the totem spirit. This idea is unfamiliar to most of us who automatically think of a totem as an animal spirit phenomenon, but totems can technically refer to any spirit that has kinship with a group or individual.

Totemism

The word *totem*, derived from the Ojibwa root word *oode*, refers to a kinship relationship, and in its strictest sense, totemism is associated with the guardian and guiding spirits of a group of people, such as a tribe, clan or village. In fact, some traditions will state that a non-human entity, often an animal spirit, is the ancestor or founder of the group, and its spirit is now the group's totem. Totemism becomes a part of both cultural and religious identity. The totem might have an individual relationship with members of the group, but functions predominantly for the group as a whole.

In the modern lore of animal totems, the animal totem is much more individually oriented. Perhaps this is a mark of the modern world, or the rise of the individualistic Age of Aquarius, though the South American shamans of Michael Harner's journey also believed in individual animal spirit relationships for healing.

In our metaphysical lore, the totem animal either embodies the natural characteristics of the animal through physical looks and behavioral tendencies, or through personal and spiritual characteristics, the "medicine" the individual is learning to embody in this lifetime. Both can be occurring simultaneously, with the physical characteristics being more inherited talents, such as a clan totem connection, while the personal medicine emphasizes individual development in this lifetime.

For example, people who look and act bird-like usually have a bird totem. You can tell the features of the face, the curve of the nose, the lightness of the build and a certain "flighty" quality. Many people can be described in terms of animalistic qualities, either in features, or behaviors. Most common are feline and canine attributes, as those are the animals most domesticated today in households. If one looks clearly enough at others, a whole range of other animal characteristics can be found. Look closely at your friends, family and coworkers. What do you see? Supporting the tradition of cultural group totem identity, you might see such animal characteristics passed among family members. This too harkens back to the idea of the medieval familiar being inherited in the family, passed from parent to child. Perhaps that is how such spirits manifest outside of a tribal context.

In terms of spiritual medicine, that can be harder to determine and distinguish. Someone who is far along on their path, whether via conscious spiritual discipline or simple chronology, can embody the spiritual characteristics of the animal totem they are learning to embrace. Take again the time-honored example of the dog, and its medicinal quality of loyalty. If a person intrinsically has difficulty with loyalty, perhaps pointing to past life experiences as one betrayed or a betrayer, dog medicine in this lifetime can teach that person about trust and loyalty. The more this person embraces the medicine and "learns its lessons," the more he or she may exhibit the qualities of loyalty, and thereby the qualities of the dog. Many do so with no conscious knowledge of their totem but life circumstance leads them to similar revelations; spiritual practitioners believe these persons are unconsciously heeding the call of the totem through dreams and instinct.

Both of these totemic modes of operating are in harmony with the Traditional Craft concept of the Fetch. Be it a part of the soul complex or a spirit-beast outside of yourself and aligned with the soul complex, the Fetch's animalistic qualities are something to be discovered, embraced, and embodied on the path to personal enlightenment.

So how does the plant familiar act as a totem? At first glance, the operations of the animal world seem entirely different than that of the plant world. But both are aspects of nature. Both open a door to a deep wisdom that cannot be found in the realm of human philosophy, but must be experienced to be understood. However, while everybody has an animal totem, because everybody is at heart an animal of flesh and blood evolved out of this natural kingdom, not everyone has a plant totem. I'm sure you've noticed that some people have a natural connection and an interest and inclination for the green realm. We sometimes describe it as a "green thumb," though I will admit that growing window plants is not necessarily the mark of someone's spiritual path, for I had the classic "black thumb" until I truly opened to my spiritual path and heard the Call of the Green. Yet my first experience of a plant "journey" in a flower essence training connected me to a spirit that was like an amalgam of the plant world, a green chimera, and it acted as guide and guardian for further journeys until my relationships with specific plants became established. It fulfilled the role of the totem and familiar before I ever began to consciously apply these terms and concepts to the plant spirits. But once the gate was open, my thumb was like an emerald and my relationship with living plants improved dramatically.

Yet in the metaphysical community, it is true that each individual is called to a different path. Some are really fascinated by the world of minerals and stones. They can't pass by a rock shop or display without stopping to take a look.

Others are called by a deep love and compassion to animals. Some seek out the more sublime teachings of the angels and archangels. Still others relate best to nature: in the wild woods, cultivated garden, or through a profound connection to the Faery spirits. I call this plant-based connection the Call of the Green. It's an opportunity for spiritual development through the plant world; to have your spiritual blood run green with the living light of plants, and to grow wise in the way the plant world grows wise. The rare person hears more than one call, and can braid and weave these multiple paths together in a manner that benefits them all.

Totemism can occur with any of these spirits, for it implies a connection and kinship with the spirit involved. While the idea of a tribe started by a powerful animal spirit is most common in native traditions, we too have creation stories linking us to the plant world. In Norse myth, the first humans were made from trees. Man was made from Ash and woman from Elm. In the myths of the desert people, such as the Egyptians or Hebrews, humanity is crafted from clay, which indicates ancestry in the mineral realm. All sorts of myths in the Witchcraft traditions tell tales that we are descended directly from the gods, the faeries or the fallen angels, granting us the "Witchblood" and our magickal and psychic abilities.

As modern humans, we live today because of the animals, plants and mineral we ingest. Mythically, they are related to us. Plant totemism is simply intensifying the connection with a particular plant, becoming blood-sap kin through ritual, ingestion, and magick.

Doctrine of Signatures

Plants speak to us in a variety of ways, just as animals do. While direct communication is ideal, it is less reliable and trustworthy in the beginning, so we look to more definable communications to start with. We learn the metaphysical medicine of the animal by looking at its traditional folklore, its habitat, and the characteristics of the animal's life cycle. We do the same for plants. In fact, one system of understanding this plant communication is known in the west as the Doctrine of Signatures. Though this system is found in a variety of cultures, in its most basic form, it tells us the shape, size and color of a plant give an indication of its medicinal value.

According to the Doctrine of Signatures, herbs that look like a part of the body are used to treat illnesses in that part of the body and act as a tonic for overall health of that organ. For example, the leaf of the lungwort looks like a lung, and is used for respiratory illness. The walnut is reminiscent of a brain, and is used in many cultures for brain illnesses and to stimulate memory. The berries of the hawthorn are the color of blood, used to heal the blood and circulatory system. Solomon's seal root looks like the spine, or ligaments and tendons, and is used to for the connective tissues, bones and back.

Other aspects of the doctrine are more interpretive and less literal. The yellow of dandelion flowers for example is an indication of how dandelion cures the yellow of jaundice from liver disease. The regenerative quick-growing power of comfrey signifies how it helps regenerate tissues damaged or cut in the body. The major changes over the lifecycle of motherwort, giving it a different look, indicates how motherwort is used in women's reproductive and menopausal health. The uterine shaped mark on the leaf of red clover also indicates its use in reproductive health.

Many of the magickal correspondences of plants used in a variety of folk traditions are not arbitrarily created, but correspond with the physical attributes of the plant. Nettles have stingers and are used in Mars warrior magick to protect, defend and to make people let go of you. Mugwort, when burned and inhaled, gives a pleasant mild euphoria and opens one up to intuition, so it is associated with psychic powers.

Asafetida is used to banish harm, and when you burn it, it smells awful; everything wants to leave the area. Myrrh is a preservative used in ancient embalming. It is also used in protection magick, to preserve a home, area, or person from harm.

Therefore, these medicinal properties, once known, can also indicate spiritual properties. Echinacea, along serving as an immune enhancement, is also used for snake bites. Shamanic practitioners can use it to remove the spiritual venom of unwanted entities, and people. Yarrow clots the blood and seals up wounds. The spirit of yarrow can do the same with wounds to the energy system and aura.

In our plant totemic work, we look even more symbolically to the Doctrine of Signatures, associating characteristics with the four elements, the astrological planets and sacred geometry. Each can give us a deeper understanding of the plant familiar's totemic quality – the wisdom we are seeking to learn from it on our path to gnosis.

The Elements

Earth: Earth plants bring stability, grounding and abundance. They deal with matters of home, health, and finance. Earth plants have strong, deep, or large roots which are often nutritious. They have an "earthy" quality or smell "earthier" than most other plants.

Air: Air plants bring the gifts of quick thinking, clarity of mind, memory, and words. They deal with areas of learning and expression. These plants are tall and thin, have beautiful, aromatic flowers, and have a relationship with the winds, particularly in terms of spreading their seeds or otherwise stimulating our imagination.

Fire: Fire plants are protective and energetic. They energize, inspire and revitalize body and soul. They can be physically hot to the tongue, being spicy, or they draw blood, being sharp and thorny.

Water: Water plants are healing. They help stimulate an awareness of our emotions. Water plants usually either contain a lot of water internally, grow by bodies of water that they need to survive, or cup and hold water after rainfall.

The Planets

Sun: Plants ruled by the Sun are typically yellow or golden in color and have a strong relationship with the Sun, above and beyond what most plants have. Plants that make one more photosensitive, that move easily with the Sun, or relate to the heart have solar correspondences.

Moon: Moon-ruled plants are those that are night blooming, white or silvery white in color, and/or enhance psychic ability. They usually have a strong water resonance.

Mercury: Mercurial herbs are those that stimulate or calm the mind and nervous system, have a lot of seeds, or grow in abundance. Mercury plants are very adaptable, and have a special relationship with air.

Venus: Venusian plants are those that work well in the feminine reproductive system. The flowers can be pink, and in general, flowers with five petals are most often associated with Venus.

Mars: The herbs of Mars are fiery. They too are spiky, easily drawing blood and are spicy. They often have a high iron content. They tend to grow at boundaries and borders, and are often good for the blood and circulatory system.

Jupiter: Spices are primarily ruled by Jupiter—anything rich and warming and fit for a king. Plants with blue and purple flowers are traditional for Jupiter, and roots that heal the liver and gall bladder are Jupiterian in nature.

Saturn: Saturn plants are usually toxic. At the very least, they are grounding and earthy. Saturn plants work on the bones and can be tenacious weeds, difficult to get rid of from a garden. Saturn flowers, like the Moon, are usually white, and five and six petals are common.

Uranus: Uranian correspondences, like all of the outer planets, are fairly new. Herbs that are stimulating to the nervous system, like coffee, are defined as Uranian. Things that have an unusual or startling nature are ruled by Uranus. Anything that heightens awareness is Uranian.

Neptune: Herbs of Neptune induce dream-like visions. Flowers that are sea-green or foam-blue can have connections with this outer planet. Many entheogens are considered to be ruled or co-ruled by Neptune. Plants fermented into alcohol have an affinity for Neptune, as well as plants that have a relationship with water, and in particular, the sea. Herbs that hold a lot of water, and fruits that hold water, such as grapes, are also ruled by the sea king.

Pluto: Pluto's herbs, like Saturn's, are most often toxic. They are the banes that can kill you. They are also the plants we are most attracted to. Some rich plants and spices, due to the rich earthy nature of the underworld, can be considered ruled by, or co-ruled by, Pluto.

A key component of the Doctrine of Signatures not usually discussed by practical practitioners and that has been brought into modern use through the disciplines of flower essence consultants is the sacred geometry of the plant, and most specifically, its flower. Sacred geometry is the study of the underlying patterns within creation, and flowers express this in the shape they form through their petals. The numerological and geometric significance of the petals can help determine the nature of the plant's inherent spirit.

Four-petaled flowers are sacred to the four directions, the four seasons, and the four elements of earth, air, fire and water.

They are concerned with the balance of cycles and seasons. Four-petaled flowers promote harmony of the four basic components, and when used with human beings, they balance the body, emotions, mind and soul. They are the flowers of the magick circle and the medicine wheel.

Six-petaled flowers are the stars of the macrocosm in the Green World. The six pointed star is a symbol of the heavens and the planets, and is used in rituals of the hexagram to evoke and banish heavenly forces. The symbol of two interlocked triangles is one of integration, and many of the six-petaled flowers are used to not only unlock the mysteries of the heavens, but to integrate those mysteries within the psyche. Flower essences made from six-petaled flowers are used to integrate changes, or bring someone out of shock.

Three-petaled flowers are similar to six-petaled flowers. They promote a sense of harmony between mind, body and spirit. Two-petaled flowers help us resolve our awareness of duality and work in healthy balance with polarity, rather than remain divided. Seven-petaled flowers seek the mysteries that cannot be easily explained.

To the Witch, the most important plants are those with five-petaled flowers, as they mimic the image of the pentagram. Five-petaled flowers are especially sacred to the Goddess Venus. The pentagram is often thought of by modern Pagans as strictly a symbol of protection, but it's much more than that. It is a gateway. Witches hold the ritual pentacle, a paten, or simply five outspread fingers up to the four directions to open the gateways to the four elemental realms. Ceremonial magicians and hermetically influenced Witches draw the five pointed star in various ways to unlock and lock the gates to the elemental realms. So while the pentagram can be used for protection, it is more accurate to think of it as a gateway. The door can be "opened" to let things in or "closed" to block unwanted energies, and talismans of the pentagram can be consecrated to block specific energies and let in other forces, as desired by the Witch or magician.

Flowers that have the same shape as the pentagram also have the same powers as the pentagram, and open and close the gates, not to the elements, but to the realm of life force, of spirit. The pentagram is sometimes depicted as the human body in medieval drawings, with the head, two legs and two arms as the points of the star. With this depiction, we realize it is a symbol of incarnation, of life force, of the spirit entering the world of form and creating the body. These flowers are some of the most powerful magickal plants, usually either very healing or very toxic, making the favorite balms and banes of Witches. They help the life force incarnate and remain healthy, or discarnate, and leave the world of form.

There is a spectrum of five-petaled flowers. On one end of the spectrum are the flowers that open the gate to life force and heal. They include Vervain and St. John's Wort. These flowers bring life and light. On the far end are the flowers that remove life force and do harm. Belladonna and Datura are among their number. And some are somewhere in the middle, like Vinca. These middle flowers are not exactly deadly, but do have some toxic qualities. Many shift their position on the spectrum depending on the dose, becoming more or less toxic. Both ends of the spectrum are used in the classic image of the Witch's flying ointment.

Fig. 6: Four-Petaled Flower

Fig. 7: Five-Petaled Flower

Fig. 8: Six-Petaled Flower

Other geometries of flowers can influence their use in magick and medicine, but the most common ones to identify are the four, five and six-petaled flowers.

Plant Gazing

Sit quietly before a plant in nature. Breathe deeply. Enter a light meditative state by being aware of your breath. Gaze at the plant. Let your eyes go into a soft focus, where you do not stare at any part of the plant, but look at it as a whole. Allow your mind to drift as you gaze at your plant. Let your mind float from characteristic to characteristic of the plant, shifting your gaze from soft focus to hard focus. Take notice of the flowers. Take notice of the leaves, the stems, and the roots. How does it grow? Where does it grow? How does it feel to you? Do you see the four elements in this plant? What is the blend of the elements like? Do you see the planets within it? What seems dominant? Allow your other senses to come into play, along with sight. Smell the plant. If it is possible and safe to do so, taste the plant. Listen to the hum, to the natural vibration of the plant. Touch the plant. What mysteries does it reveal to you?

When you are done, thank the plant and ground your awareness in day-to-day consciousness.

The Three Kin

In my exploration of plant familiars and their totemic qualities in my Craft, I have experienced three types of allies from this realm – what I see as three types of "kin." While all of our human relationships are individualized and unique (and we could say the same about our green spirit allies) we can characterize our human relationships in categories. The relationship people have with their mother is generally different from that of a sibling, uncle, cousin or offspring. Likewise, the relationships we have with different plants can be looked at in terms of familial categories, yet have very different purposes and qualities. The three primary categories we can have with the plant world is determined by the plants' general qualities. I use the terms *balm*, *bane* and *tree teacher* for the relationships I've experienced. The plant spirits themselves suggested these categories to me.

Balms

Balms are the traditional healing herbs of folklore and magick. They are the ones that generally bring healing and blessings in magick, and in medicine they tend to be the most powerful healers. Some we understand scientifically. These plants have potent chemicals that act as medicines in the bodies of humans and animals. Their active constituents also give us clues about their magickal properties, as the two usually share a common thread. The balms have become the staples of medical herbalism, and are considered powerful plants in magickal traditions as well. While all plants can have spiritual properties, these are the plants that stand out the most in our medicine traditions and have a lot of lore around their origin and use. One could say the plant spirits of these balms are very active and bright. They enhance life force. Sadly, many are considered weeds, and while being very healing, they live on the edge of society, not in the heart of the community, like the archetype of the European Witch.

Banes

The banes are the dark twins to the balms. They are the toxins, the plants that can bring sickness, madness and death to those who are not careful. Their active constituents are poisons to humans and some animals. Some are purgatives, making us vomit. Others are intoxicating or made into alcoholic sacraments. Alcohol, while we can process it in the body and it can make us feel good, is technically a toxin made from plant matter. Banes can be true psychedelics, inducing otherworldly experiences, and most are simply toxins; the entheogenic effects of some banes stem from their toxicity. Like the balms, they too are surrounded by lore, and are often associated with Witchcraft, magick and shamanism. Banes were traditionally used in the classic medieval versions of flying ointment. We now speculate that certain other ingredients inhibited the more lethal aspects of the toxins, or the medieval Witch knew exactly what dose to give. While banes remove life force, they also truly help open the gates to the spirit world. They are the teachers of the mysteries, and through their partnership and careful use, a Witch can gain knowledge and perhaps even wisdom.

Tree Teachers

The trees are in some ways the most important of the plant spirits. While the balms and banes act as guides, the trees are the teachers. To the plant world, they are the high priests and high priestesses of the green. They are the teachers to the plant world and, if we're lucky, our teachers as well. They can act as guardians. They are also the keeper of the records of our planet, or the records for at least as long as cellular life has been here. They can work in tandem with stone and land spirits. Much of our magickal lore is associated with trees and their spirits, from the famous poetry of Oak, Ash and Thorn to the descriptions of the world tree as the center of the universe. The Norse mostly likely saw the world tree as the ash or yew, both sacred in the Northern Traditions. The Celts immortalized the trees in their Ogham alphabet, with a set of correspondences relating to the Celtic trees and referred to as the Tree alphabet. The Druids most likely take their name from duir, the oak. Trees are seen as symbols of wisdom worldwide because of their longevity, their ability to connect heaven and earth, and their power of regeneration, protection and medicine.

These designations of spirits are poetic, not absolute. We could in turn distinguish plant spirit families within the lines of botany and science. The dividing line between balm and bane is not always so clear. In essence, dosage is what makes the difference between toxin and medicine. The famous physician-alchemist Paracelsus is often quoted for saying, "The dose makes the poison." In actuality, he said, "All things are poison and nothing is without poison, only the dose permits something not to be poisonous." In homeopathy, dangerous plants, like aconite, are standard remedies. Paracelsus believed that "evil" or "poison" can cure its like by expelling it. Some blessed medicines do great harm with improper use, application, or dose. But the general character of the plants can be divided into life giving, life taking, and teaching. Befriend a plant spirit in each of these categories and you will be far on your way to walking the Green Road.

Part Two:
Entering the Garden

Chapter Four:
Cultivating Your Allies

hile working in the green realm, it would be easy to think of cultivation as simply gardening, but when I talk about cultivating your plant spirits, I'm talking about both an outer world and an inner world process. The surface meaning of cultivation is agricultural improvement, to establish and maintain the ideal conditions for growing plants, usually in a garden. But if you truly observe the plants best known in Witchcraft and healing, many of them thrive under non-human conditions. They grow wild. They grow where we don't want them. They appear in brambles and become what most humans think of as weeds, as nuisances, or as something "wrong" destroying the perfection of the garden or yard. No wonder they are the herbs of Witches, as historically people have felt the same about us. Once we began to judge "good" plants in the garden and weeds as "bad" invaders, we saw people much the same way and divided them into acceptable and unacceptable. So while we can literally cultivate some plants in our gardens of soil, some of the best

Witch gardens look rather wild, atrocious to the civilized gardener. And our next step in cultivation is in the garden of our souls.

Building Relationships with the Plants

Cultivation is, in essence, spending time and attention on something to improve it. While many humans arrogantly think that our placement and care of plants improves them from their state in nature, the improvement I speak of is the improvement of the relationship between the Witch and the plant spirit. Plants are fickle, particularly our power plants in the form of balms and banes. They grow as they will, disturbing our best laid garden plans. Plants react and respond to our thoughts, to our voices, to our music and environment. In essence, they respond to the energy of our consciousness and the environment we create around us. In many ways, they are more honest than people. They do not hide how they feel. Their health immediately reflects their experience. While they can be forgiving for the lack of water or food at times, their patience is not eternal. They feel joy and pain and sadness. As you grow more sensitive to the green spirits you will see this, if you haven't already.

Plant spirits are just like the plants they inhabit. The physical visible vegetation is an expression of the greater green spirit, just as our bodies are a physical manifestation of our own consciousness. Plant spirits are honest, fickle, and have their own needs and wants. In our day and age of relatively modern spiritualism and metaphysics, many have the idea that the spirit world, and by extension the animal, vegetable and mineral realms, are here to serve us. Due to the prevalence of a particular worldview espoused in our Western culture's dominant spiritual text, the Bible, many believe we are given dominion over the Earth and all in it:

*And God said, Let us make man in our image, after our likeness:
and let them have dominion over the fish of the sea, and over the fowl of
the air, and over the cattle, and over all the earth, and over every
creeping thing that creepeth upon the earth. So God created man in his
own image, in the image of God created he him; male and female created
he them. And God blessed them, and God said unto them, Be fruitful,
and multiply, and replenish the earth, and subdue it: and have
dominion over the fish of the sea, and over the fowl of the air, and over
every living thing that moveth upon the earth. And God said, Behold, I
have given you every herb bearing seed, which is upon the face of all the
earth, and every tree, in the which is the fruit of a tree yielding seed; to
you it shall be for meat. And to every beast of the earth, and to every
fowl of the air, and to every thing that creepeth upon the earth,
wherein there is life, I have given every green herb for meat: and it was
so.*

– Genesis 1:26-30 (King James Version)

Today many people, even some studying Witchcraft, assume
that all the Earth is here to serve humanity. The concept is
prevalent in our culture, and much of our modern spiritual
work is in breaking the programming of this dominant
worldview that no longer serves, in order to go back to primal,
Pagan traditions and renew our relationship with the land and
gardens of life in cooperation, not dominion, for we are all
children of the Mother Earth and Father Sky. No one child is
given to another to do as they please. All live together in the
garden. Though life feeds life and there is a cycle of birth and
death, it is only in the human world where we take more than
we need and we damage more than is necessary. I believe this is
due, in part, to the programming of this Biblical teaching.

Many assume dominion equates with domination, and in
some definitions it is solely about control, but in essence
dominion is about lordship, about sovereignty. A sovereign, one
who reigns, is really a servant, a steward. In the ancient Pagan
traditions of Europe, the King was an embodiment of the

divine god, the animal god and/or grain god. The King was married to the Land, and when the Land did well, it was because the King, and through the King, the people, were in right relationship with it. When the Land suffered, it was the King's job to correct it, and Kings were sacrificed for the good of the Land. The King and the Land are one. One title for the Goddess of the Land in the Celtic traditions translates to Sovereignty, She who Reigns. While we think of the King as all powerful, having dominance over a territory, he is really a humble servant when working in harmony with the Land, the Goddess, and the people.

So those of us who seek personal and spiritual sovereignty are really seeking to be servants. Dominion is really about care-taking, about stewardship, rather than control and domination. I think this is the true teaching of the earliest versions of Genesis, distorted over time. Many progressive Christians are returning to this true teaching, seeing environmentalism as a part of their spirituality. When we look to ancient Pagan traditions and current indigenous tribal traditions, we clearly see a partnership with nature, a familial tie and ultimately a sense of care-taking between nature and humanity. This relationship is one of reciprocity, for in these traditions, both matter and spirit are sacred, being simply different expressions of the same divine force.

For those just starting on the path of the green, the idea of serving plant spirits seems strange. Most metaphysical literature is written from the perspective of what the plants, animal, faeries, angels and gods can do for us. Many texts are written on how they can help someone find a job, love, protection and healing. But few texts ask, what can we be doing for them? Why would such non-human spirits serve the human world?

When I asked my own guides about this, they said the spirit world aids humanity so readily because we are in a crisis state.

The old reciprocal relationships are no longer present. Our survival, not just our success, is dependent upon a mutual cooperation that is now minimally maintained by a few traditions that have not been overrun or made bankrupt by political and religious dogma. The spirit world will reach out to support anyone who calls on them at this time in the hopes that when the human's basic needs are met – love, success, health and protection – then the bigger questions will be asked of them, such as: What can I do for *you?* How can I serve? It is the essential mystery question of the ages, characterized by the "Grail question." The Grail Knight on the quest simply needs to ask, "Whom does the grail serve?" to restore the kingdom, but rarely does the seeker ever ask. The same is true today. Our ancestors have given us a potential key to solve our current crisis: service.

Reciprocity is the basic foundation of relationship, of any social or business relationship. True shamans, magicians and Witches understand this and enact it in their work. So our first step in green cultivation is to cultivate the proper attitude and relationship between us and nature. We must transmute the lord and servant mode of our thinking to a co-creational partnership where both parties enjoy and benefit from the relationship.

Gardening – While many of the Witch's herbs tend to grow best in the wild, quite a few of these herbs also do well in gardens and pots, and have become staples in herb, vegetable and flower gardens. Stewardship over a group of plants from the start of their life cycle to the end is quite a powerful way to know all aspects of the plant, and gives the gardener ample opportunity to experience them directly on a daily basis.

Wild Walks – For those who do not garden, and for those plants that do not like to be tended, walking in the fields and woods is an excellent way to encounter and experience the plant allies. Many of my favorite green spirits are wild weeds found all along roadsides and forest edges when walking. Encountering them in the natural habitat helps us understand their own spiritual nature, for the places in which they grow reflect quite a bit about the plants themselves. Look for the amount of sunlight, water, and exposure they are receiving, whether they grow near trees or roadsides, in the light or dark. Interestingly, some of the darkest-natured plants thrive in the light, as they help bring the light into the darkness.

Speaking – Simply talking to plants, be they houseplants, garden plants, or wild weeds and trees, establishes a harmony between the individual and the plant as living, conscious beings. Though much of the lore, both fact and fantasy fiction, will describe many of the trees as having "slow" minds, I've found that once communication is established, which is usually not in words anyway, it's possible to have a fairly normal exchange of information, emotion and energy. Simply speaking words to the plants, with or without direct psychic response, creates a familiarity and bond between human and plant. Singing to the plants is an excellent way of establishing rapport, and is fun for both you and the plants.

Meditation – Deeper communion with the Green World can occur when meditating with, near or under a plant. Shamanically considered to be "dreaming" with the plant, it is a method of journeying to, or journeying with, the plant spirit. Simply entering a trance state while in the presence of the plant's living energy field can help attune you to it.

Harvesting – Rituals of harvesting the plant are some of the most intimate ways of attuning with its spirit. Traditionally permission is asked, and if you are given a positive response, an offering is made. Offerings can include a few coins, water, cakes, beer, wine, honey, milk or bread. Traditionally the offerings are something native to your own land, culture and traditions. I was taught to offer a strand of your hair, i.e. if you take a part of them, you leave a part of you. Traditionally, and particularly for magickal purposes, iron is not used for harvesting, but rather a "faery friendly" metal such as silver, copper, brass or bronze, or simply your hands depending on the harvest. My teachers were practical herbalists at heart, and used scissors. To encourage magickal, and subtle properties in the herb, harvest with the herb in your non-dominant hand, usually the left for most people, and cut with the right. To encourage medicinal properties, harvest with the herb in the right hand, cutting with the left. Traditional astrologically oriented herbalists will choose an appropriate moon phase, moon sign, day of the week and planetary hour for harvesting, based upon the use of the plant.

Consumption – Eating the plant as food, beverage or medicine, creates a strong sympathy with the plant spirit. Having a bit of it within your body helps facilitate the communication and relationship between you and the green ally.

Respect – While all these physical actions have tremendous impact upon your work with the Green World, having a conscious respect and love for the plants is the most important thing you can do. All these rituals help generate this state of consciousness. Some people simply know, feel and acknowledge the power and wisdom of the Green World, and the Green World, in turn, acknowledges them.

Offering – Rituals of offering to the plant world, be it nature spirits in general, or to a specific tree or plant, can help build a relationship. Offerings are similar to faery offerings – a bit of beer, wine, mead or other alcohol, milk, butter, bread, honey, pastries, candy, cocoa leaves, cornmeal or tobacco can all work.

Sacrament – A shared sacrament, an offering in which you both partake and share a portion with the land and plant spirits, is an excellent way to bond with nature's spirits. By allowing the plant to absorb a portion, both energetically and chemically, while at the same time you are consuming a portion of the same material, you create a link between yourself and the plant.

The Huzel

Sacramental meals and offerings are found in many Witchcraft traditions. Most common are the rites of Cakes and Ale in Wicca. While many today use the ritual of cakes and ale in a simple celebratory manner, and as a method of grounding the energy into the body via digestion, it is traditional to offer a portion to the gods and spirits. In fact, it is most traditional to offer a portion to the spirit world before any human consumes the sacrament. In the Northern traditions of Paganism, we find the ritual sacrifice offering of drink and food in the *blót*. Technically, the word blót is closely related to blood, and can mean a ritual meal from a sacrificed animal, though most today use it to mean any type of sacrificial offering of food or drink to the gods. *Húsel* is another term for sacrifice, sometimes used instead of the word blót, as it can refer to non-animal sacrifice. A *symbel* is a similar ritual, usually a ritual feast of both food and drink, consisting of boasting and oath making with offerings of mead from a horn. These Northern traditions have influenced other forms of the Craft, as many today make use of a Húsel rite. I prefer the spelling Huzel or Houzle to distinguish it from the Northern reconstruction traditions and place it more in the realm of modern Witchcraft.

In Traditional Witchcraft we find the concept of the "Red Meal"— a meal consisting of red bread and red drink, usually wine. I first came across the concept in the work of Nigel Jackson, especially in *Call of the Horned Piper* and *Masks of Misrule* and later expanded upon in the work of Robin Artisson. The concept of a similar sacrament is also found in the writings of Robert Cochrane, William Gray and Doreen Valiente. It obviously has associations with ritual sacrifice of flesh and blood, like any good Eucharistic meal, but it is done most often with bread. Some also think of the dead as eating "red" food such as the apple or pomegranate seed.

When I first experienced a Red Meal-Huzel with Traditional Craft practitioners, it consisted of breaking the bread partially and pouring wine into the break, and offering a bit to the spirits of the land and consuming a small portion for ourselves. They alluded to reddening the bread with other fluids, but for my sake that night it was wine as I did not have that blood bond with them.

While this rite can be performed as the sacrament in a larger ritual in a formal sacred space, such as the Green Circle of Chapter Six, it can also be done alone as an offering in the spirit of love and communion to the Green World. To perform the rite, obtain a dark bread or cake of good quality and red wine. If you can bake the bread yourself, all the better, but a good quality commercial bread can do. Pour the wine onto the bread, or dip the bread into the chalice/horn of wine. Blow upon the moistened bread three times with intentions of love, power and wisdom – one for each breath. You are giving a bit of your life force in each breath, and in turn might receive a blessing from the Green World. Recite these or similar words, naming the specific plant you want to work with in the blank, or simply saying "Spirits of the Land" for a general offering:

Beloved Mother,
Both Cruel and Kind.
Watchful Father,
Of Tide and Time.
We share this meal in your name,
In your heart and in your mind.
We share this meal with the spirits of _____.
Spirits of the love and trust,
May there always be good will,
May there always be peace between us.
Blessed be.

Break off a larger portion and place it on the ground, near the plant or tree to whom you are making the offering. Take the smaller portion and eat it. Back away from the offering you leave, to allow the spirits undisturbed time to consume it. Thank the spirits in your own way and either continue your ritual, or say farewell.

If you are working with specific gods, you can use their names in place of "Mother" and "Father" or adapt the working to suit your own style.

The Green Man

When examining the trial transcripts of the witchcraft persecutions, modern Witches seek to find threads of truth among the propaganda, lies and repressed sexuality found throughout the material. One of the beliefs among some modern Witches when looking at these patterns is that the "Devil" or from our perspective, the Horned God, is the "giver" of animal familiar spirits. Known by many names, the Horned God is both the hunter and the hunted, and is considered the master of animals. One of his depictions is considered to be the Celtic Cernunnos on the Gunderstrup Cauldron, which shows him in a meditative position, handling a snake and surrounded peacefully by wild creatures. The Horned God image became corrupted into the image of the Christian Devil, but his mastery over animals was retained in bits of truth, as the one who would provide animal familiars to the budding Witch. He can be considered a spirit teacher, helping the Witch who practiced the vestiges of a European shamanic tradition. The Horned God gave the deeper instructions into the masteries of the familiar-fetch.

In my own teachings and personal visions, I see the God of Witches as two-faced, like the Roman Janus. On one side he is the lord of death and darkness, Lord of animals, the underworld, Bearer of Horns. His colors are black and blood red. One the other side, he is the lord of life and light, Sun Child and Grain King, Green Man and Plant Lord. His colors are green and gold. Together, these two faces hold the gates of life and death, opening the way for the Witch to travel in spirit, as a guardian and gatekeeper. He dwells at the threshold of the mysteries. So while the Horned God is the master of flesh and blood, giver of animal familiars, the Green Man is the master of sap and root, the giver of plant familiars.

As all things have their opposite and compliment, in the realm of the God, the Green Man is the flip-side of the more familiar Witchcraft figure of the Horned God. In the journey of the Wheel of the Year, he manifests first as the new born sun in the heavenly overworld. He descends to the world upon rays of light absorbed by the new vegetation and is reborn in the world as the Green Man. He grows to maturity as the "corn" grows from green to gold, becoming the Grain King. He then gives up his rule to the dark lord who rises at Midsummer from the underworld. He is sacrificed, and the light begins a journey down to the underworld to await rebirth as the new Sun Child.

The Green Man is found in Catholic Church iconography as well as in the lore of the Sufis, as the hidden prophet Khezr, the immortal adept of vegetation and the secret master of the waters of life. He is found in the mythology of agricultural gods across the world, such as Osiris in his green form of vegetable life.

As the Horned God is the master of animal familiars, the Green God is the master of the plant familiars. He too has a benevolent side, expressed in the balms. Here we see the Green Man in his familiar leafy face, often hidden in carvings within Christian Churches. While the relationship between the Green-faced man in the carvings and Pagan fertility and vegetation gods makes quite a bit of poetic sense, we don't know for historic certainty if the image of the leaf-faced man was truly a part of any ancient Paganism. But when we look into the poetry of our hearts, we know it's true. And we return to it now in modern Paganism.

In my own visions, I know the Green God also has a dark side, if not malevolent, depending on how you approach him. I have been instructed to call him the "Green Devil." He shows us the shadow of forest and the shadow of our own souls. Not all things in the Green World are bright and beautiful, or completely safe. Vegetation has a dark side, expressed in the banes of the Green World. Here we have the Witch's garden of wild hedge herbs, those used to induce spirit flight in the ointments of old. Here are the toxins and poisons, warning us of the dangers of the green. Perhaps less obviously ferocious than a wild animal charging towards us, but no less deadly in result. Just a different kind of death.

The blessings of the balms and banes are united in the leaves of the trees, thereby opening the gate to deeper wisdom and teaching. The Green Man is seen in oak leaves, for the oak is one of the most sacred trees, particularly to the Druids. So his wisest and most balanced form is expressed in the tree teachers. While some trees contain medicines and food, like oak, hawthorn and apple, others are a danger to humans, like yew and blackthorn. Some contain a paradox of both. Blackthorn, one of my favorite trees, is associated with poison, hexing and injury, as the long and sharp thorns easily cause infected wounds, but the fruit, the sloe, is quite delicious and used to flavor gin. The Green Man holds this paradox within him as virile flowering youth, rotting Green Devil, and the balance of the wise tree.

Breathing the Green Man

The primary bridge in the relationship between animals and plants is through the breath. We exchange breath with each other, and with that breath, we exchange energy, our very life force. In tantric sexual practices, breath and energy exchange between partners is a foundational step to developing further communion. While we might not take our relationship with our plant allies in that direction (see Chapter Nine) it can still be a piece of our foundation in relating to the Green World and its gods. A green breath can transform our understanding of the plant world.

Go out into a place of nature. If possible, surround yourself with plants. The air around them will be oxygen rich, and might make you a little giddy if you slow down enough to truly feel its effects. Invite the spirit of the Green Man to be with you. If you would rather work with a specific plant ally that is before you, you can invite the spirit of that specific plant.

Oak leaf faced
Man of the Green
Standing on this side of the gate
Standing between
Be here with me
Come and be felt
Come and be seen

Breathe deeply the air around you, and feel you are drawing in the exhalation of the plants around you. As you exhale, feel that your breath is feeding, is being inhaled by, the same plants. Exchange these breaths consciously. Begin to breathe through your energy centers, from the chakra power points within your body, or simply the three points of the belly, heart and head. Breathe through the souls of your feet and the crown of your head. Breathe through your palms. Notice where the energies are entering and exiting your body.

In the presence of this breath, feel the Green Man. Feel the lord of all the plants around and within you. His consciousness is in the light absorbed by the plant's cells, forming the green chlorophyll. His consciousness is in the breath and energy radiated and absorbed by you and the plants. Commune with the Green Man. Nature is the great healer, and this breathing can do wonders to restore health and vitality, and even banish illness.

If you do this exercise along with Plant Gazing, perhaps looking into a leafed canopy as if scrying into a dark mirror or fire, you might see the face of the Green Man take form in the trees and leaves before you.

The mystery of the Witch's God, embodiment of both sap and blood, holds the key to the relationship between the animal and plant world. Both are dependent upon each other, and are ultimately dependent upon the Sun, our very own starlight, for life. Animals feed on plants, which in turn feed other animals, yet the decaying body of the animals also helps feed the plants. The in and out breaths of carbon dioxide and oxygen show the reciprocity of the God; nothing is wasted. All things serve. Modern stewards building new ways of living with the land, animals and plants, are exploring the work of Rudolph Steiner in regards to biodynamic agriculture, using previously buried animal horns to become catalyst material to regenerate the land, further showing the relationship between the Horned One and the Green Man. They work as one. The secrets of life and our relationship with the planet are simply waiting to be discovered by those who have the eyes to see and the ears to hear.

You can adapt the exercise above to exchange breath, and energy, with a single plant. Imagine sending your breath and energy to the plant, and specifically having it absorb your energy from the roots. As it "exhales" from the leaves, it beams the life force to you. You "inhale" it not only through your respiratory system, but through your energy centers, and specifically the top of your skull and base of your spine or the soles of your feet. The exchange can give you insight into the nature of the plant's magick and medicine, and makes a good preliminary exercise prior to working with that herb spiritually.

Journey Into Verdant World of Spirits

To the one who has opened the gates to spirit flight, to the shamanic journey or visionary quest, there are many worlds to explore. They are mostly described in terms of overworlds or underworlds, or in the language of the Tree of Life from Qabalistic texts. They are usually described in terms of being "away" from the physical world, yet many Earth-based explorers know there is an unseen, untapped spiritual world all around us. Beneath the visible exterior of our world is the Middle World, containing all that we seek and all that is unseen, all space and time, all past and future. There beneath the veneer is the original garden, the Eden or Hesperides that we never left, but simply forgot how to see. It awaits us, filled with the spirits of nature.

In this garden all the plants, animals, insects and fungi can commune with us. Animist in our theology, the living places seek to know us, to enter into right relationship with us, and us with them. It is here we do the true work of the green, in the world and beyond the world simultaneously, in a paradox of both flesh and spirit.

My first experience with this work came about during the more esoteric portion of my flower essence training. We were sent on a journey into the Green World to find a spirit to act as an intermediary between us and the plant world. We had spent the afternoon seeking out flowers, communing with them, and making essences from them. It was now the evening time and we were being given a chance to deepen our relationship with them. Through visionary cues given to us by the teacher while in a sacred space established by crystals and bowls of flower essences to "hold the vibration," I experienced a kaleidoscope of colors that reminded me of descriptions of LSD experiences.

I have never seen things quite that way before or since, even though I've continued to have profound plant experiences. When the tunnel of colors faded, I was in a bright and vibrant garden, as if each plant was lit from within. It looked more like something out of a futuristic television show than real vegetation. In that realm, a spirit with an almost unpronounceable name appeared, in an amorphous body, to be my guide and intermediary. It was a composite of several different plants and trees, never keeping its shape long enough to establish itself. It was like a green fluid, a quicksilver reflecting vegetation until it gained enough shape and form for me to commune with, but only enough shape for that. It never became solid. It took me around the garden and introduced me to plants. Sometimes it was very formal, and other times it was as if it pushed me into the plant, to touch it, feel it and be absorbed by it, and in turn absorb it. It was a strange little journey, but the plant world became much more open to me after that.

While my shapeless ally appeared to me several more times after that initial meeting, eventually it faded into the background as I established my relationships with specific plants. In a subsequent experience, while creating a talisman for a composite plant familiar (see Chapter Eight) it seemed to return to inhabit the talisman, but established itself through the composite plants that I had chosen, the ones with whom I had established a relationship.

The Crossroads of the Green

Many traditions signify the importance of the crossroads. The triple way, where three roads meet, is particularly sacred to Hecate, Goddess of Witches. There the Hekation would be established, a beautiful and primal construct serving as both altar and statue, consisting of a pole, three masks, three keys and offerings at the foot of the pole. In other traditions, the four-way cross roads, where two roads cross, is sacred. To many, this is the place of Hermes, the messenger god, also having associations with magick and journeying. Hermes is the psychopomp, the guide of souls as well as being the messenger, and eventually his name was leant to the alchemist-philosopher Hermes Trismegistus.

In the Celtic faery traditions, crossroads are also considered a meeting place of the spirits, and a place of danger and power, along with burial mounds and thresholds or liminal places. Any place where natures mix, such as a shorelines or swamps, are considered gateways. A crossroads is where roads mix, so they too, are gateways to magick.

Additionally, four-way crossroads are sacred in the magick traditions of the American south as well as African diasporic magick. Various images of the Man in Black or the guardian of the crossroads and opener of the way can be found there. One tradition says that you can seek out the "Devil" at the crossroads and he will give you mastery over your particular skill. Supposedly many talented jazz or blues musicians gained their skill in this way, as the Devil would tune their guitar and teach them how to play. In essence, this is the crossroads god, not the Christian Devil, but in Christian society, the Man in Black was interpreted in that manner.

Both the three and four-way crossroads are places of magick, where spells are done and undone, where spirits meet and all things are possible. The image of the crossroads can be quite helpful to establish yourself in sacred space, between the worlds. The gods of this place, be they Greco-Roman, Celtic, African or anything else, help open and close gateways, much like the two faced god of Witchcraft and the green god who is both verdant youth and green devil. It's not surprising to think of the goddesses and gods of Witchcraft as associated with the crossroads.

In my own visions, I was led to a realm of plant spirits where there was a five-way crossroads. Initially looking like a five rayed star, each path held a different type of plant spirit. On the left, the two paths actually formed a loop in the realm of the banes and the hedges. On the right, likewise two paths looped through a sunny field into the balms (see Fig. 9, Plant Spirit Journey Sigil). The path forward was the only way in and the only way out of the forest of tree teachers. That is the image I most often use when teaching this work.

Dreaming with the Plant Spirits

While this "dreaming" journey can be done anywhere, it is best performed in nature when communing with the nature spirits. Establish a comfortable place to journey in, perhaps sitting up with your back against a tree, gazing into greenery.

Look for a natural "gate" in the setting. This gate can be a hole in the ground or rocks, an opening in the roots of a tree, or, particularly useful for this exercise, a dark space framed by branches, vines or other vegetation, creating a " window" or "door" to gaze through. It might be similar to where you "saw" the Green Man's face through your breathing of the forest. This window provides an excellent opening into the green realm by projecting your life force both in and through the plant spirits.

Relax your body, breathe deeply and enter a trance state. Those who do well with music or drumming may use these assistants. Bring your attention to your opening and when ready, close your eyes. Hold the image of the opening in your mind, and imagine entering it. Find yourself in the green realm. You may experience the Green Man there as your guide, or subtly feel his presence in all that is there.

Everything is brighter than you imagined. You find yourself walking into an unusual crossroads, a place where five paths meet, like the five points of the pentagram. Look all around you. To the right seems to lead towards a clear and bright path. You know that is where the balms are most likely to be. To the left is darker and more crooked. The path is rougher and wild, toward a hedge. There lies some of the banes and the wilder plant spirits. Before you the path leads deep into the forest, where the trees are.

Choose a path consciously, or let intuition alone guide you and seek out your plant spirit. Commune with the plant or plants you find. Understand what their nature is through spirit exchange and observation of their signature. What personal messages do they have for you? Spend your time with the plants and learn their mysteries.

When the experience is done, make them an offering of energy as a thank you for this time and experience. You can envision a specific offering or pure energy to the plant spirits, and perhaps follow it up with a physical offering when you have returned your awareness to the flesh.

Follow the path back to the crossroads. Say thank you to the spirit of the place, of the crossroads, and to the Green Man. Find yourself returning the way you came, back through your gateway and bringing your awareness back to your flesh and blood, breath and bone. Ground and clear yourself as needed, and I suggest journaling about the experience while the details are still fresh in your mind.

To connect with a specific plant spirit, if you can find a living plant, sit with it. If not, having some of the dried herb, tincture/tea with you is helpful. If it is not toxic, consuming a little bit to attune you to that specific plant also works well.

Fig. 9: Plant Spirit Journey Sigil

Once I had explored all of these paths I was given this symbol for the green journey with a five-ways crossroads. Each side of the infinity loop was for either the balms to the right or the banes on the left, with the remaining path to the grove of trees. For some reason the last path was triple branched like a trident or pitchfork, or one of the Elder Futhark runes. I've found drawing or envisioning this symbol, for myself or when guiding others through this meditation, helps establish the connection.

The Soul Garden

The Soul Garden is where your own personal inner world interfaces with the Green World of nature. Various traditions have a personal inner temple, a soul shrine or inner abbey where you go for insight, rejuvenation and magick. The garden is a place where you can safely cultivate a relationship with the plant spirits in your space. For people oriented towards plants as their primary spirituality, the entire inner temple could be a garden shrine. For others, it is a small cultivated part of the inner sacred space.

For those looking at the inner world as simply a metaphorical space for the practicing of self-help techniques, the garden is only established as a place to plant "seeds" for the future and "grow" the wishes and dreams of your life. Yet for the magickal practitioner, it takes on a deeper role, becoming a place to invite in and establish relationship with your own plant allies. Practitioners can find a special tree takes shape without their conscious intention, or plants appear, as "signs" of whatever work or healing needs to be done.

In my own tradition, the practitioner establishes an "Inner Temple" on the inner planes where she is sovereign, and the temple becomes her reflection through the process of spiritual development. We plant in the garden both metaphorical seeds and the seeds of the plants with which we wish to cultivate a relationship. Often the "weeds" of the garden are healing herbs and power plants we need on our journey. In this manner, both the plant spirits and the temple itself become our teachers.

Journey to the Soul Garden

Relax your body, breathe deeply and enter a trance state via your preferred method. Envision a great tree, the World Tree or central axis of the cosmos. Bring your awareness to it, passing through the veil of your mind to step before it. Hear the wind through its branches. Smell the earth where the roots dig in. Touch the bark and feel its texture. Hold the intention of visiting your Soul Garden, a place of nature within the otherworld where you can attune, find spirit medicine, and grow. The roots of the great tree will open up for you and form a tunnel that will to lead you to the Soul Garden.

You will find yourself eventually in a great garden, forest or grove, where many of the plants that are special to you reside together. Some will be new and surprising for you. But the plant spirits that desire a relationship with you will be growing in this garden. Take the time to commune with some of these spirits.

When ready, just sit in the center of the garden and attune to the general vibration, the overall spirit quality of the garden. Let it feed and nourish you. Just as you breathed in the forest of the Middle World, where your breath fed the plants and their breath fed you, let the vibrations of the garden nourish you, and let your vibrations nourish the garden in return. Feel changes subtly taking place within your consciousness and energy body. The journey will be different for everyone.

When you are finished, find yourself returning the way you came, back through your gateway and bringing your awareness back to your flesh and blood, breath and bone. Ground and clear yourself as needed and journal about your experience.

The soul garden can lead us to a variety of otherworldly gardens in the realms beyond. I'm fond of visiting a garden on the "dark side" of the Moon as it hangs in the underworld. There I pick the spirits' herbs for my spirit remedies to heal those who need not only physical healing, but soul healing. Students in class with me have journeyed to the gardens of mist in the clouds of the upper world. All manner of terrain can be found in the subtle inner and outer spaces we travel during soul flight.

Many plants exist in the realms above and below that have either passed or not yet manifested in the world between where we dwell. The hunt to identify plants in our realm from our spirit vision can be rewarding, but also frustrating. Trust your experience. Trust the plants. Trust your own results. They will lead you. You might even find yourself returning to the first garden, the primal garden, our Eden, Avalon or Hesperides where the fruits of life, knowledge and immortality grow.

Plant Gateways

To our Pagan ancestors, nature was not just an expression of the divine, filled with spirits and powers, but a gateway to the spirit world. Just as in the last exercise, where you used the frame of branches to be a potential "doorway," and as in other shamanic traditions that use the image of roots in a tree or a hole in the ground as a natural gateway, there are some hidden openings among the plant world.

One of the easiest ways to open the gates as part of a plant journey is through the use of an ecstatic body posture. Research from the Cuyamungue Institute has shown certain ancient artistic positions can induce particular kinds of trance journeys when held while listening to a fast repetitive shamanic beat of roughly 160 beats per minute (bpm). One posture well known to modern European tradition Witches is that of Cernunnos from the Gunderstrup Cauldron. Those who hold this position, sitting with the right heel towards the groin and the left slightly outward from the right, with the back straight and arms held in a "V" with the fingers curled forward as if holding a snake and torc neck ring, are brought into a shapeshifting and transformative trance. From the Gunderstrup image, one might think it would induce the wisdom of animals, and it can at times, but more often it brings a journey that is more green, with plants merging and shapeshifting with the practitioner. While depicting an animal horned god, it seems to more often bring us to his twin the Green Man and his plant mysteries. I highly recommend experimenting with this posture while listening to a drum or rattle, real or recorded, to attune to the plant consciousness of our world. Use it with simple ritual, such as honoring the directions.

Fig. 10: Cernunnos Position

Once you have attuned to the plant world in a generalized way, you will find that particular plants and their arrangements can open other specific gateways of consciousness. Below you will find some gateways that I've experienced, but they are by no means the only ones available to you. Use them with simple ritual, and as you are asking for aid from the plant spirits, an offering of some sort, such as the ritual meal, is always appreciated and will aid you in your work. I also highly recommend that you first make contact with your own personal plant familiar, and evoke that plant familiar to aid, inform, guide and protect you during these journeys. Just like an animal familiar, it will guide you in unfamiliar territory and protect you from harm. Some might even experience the plurality of being guided by both plant and animal familiars, among other spirit guides. Explore with your spirit ally and use the information you receive from your "Cernunnos" posture journeys.

Floral Circle for the Lady of Flowers

A simple plant gateway is to gather a number of flower blossoms that are just past their prime. I hate to pick flowers, preferring they go to fruit, so it could theoretically be done in a big flower garden or field in bloom, without necessitating the picking of blossoms. Basically you want to create a circle of flowers around you on the land. They can be in a simple geometric design like a modern stone healer's crystal grid – four flowers at the four directions, five flowers in a pentacle formation, six flowers in a hexagram formation, eight flowers for the wheel of the year and so on. Use a geometry that speaks to you. Or, with an excess of flowers, or flower petals, you can create a complete ring of flowers rather than a geometric shape based upon individual flowers. This is similar to the strewing of rose petals to create a space for handfastings and blessings.

Lady of the Flowers
Lady of the Bloom

Lady of the New Life
And Lady of the Tomb
Open the way to your Mysteries
Please open your gate
Through this living circle
Show me the turning wheel of fate.

A meditative journey in your ring of flowers will bring you to the Goddess of the Middle World, often described as a Lady of Flowers. Old Craft traditions, such as the Kent Tradition, suggest that the Goddess doesn't simply rule over flowers, but her very essence is found within the flowers, sharing some kinship with myths such as the Welsh Blodeuwedd. In this form, the Goddess can be both cruel and kind, but very enlightening and empowering if approached in the correct spirit.

Gateway of the Oak

The oak tree is known as a gateway, a door, into the Green World. Find an oak tree that resonates with you. While I love white oak, I've found personally the red oak is more favorable to me. Sit close before the oak and gaze into its roots. Let your focus go soft, and knock on the oak tree, as if it were a door. Ask the oak to open its way.

Duir of the Oak
Door of the Forest
Knock, knock, knock come I
Will you let me in?
Will you let me pass?
I come in Love and Trust with Gifts in Hand
And seek to pass through your dark eye.

Feel yourself gently pass through the roots of the tree, as if the tree were truly a door. Your eyes might close or remain open. The oaken door can truly take you anywhere within the

Green World. Have a clear intention of what kind of journey you wish, or where you want to go before opening the door. Make sure to return the way you came, close the door and thank the oak tree for the journey. You can later use this memory as a future gateway for other journeys through the world tree.

A variation of this ritual can be used with the ash or yew tree, though the journey may be more vertical with these trees, ascending to the heavens or journeying to the depths. Oak's journeys seem to be more based in the overall middle world of the plant realm. Make sure to leave your offering to the tree spirit.

Crossroads of the Branches

Witchcraft is known for its rituals at the crossroads, be it a gathering of three ways or four. A similar magick can be created by making a crossroads with tree branches. Choose two branches whose nature is appropriate to your intention for the journey. If you are a more formal ritualist, they can be two wands, rods or staves, but they should be roughly of equal size and power. Look to Chapter Five for specific tree spirit descriptions. Sit in nature or your temple with your two branches. Ask the spirit of each wood to help open the crossroads, a magickal vortex for you to commune with nature and with all plants, and the Queen of all the Wise who is the source and end of all plant life. Then cross the branches, forming an "X" before you. Gaze at the X and close your eyes. Feel the energy and opening generated by your prayer and the mingling of two place spirits. The three of you together create a synergy greater than your individual parts to create communion and bridge the gap between the human and plant worlds. With such a vortex, you may find communication with your plant familiars more clear and direct. When done, thank all spirits involved, including the two woods, and uncross the branches to close the gate.

Council of Trees

The Council of Trees gateway is very simple. Find a grove of trees, an opening in the forest where you have some space to sit, yet are generally surrounded by trees. Imagine expanding your awareness outward while sitting in a meditative trance state, to touch all the trees. Your mind, heart and soul reach out to the mind, heart and soul of not just one tree, but all of them together. Ask to be brought into their council, into their communal consciousness. Any poetry recited should be specific to the types of trees present in your grove, so it is important, and respectful, to learn to identify them before you do this work. There in council, they will often commune with a human as a group of tribal elders may commune with a young member of their tribe. Their lessons take place in story form, not linear messages. They will share tales with you that may or may not have direct relationship with you personally, but will have bearing on the land, their own lives, and how we all relate together.

Gateway to the Elder Queen

Probably the most difficult of all these gateways, and one to be approached with caution, is the Gateway to the Elder Queen. Wiccan poetry says, "Elder be the Lady's Tree, burn it not or cursed ye be." There is much lore and prohibition around the Elder, for it is the dark queen, the underworld White Goddess, the Faery Lady, who is in alignment with the Elder tree. She is only to be visited when there is a reason for doing so. She can heal those who are gravely ill, or ease their transition to the otherworld. She can initiate and bring wisdom, but she also asks a price. She forces you to face the dark, the cold and your fear before you truly receive her blessings and gifts.

Find an elder tree, ideally one standing alone rather than in a bunch. The season when this is attempted will alter your experience with it. Some believe the flowering time is when she is at her most gentle, but often things are opposite in the spirit world—our summer being their winter—so others would say winter is when she may be most gentle. I like to approach her in the fall, when the flowers have turned to dark berries. Make sure to make your offerings to her at the base of the bush. Lie down beneath her with your head gazing up through the branches and leaves. Allow the light to diffuse through it and put you into a relaxed state of consciousness. Recite these or similar words:

Blessed be the Lady's Tree
Elder wise and Elder Key
Dark eyes who only see
Spirits fly and spirits free
White lady who guarantees
Life in death for you and me
Two in one and one in three
Please share with me your mysteries
Gracious Lady of the Elder Tree
Elder wise and Elder Key
Open the way and come to me.

Feel the Goddess of the Elder come to you. Commune with her. Be direct in your intention. "Talk little and listen much," for she has much to share and little patience or time. Don't miss opportunities by being too mired in your expectations of how the meeting should be. Have intention for your visit, but be open to how it may manifest.

When done, thank the Elder spirit and say farewell. Ground yourself and return to normal consciousness.

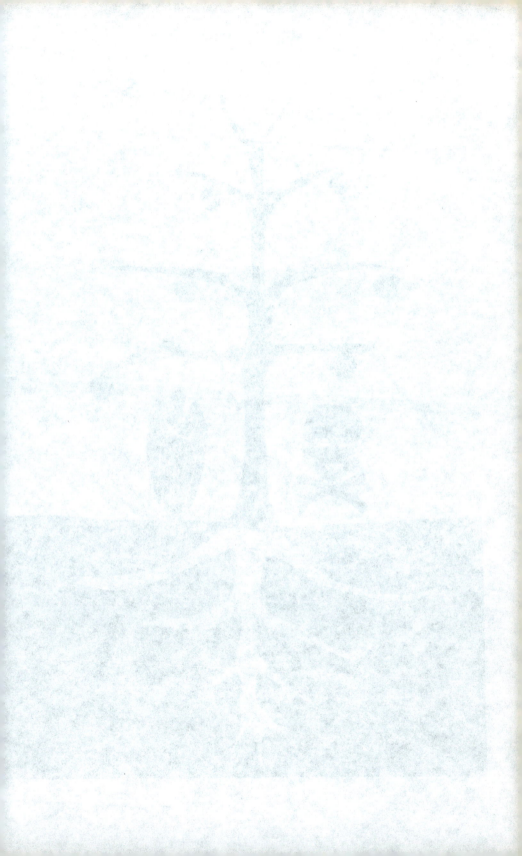

Chapter Five:
Balms, Banes
& Tree Teachers

 o walk the path of plant magick, you must journey deeper into the realm of your allies. You must meet with them. You must get to know the spirits of the green as you would any friend or family member. Like growing a plant in your garden or windowsill, it takes time, nurturance and love to grow these relationships. While we would like the fruits of our magick to be instantaneous, more often than not they must grow organically, just as things grow in nature.

Now that you know how to open the gates, it is time to work with your allies individually, to know them as spirits in their own right.

Healing Herbs

The work of the herbal healer and the Witch overlaps. Plants with powerful medicines to heal the body also have powerful spirits to heal the soul. There is a correspondence between chemicals and energy, though there are many powerful plant spirits that are not used in herbal medicine today. It is my belief, and the belief of many spiritual herbalists, that all plants have a healing power. Sometimes that power is not directed toward humans, but may be toward other animals, other plants, minerals or toward nature itself. Each plant is an important part of the web of life and plays a role in the greater organism of the planet, and thereby the universe.

Rose – Rose is the preeminent plant of the Western Mysteries. Traditionally viewed as a plant of love and romance, it is also the plant of spirituality and regeneration—the center of the Rosy Cross and the plant that blooms in the wasteland in Arthurian myth. It is sacred to the Goddess as Aphrodite-Venus, Earth mother, Witch goddess, enchantress and keeper of the morning and evening star mysteries. Rose's magick elevates the vibrations of any person or place, and can be used to heal, bless, love, and to open the gates to the Mysteries.

Mugwort – Mugwort is one of the plants sacred to Artemis, the Moon huntress. Growing wild and abundant in many areas, it is used to increase psychic ability and divinatory prowess. It is most effective as a tea, incense and oil. Its spirit medicine opens the third eye, bringing in more psychic light, as well as helping you feel and listen to your gut instinct. Burned mugwort is also considered protective, helping to chase away the spirits of sickness and misfortune.

Angelica – Angelica is said to be a gift from the angels, given to a monk in a dream to help humanity with the Bubonic plague. It is considered heavenly medicine, and a panacea for many different illnesses. Any plant with a hollow stem like angelica's is used spiritually for journey work and travel, and with this plant, specifically for traveling to the overworlds and angelic realms. It helps us with the magick of all transitions, particularly birth and death, and increases our ability to commune with angels and spirits. Its spirit is protective and nurturing, particularly when we feel isolated. In magick, the powdered root is used for protection and in incense and powders for blessings. The spirit of Angelica is very helpful and active in the human realm.

St. John's Wort – St. John's Wort is at the healing end of the spectrum for five-petaled flowers. Most magickal practitioners who find this flower immediately feel both its medicinal and spiritual power, despite its being an unassuming little herb. Its purpose is to bring the light in, both through its bright yellow flower and through its leaf, perforated to let more light through it, hence its Latin name *Hypericum perforatum*. As a tincture and tea, it heals depression, letting spiritual light uplift the user. As an oil, its blood red color heals trauma and injury, those physical darknesses that enter the body. As a flower essence it heals nightmares and depression. As a spirit, it does all this and more. It is protective, blessing and healing on all levels. St. John's Wort is at the peak of its power near Midsummer.

Comfrey – Comfrey is a plant of regeneration. Herbally it is used in poultices and oils to heal damaged tissues and bones. Magickally it is protective, but also helps you return home, and assists in the returning home of your luggage and valuables as well. Spiritually it helps you regenerate when you feel you've lost something, as well as helps you find your home. The flower essence is also good for helping kindle past life memories of previous homes and incarnations.

Cinquefoil – Cinquefoil is commonly known as Five Finger Grass, and its leaf, which looks like five or seven fingers, is used in counter magick to break curses. It is considered protective against all forms of malicious magick. Cinquefoil is a common ingredient in classic flying ointments, though it is not known for any particularly narcotic or psychotropic properties. As a flower essence, it helps clear unwanted imprints and protects us during psychic experience, which may explain its use in flying ointments. Generally the spirit of cinquefoil tends to energetically support us in whatever we do.

Lemon Balm – Lemon Balm's blessings are for aid and ease. Added to any mixture physically or spiritually, it aids the overall working. On its own, it brings a gentle calm and steadies the body and mind. Its spirit medicine makes things easier and helps you find synchronicity and blessings already present. Ruled by both Jupiter and the Moon, it is honored as a primary plant in alchemy.

Peppermint – Peppermint is beloved by humanity, and in turn loves humanity too. Its historic uses range from a sacramental herb in the rites of Eleusis to a flavoring for candy. Its nature power is one of enhancing communication and awareness. Peppermint sharpens and clears the mind. Magickally it's a mercurial all-purpose herb, used for psychic awareness and information, protection and purification.

Lady's Mantle – Lady's Mantle is the preeminent herb of the alchemists, said to be a wise teacher helping to unlock the secrets of nature and the herbs. Some consider it feminine, as herbally it heals the reproductive system, while other see it appear magickally as a wise old man, a hermit mentor. Lady's Mantle helps us align our bodies with our own feminine energy, and align both our own body and energy with that of the Earth. It helps our hearts beat in tune with Mother Earth's heart and have a greater sense of the eternal Garden of the Gods before time began.

Solomon's Seal – Solomon's Seal and similar plants related to it embody the most benign aspects of Saturn. They are protective and blessing. The six-petaled flowers that hang down from its stem embody the hexagram of the macrocosm, the power of the magickal planets. With the Star of David imagery, the plant is associated in folklore with King Solomon, who bound demons to help him build his temple. This imagery implies the root's power to protect and control the demons of our lives, and set them to useful purposes. Being a king, it is also associated with riches and success in folkloric magick systems, like Hoodoo. The root looks like a spine, or sometimes like the connective tissue of a joint. Medicinally it is used to treat injuries of the spine and connective tissues, particularly helping to loosen overly tight ligaments and tendons, or tighten those that are too loose or traumatized. Its spirit helps us be flexible when we are too rigid or too willful. Solomon's Seal helps with issues of pride, arrogance and ego, assisting us in seeing the larger picture of the macrocosm. It helps us find our life's purpose and work in the world, and manifest it.

Yarrow – Yarrow is a powerful plant, recognized the world over for its herbal and spiritual properties. It's considered a potent love herb, though the planetary attributes can be variably Venus, Mars or Mercury. Yarrow is used in love spells and potions. The Taoist traditions used yarrow stalks for the I-Ching before coins became more fashionable. It is associated with the faeries, and thereby fate, as well as with the boundaries of gardens and roads, growing well on roadsides. Medicinally, yarrow is used to treat wounds, stopping the flow of blood and sealing up a cut. Spiritually it helps us with all sorts of violations to our boundaries, sealing holes in our auras, adjusting the aura's size and helping us discern what is and isn't good for us. It gives us a sense of protection, can aid in reducing our anxiety levels, and help our energy "flow" better. Yarrow tea, along with being a good tonic for the blood, is said to increase perception and psychic awareness, perhaps because it enhances our aura and the way we receive information.

Dill – The plant spirit of Dill is one of multiplication. The signature of the seeds show us that its gift is in abundance.

Abundance is not necessarily success. It simply means a lot of anything. Dill can help you do and make a lot. It is used in protection, love and money magick for that reason. The tea of dill seeds in a bath is said to make the bather irresistible. It's an herb of Mercury, of the mind and thoughts, and as such the seeds are also indicative of many thoughts and ideas. It can be used in potions and incense for knowledge, information and creativity. Its long-lasting aroma is used to aid in concentration and mental clarity, and so is great for study charms. Folklore says that Dill "robs Witches of their will" because it is was to heal babies with colic in an age when colic was believed to be caused by Witches cursing a family, but I can say that I know many Witches who work quite well with Dill and still seem willful.

Nettle – Nettle is a powerful but prickly ally, not always conforming to what we expect of it. Its spirit helps us in many ways. It helps us let go of harmful people and things to which we insist on clinging. Herbally it nourishes the entire body and helps our bodies relieve stress without sedating us. Magickally it is an herb of Mars and can be called upon for protection, similar to thorny briars. Its sting, however, can be used as a gateway into the realm of Faery. The pain of stinging nettle moving up to the back of the head can effectively open the gates.

Burdock – Burdock is considered a weed by most, with its aggravating little "burs" that catch on everything – clothes, hair and our animals. Yet it's in the power of those little burs that you find its magick. Herbally, the roots and even leaf are used to draw toxicity out of the body. Spiritually, burdock is a detoxifier. It draws things out of energy bodies as well as the physical body. It clears the mental body of energy forms that distract us or keep us clouded, and it clears the emotional body of toxicity. It helps us detoxify harmful emotions and thoughts, particularly issues of anger that cling to us like burs, pricking and wounding us as we lash out at others. Burdock is actually a healer for people whom we would describe as "prickly" or "spiky." It regenerates and rejuvenates us. It also helps us to remain focused. When we are overwhelmed by toxic emotions but don't want to act in a toxic manner towards others, many of us choose to disassociate and become very ungrounded. Burdock's tenacious root is an indication that its spirit helps us tether to the Earth, be present and fulfill our goals and commitments. Burdock root can be hung like a charm to aid in creativity, study or enhance any skill or talent. The root is also used as a protective charm.

Basil – Basil is a magickal plant of love and success. It's used in love magick, particularly in food-related love spells, as well as in money magick, as the fresh leaves resemble shredded cash. Spiritually, Basil aids us in balancing our sexual energy, particularly more projective, or male, sexual energy. The flower essence is used to help people with issues surrounding sexuality, desire, control and sexual identity. Its spicy and warm energy helps our life force flow into all areas of our consciousness, including the carnal, and bring them back into alignment with our full awareness.

Rue – Rue is a powerful herbal ally stemming from the Mediterranean traditions of magick, and most notably Stregheria, or Italian Witchcraft. Charms based upon the sprig of rue—known as *Cimaruta* among the Strega, meaning simply "sprig of rue"—are worn for blessings and protection. Once introduced to Rue, Central and South American practitioners immediately recognized its power and adopted it into their own practices. Rue not only protects the user from harm, but also brings blessings of health, wealth and happiness. Spiritually it is said to bolster the life force and its union with the soul, so you can manifest your soul's will, your Higher Will, in daily life. The oil within rue can be caustic to the skin of many people and in concentrated forms it is most definitely an irritant. This irritation principle can make Rue, especially in its flower essence form, an effective ally in spiritual work involving the removal of parasitic and vampiric people and entities. Rue causes such unwanted attachments to release, allowing the user to more clearly use his or her own life force. As a homeopathic remedy, it is indicated for those who suffer from anxiety, depression, panic or paranoia, and physically it works to ease the stress of muscle and connective tissue strains, aches in the joints, and eye strain. Medicinally rue should be used with caution, especially by pregnant women, as it is a known abortificant.

Baneful Allies

In the world of baneful allies, Witchcraft is primarily concerned with three groupings of plants. While banes come in many shapes and sizes, and often their status as "baneful" is only determined by dosage, three groups take precedence in Medieval recipes of flying ointments and should only be approached with the utmost care, spiritually and medicinally. In fact, I urge most practitioners to only approach them medicinally with the aid of an experienced and wise mentor. Other less potentially deadly plants can be considered banes for our magickal purposes, but will pose less risk to your health and life expectancy.

The three traditional baneful groups of herbs are Solanum, Ranunculaceae and Apiaceae. The Solanum are perhaps the most well known, and include the five-petaled banes associated with Deadly Nightshade and Black Nightshade, as well as Henbane, Datura, and true Mandrake. Belladonna itself is named for Atropa, one of the three Fates of Greek myth—the one who cuts the thread of life. The Ranunculaceae comprises the buttercup family, which are all very magickal plants, but Ranunculaceae also includes the Aconites, such as Monkshood and Wolfsbane. Apiacaea includes the deadly Hemlock, not to be confused with the less fearsome Hemlock tree. Apiacaea also includes Queen Anne's Lace (Wild Carrot), Parsley, Dill, and Celery.

These three groupings, along with a few others, are the most popular plants found in traditional Witchcraft lore. Some plants, not chemically deadly, have also been included amongst the banes due to their spiritual nature, if not their relative toxicity.

Belladonna –Belladonna (*Atropa belladonna*) is a powerful plant, associated with Witches, the frenzy of battle, sexuality, seduction, protection, and death. In my experience , Belladonna is called upon to open the gateways to other realms of consciousness, dream states and parallel worlds, as well as to cut the cords attaching us to toxic, deadly people, places and times in our past. Belladonna is also known as Deadly Nightshade. It is believed that the name Belladonna refers to a time when Italian women used it to dilate their eyes, giving it the additional nickname Beautiful Lady, though it could also be associated with the goddess Bellonna. The plant spirit can manifest as a beautiful, dark-eyed, dark-haired faery-like woman who teaches the Witch about the magick over which she rules.

Nightshade – Although Belladonna is known as Deadly Nightshade and the Solanum genus is known collectively as the Nightshades, which includes many of the banes here as well as potatoes, tomatoes, eggplant and tobacco, the name *nightshade* is associated with a whole collection of different plants that share similar features and magickal properties, if not all the same botanical properties, and can include Black Nightshade (*Solanum nigrum*), Common Nightshade (*Solanum americanum*), Bittersweet Nightshade (*Solanum dulcamaru*) and Enchanter's Nightshade (*Circaea lutetiana*). Due to the confusion surrounding their names, they have a tendency to get mixed up. Black Nightshade has different *chemical* attributes than the Belladonna/Datura/Henbane group, but shares similar *magickal* attributes with Belladonna. Black Nightshade is less sexual and more associated with the Dark Goddess and the Crone, and has historical associations with Hecate. It's great for aiding us in breaking past life cords and connections. Bittersweet Nightshade has the power to bind one's enemies. Common Nightshade is good for protection magick and in my relationship with her, she often pops up to warn me of psychic danger in my life by growing close to my home, office, or wherever I will notice her. Enchanter's Nightshade is related to Evening Primrose, not the Solanum genus, and has a two-petaled flower. Its magickal properties include balancing duality and assisting the magician in seeing things clearly.

Datura – Several different species are known as Datura, each with similar magickal and chemical properties. Known commonly as Jimson Weed, Thorn Apple, Devil's Weed, Devil's Trumpet and Witch's Thimble, Datura is intimately associated with magick, Witchcraft, the underworld and the dark goddess. It has been historically used as a potentially dangerous entheogen, topically as part of flying ointment recipes or via inhalation by smoking the seeds and leaves. As a homeopathic remedy, it aids restlessness and cures nightmares. According to Castaneda's work, Datura can be used to help acquire the power of divination and flight. Spiritually, Datura is a powerful ally in opening the gates of the other world. She told me that she opens the gates vertically, while her sister, Belladonna, opens them horizontally. If you have spiritual "wings" while traveling shamanically, you can fly with Datura to the heavens of the overworld or the realms of the underworld. Those who use her recreationally end up opening the gates and falling into hell, because they lack "wings," experiencing nightmares and the spirits of the dead in unpleasant ways. She awakens the crown and third eye, helps us deal with the process of dying and accepting death with others, brings clarity and insight to dreams, and heals anxiety and fear by helping us face our fears.

She can help us relax and be at peace with who we are and what our purpose is. Like an inverse of her sister Belladonna, she can appear as a white-haired, white-eyed faery lady.

Mandrake – Like Nightshade, the name Mandrake brings up a whole host of plants not necessarily related to each other magickally. True mandrake's Latin name is *Mandragora officinarum*, though there are a few similar species. True Mandragora is the root that looks like a man, classically found in European Witchcraft. It has powers of protection, domination, sexual stimulation, blessing and cursing. Rituals involving Mandrake can include waking its spirit to be a familiar or homunculus. The plant spirit of Mandrake can help us find our true spirituality and break away from religious dogma. It tends to heal us of sexual wounds and the disconnection between sexuality and spirit. It increases clairaudience, allowing us to hear the spirits and guides. Some consider it the master of the plant realm. Due to the difficulty in obtaining true Mandrake, as it grows best in Central and Southern Europe, other plants have been associated with it and used as Mandrake substitutes. White Bryony is known as English Mandrake or False Mandrake. It has a somewhat similar root with a man shape, though it would be dug up, shaped through carving, and then put in the ground to heal and then dug up again and sold at a higher price by those passing it off as true Mandrake. Magickally it is said to have similar properties to true Mandrake. In homeopathy white bryony is used to treat muscle and joint pain. Lastly there is American Mandrake, also known as May Apple. While probably only associated with Mandrake due to its apple-like fruit, May Apple's spirit does have some attributes in common with true Mandrake. It helps us go deeper within ourselves and the underworld, and balance our personal, psychological and magickal imbalances. It also has some of the same sexual associations as Mandrake, as it has been made into a remedy for sexually transmitted diseases.

What most American Witches buy as Mandrake is really May Apple.

Monkshood – Monkshood is a powerful bane. Its flowers come in a variety of colors, and while there is a tendency for some people to associate various flower colors specifically with folk names such as Wolfsbane, all the flowers, often blue, purple or yellow, belong to the Aconite genus. Historically, Monkshood was used to make a poison that would kill off wolves that attacked the village. It has since become associated with werewolves, shape shifting and lycanthropy. Greek mythology tells us it grew up from where the spittle of the underworld guardian Cerberus dripped to the ground. The flowers look like little hoods, and therefore the spirit of Monkshood is associated with spirituality, introspection, and withdrawing the senses from the world of form to focus on the inner reality. As a flower essence it helps build spiritual leadership qualities and spiritual integrity, as well as to develop psychic abilities.

Wormwood – Wormwood, or Artemisia Absinthium, is brother to the more well-known Mugwort. While Mugwort opens the psychic senses, Wormwood is used to call spirits and summon those entities with whom you desire communion. It can be protective, warding off unwanted spirits just as it medicinally works to ward off parasites and other unwanted creatures in its role as vermifuge. The Spirit of Wormwood is fiery, and sometimes trickster-like, appearing to some as a devilish figure, unless fashioned into the drink absinthe, when it appears as a Green Victorian Faery. My own vision of absinthe's spirit fit neither image, and manifested as, or possibly summoned, a small gaggle of impish spirits who circled around the house where we were drinking.

Foxglove – Foxglove blossoms were originally called "faery gloves" by people who believed that the little folk wore them as gloves, and somehow the name transitioned from faeries to foxes. Foxglove is the herb of the heart. While a potentially deadly poison, and is not to be consumed, its medicine affects the cardiovascular system and its spirit affects the heart and emotional body, imbuing it with love, particularly in those who feel unloved and abandoned. Foxglove is powerful, but kind to those who call upon it.

Parsley – While Parsley is a common household herb and perfectly safe to consume, many feel it has a sinister spirit. It has been referred to as the "Devil's Weed," either because of its power to summon demons, devils and malevolent spirits, or because of its power to protect you from them. Spiritually, Parsley is often a key ingredient in flying ointment recipes, and being a Martian herb, has a strong masculine and sexual power to it. Perhaps these sexual overtones are what led to it being classified as a sinister herb. As a tea, the herb is supposed to increase your "cunning" both in knowledge and in the clever wiles of the Trickster. I find it quite powerful as a ritual sacrament and it was the first herb to ever really "speak" to me as a child, encouraging me to take those first tentative steps towards herbalism.

Vinca – Vinca is known as Periwinkle or Sorcerer's Violet. It's a small creeping vine with five-petaled purple flowers. The spirit of Vinca helps us open our third eye while remaining grounded. It also has associations with the dead, and is known as Tomb Vine in some places for its propensity to grow near graves. Italian traditionalists also use it in love magick, as it can be used to both kindle love and bind people together.

Mastery of the Trees

The trees of any land are the ministers of the plant world. They are the priestesses and priests mediating the energy between the heavens, Earth and underworld, and between the world of the green and the world of flesh and blood. They are lungs of our planet.

While all trees are magickal, wise and special, in the traditions of European-based Witchcraft, those trees associated with the Ogham script usually take priority. Ogham is a Celtic script found on markers and manuscripts throughout Britain and Ireland. Each symbol is associated with a tree, giving rise to the idea that it is a Celtic Tree Alphabet. Technically each symbol is associated with a long list of correspondences, including trees, colors and birds, but the tree aspect is what has fascinated modern occultists and Witches the most, even leading to the creation of a Celtic astrological system based upon Ogham "tree signs." Some believe the name "Ogham" refers to the Celtic god Ogma/Ogmois, the script's potential creator. Today the symbols are used in magickal talismans and divination systems, many of which have been inspired by the sometimes controversial work of Robert Graves and his book *The White Goddess*. Much of the magickal meaning in each symbol is based upon the tree's lore in magick, medicine and mythology. Ogham therefore provides a ready-made body of tree lore for the modern Pagan movement.

Oak – Oak is the tree of the wise, often seen as the World Tree by Celtic practitioners. Folk traditions tell us that the name of the oak in Ogham, *duir*, is the basis of the word Druid, the priestly caste of the Celtic people. While etymological sources disagree, the oak is still a primary tree of Celtic spirit practices. It confers strength to the individual in difficult times and is considered a door or gateway to the world of spirits. Witches often see the God of Life as the Oak King or Green Knight—a further testament to this tree's power and importance.

Apple – Apple trees are related to roses, and this gives them an important place in the pantheon of trees, being very spiritual and otherworldly. The five-petaled white flowers with the five-seeded red fruit play a huge role in the lore of the Faery realms and Witchcraft. In terms of healing, apples help us align with the body and understand the pains and illnesses of our bodies as part of the cycle of life. Apple trees open the gates of enchantment to the Faery King and Queen. The Silver Branch, a mythic wand made from apple wood, is seen as the Northern equivalent of the Southern Oak Golden Bough, a gateway herb. When the silver "apple" bells ring on the Silver Branch, the gates open to the other realm.

Hazel – Hazel is the tree of wisdom. The nuts are said to be the source of wisdom for the Celtic Salmon of Knowledge, for it feasts on the hazel nuts that fall into its pool. Hazel is the wood of the magician, and powerful wands can be crafted from its wood. It grants eloquence and the understanding of languages. In healing work, Hazel grants a heightened perception of time, including time beyond linear perception. It can shift the user into the past, present and future, or allow the user to step out of time entirely for a short duration.

Birch – Birch is a magickal tree, with its white and silver trunks showing up brightly against the brown grey trunks of the rest of the forest. Its bright color is associated with the light of the Sun, as well as the otherworldly brightness of the White Goddess. The birch tree is known for its fertility, yet it bears no fruit. It still "somehow" multiplies in the forest, being quick to grow, and can show us how to multiply our blessings and be fertile in new and creative ways. Birch paper is used for spells, and any wish made with birch paper is blessed with the power of the tree spirit, though I've found fallen birch paper to work just as well if not better than harvested or processed paper, as the tree appreciated remaining whole and protected from parasites. It will easily shed paper for those who ask kindly.

Rowan – Rowan is a tree of protection. Its spirit protects the journeyman and traveler, and in particular the mountain climber, for it is known as Mountain Ash as well. The red berries are considered a cure for "bewitchment," and a tea made of the berries will break curses. Five-pointed stars appear where the rowan stem attaches to the berry, and thus Rowan can be used to "block" harm with the power of the pentagram. The berries or twigs can be placed into charms or threaded into necklaces. The twigs are used in protective charms wherein they are tied into a cross with red thread. The spirit of Rowan is a great ally against any form of magickal attack or curse, as well as in helping us to remove self-attacks and self-sabotage we may perceive as magickal attacks.

Maple – While Maple is not found among the Ogham script trees, it is a powerful and vocal ally to those who know it. Maple is a tree most associated with its syrup—with sugar and sweetness—though not all maples produce sap for maple syrup. Yet all maples can help us find the goodness, the sweetness, of life. They help us find happiness and the bright side in any dark situation. In healing work, Maple helps us balance the left and right side of the body, as well as the yin and yang qualities of our energy fields. In that balance we can find the peace and happiness that was eluding us.

Pine – Pine is a tree of leadership and endurance. Pines, being evergreen, last throughout the winter. Some associate them with the Goddess, being an eternal principle even in the depth of winter, while others see them as an immortal aspect of the Green God. The cones are seen as phallic images of the God. The god Dionysus was represented by a thyrsus: a fennel stock with a pine cone affixed to the top with ivy wrapped around it. In either case, the Pine helps us persevere through the darkness and coldness of life, as it perseveres through the darkness of winter. As pine needles and sap are used in purification and healing rituals, so too does the plant spirit of Pine help us heal and purify.

Plant Spirit Medicine

The practice of plant spirit medicine is the spiritual ingestion of the plant's energy, its vibration, or in older terminology, its virtue. Today it is performed by a shamanic practitioner who offers the spirit medicine through ritual to a client. Such healing rituals usually require the shamanic practitioner to have made contact with the plant spirit, and developed a relationship with it as an ally. Alternately, plant spirit medicine requires the practitioner to have a spirit ally that acts as an intermediary, brokering a deal between the new plant spirit medicine ally, the practitioner, and the client.

For green Witches, one of the best ways of working with a plant's medicine is to work with its spirit directly. This can be through ingestion of the plant spirit as a tea, tincture or flower essence, and followed by spiritual communion through trance. Contact can also occur with no plant material present whatsoever, but simply via a sincere desire to commune with the plant's spirit. My favorite way, by far, is to work with the living plant, when in bloom if possible, and to build a direct living relationship with the plant, and thereby nature. Nature is the great healer, and the plant spirits are connecting us to the healing powers of Nature.

With the living plant in mind, I've designed a number of medicine rituals to be done with plants. If the living plant is not available to you, simply use intent, or an herbal preparation, when dealing with non-toxic herbs. If you are on any medication or have any health concerns, consult your doctor before taking such preparations. An advantage of working with the herbs only spiritually is that such experiences won't hinder any health issues, and can even, at certain times, promote temporary or even permanent relief from them.

The Cup of Digitalis

The Cup of Digitalis is a late springtime ritual, when the Foxglove, Digitalis, is in bloom. The name of the ritual is misleading—literally drinking a cup of digitalis without the supervision of an expert is not advisable, as it stimulates a strong cardiac response in the body. The "cup" I refer to is the bloom itself, a bell-shaped flower that can actually be used to contain water or wine. These blooms can act like little containers. Too small for human gloves (as they cover no more than the finger tips) for rituals, they make wonderful tiny chalices. Do not fear: what little chemical can be transferred by this simple ritual should not harm anyone. The dose is more akin to homeopathy levels than pharmaceutical ones.

I perform this ritual as the garden is truly coming into bloom, to attune my heart spiritually with the green heart of the land. The years when I do catch the foxglove in bloom and remember to do this rite are much more vibrant and communicative with the plant spirits than the years I don't. I think of the Cup of Digitalis ritual as a subtle yet powerful communion with nature that lasts until the winter.

Begin by simply making an offering to the plant spirit itself. Venusian offerings are appropriate, such as honey, brown sugar, rose water or sweet bread. Have a small container of spring water or well water with you—local water if possible. If the water of a nearby stream or river is drinkable, then by all means use it. Ask permission of the plant spirit to pick a whole and hearty blossom. Permission might be received as an intuitive impression or inner knowing. You can also use a pendulum to determine a yes/no response; a "yes" is typically a clockwise circle.

Tip the bloom upright so the opening is up, and fill it with water. If you take care not to damage the bottom when picking it, the blossom will easily hold a tiny sip of water. Sit. Meditate. Attune to the power of Foxglove and the garden or field. Feel the pulse of the flower and water. Recite the following:

Cup of Digitalis,
Faery Bell.
Open the Heart,
Please open it well.
Grant me communion with the Living Green,

Communion with the Living Light.
Make me one with your own heart.
Put our relationships right.
Blessed be to you and all your kin.

When you feel the time is right, drink the water. You can slowly sip, or take one gulp. Then truly meditate, feeling the power of Digitalis open your heart to the heart of nature. Commune, not necessarily in words but in feelings, in love, with all the plants around you, starting with Foxglove.

When done, say your farewells, and return to your normal day. But be sure to note the effect of the Foxglove attunement throughout the growing season.

The Armor of Yarrow

As Yarrow is an herb of boundaries, both physical and energetic, it's an excellent herb to aid us in strengthening our psychic shields. Though I've done this ritual several times with a more Martial warrior quality, as Yarrow influences the flow of blood herbally and the flow and boundary of the aura spiritually, I was recently reminded of the dual nature of Yarrow. Because it controls flow, some regard Yarrow not as a Martian herb, but as a Venusian one, and use it in love spells. In crafting this psychic armor rite with Yarrow, this dual nature came out. What I usually see as the faery "Prince of Yarrow" instead spontaneously transformed into the divine androgyne, a Prince/ Princess with balanced qualities. This spirit taught me that the power of protection and shielding is in both boundaries *and* flow, giving *and* receiving, male *and* female.

If possible, locate living yarrow at the edge of a field, road or garden—someplace where you can safely lie down and be undisturbed for a time. Make your offering to the plant. In my last encounter with Yarrow, I had dried meat available in my bag, and made an offering which was summarily rejected. I thought it would be perfect for a warrior plant, but I clearly felt that it wasn't accepted. Due to the dual nature of this particular plant spirit, I now understand that I needed something more Venusian, so I offered a penny. Even though modern pennies are made with less copper than they used to be, the color itself seemed to satisfy the plant spirit. It also asked me to pick up the trash near and around it and remove it. There were bits of shredded soda cans littered about, so I did.

Then I evoked the power of the plant's deva, its oversoul, the consciousness of the individual plant, and the Archfey Lord from the depths:

Yarrow of the Heavens, I call to you.
Yarrow of the Land before me, I call to you.
Yarrow Prince of the Depths below, I call to you.
The Three Who are One, gird me in your strength and love.
Above, below and between,
So mote it be.

Lie down with the yarrow plant at your crown. Gaze up at the sky through the leaves and flowers. Be aware of your body and your energy bodies. Everyone will work with the plant spirits differently. In my experience, I felt my skin profoundly, the sticking of dry grass, the sensation of bugs near my skin and the feeling of my summer clothes. I felt my aura expand, turning green and white as if it were made of yarrow, and I felt the bugs go away. I was surrounded soon in white flowers and white flame, healing my aura and clearing it. I started to sweat, as yarrow herbally can be a diaphoretic. I then psychically sensed white flowers in my blood, purifying my blood of all toxic forces. Poetry raced through my mind as I saw the feminine side of the "Prince" of Yarrow, becoming something like a spoken charm known as a lorica, a breastplate protective verse used to align the individual with divine powers. Most famous is the Lorica of St. Patrick in the Catholic and Celtic Christian traditions, though there are many other forms in both ancient and modern traditions. Here is a close reconstruction of what I received:

Borders and boundaries
I'm guarded like a garden
Gates will open
Gates will close
Gates will open again
Fern and flower
Flow and ebb
All things come
And all things go again
Male and female
Venus to Mars
Attract and Repel
I move like a magnet
Wings of hidden force
Warrior and Seducer
Princess and Prince am I
All things in that do serve
All things out that do harm
As I hold the borders and boundaries
Yarrow am I

When we were done, my awareness returned mostly to normal, though my energy body felt bigger and clearer. I thanked the three aspects of Yarrow – oversoul, plant spirit and Archfey. I saw before my face a gaggle of "faery bugs"; tiny, nondescript insects in a little swarm. I swatted them away and Yarrow seemed angered by this. They later returned and were almost playing with me, like tiny Victorian-style "Tinkerbell" faeries. I'm not sure of their connection to Yarrow other than the balance of work and play, but they seemed important in the experience.

Yarrow has inspired other herbal Loricas and prayers in my practice, particularly protection and blessing prayers that involve many of my plant, animal and stone allies.

Beauty of the Lady's Mantle

Lady's Mantle is known not only as a tonic for women, and as the herb used by alchemists seeking to unlock the secrets of nature, but also as the granter of eternal beauty and wisdom. Folklore tells us to wash in the dew of the Lady's Mantle leaf—the center of it collects dew like a tiny cup—and you will remain forever beautiful. This teaching typically comes from elder herbalists past their physical prime, who urge us to start this practice now to retain our youth and beauty, as they neglected to do so.

Seek out Lady's Mantle in the hours of the early morning, when the dew is still fresh and cool. May 1st, or Beltane, is an appropriate time. Be sure to ask permission of the plant spirit to do this work. Lady's Mantle is quite gracious and almost always gives permission. Offerings are always accepted, particularly milk and honey. Picking the leaf is not necessary. I've found the best method is to get on your hands and knees before the plant and stick your face right in, getting it all wet with the dew. Then rub the water into your skin. Gaze at the rising sun and say:

Lady's Mantle, Alchemilla, Lady of the Elixir of Life,
Please grant me eternal youth and beauty, inside and out.
Grant me health and well being,
So I can continue to walk the path of green till the end of my days.
So mote it be.

Once the dew has dried on your face, thank Lady's Mantle and resume your day.

The Light of St. John's Wort

St. John's Wort's humble power is a catalyst for spiritual change. It helps bolster the energy body with light, and I try to work with it whenever I am preparing for a bigger ritual or transformation. It is also very healing after any type of trauma or injury, to body or spirit. This ritual helps us let in more light and more consciousness, and works well if done soon after the Yarrow Armor Ritual. Yarrow will help you build the container of your energy body and St. John's Wort will help you fill the container with light. They both tend to grow near each other and bloom at roughly the same time, near Midsummer.

Locate blooming St. John's Wort and sit before it. Make an offering. Like Lady's Mantle, this is another very generous plant, and while it has told me no offering is necessary, I've found offerings of simple cool water to be very welcomed by it. Ask permission to take a leaf, and when you have it, hold the leaf up to the sun. Gaze through the pores of the leaf. Named *Hypericum perforatum* because the leaves are "perforated" or seem to be so; they let tiny pinpricks of light through them, yet the leaves have not been damaged at all. Thus, St. John's Wort lets more light through your own energy body without damaging you.

Gaze at the blooming yellow flowers, five-petaled, like the Witch's Star. Bow your head before St. John's Wort. This is truly the Sun God in one of his many plant forms. This is one of his most humble and powerful forms, overlooked by the unwise as a weed. Bowing our crowns toward it helps us emulate its own humility. Feel the light of the flowers flow into your crown. Feel the light open up your own psychic "pores" in the aura and body, like opening window shades. St. John's Wort doesn't destroy boundaries or create holes, but rather clears windows for light to pass through freely wherever it is needed. The aura fills with light. Any area of illness or "dis-ease" fills with light. You become a miniature sun.

I've found this ritual to be so simple and profound that it is beyond words for me. The communion is through energy and intention. I have noticed that afterwards I tend to attract bees, though none have ever stung me. This ritual conveys a feeling of optimism and brightness. Everything is going to be all right, no matter the outcome. It is then our duty to carry that optimism out into the world, to be a beacon of light for others to see and from which find inspiration.

The rituals above tend to focus on the balms, a safer place for most of us to start. Use them to inspire similar rituals amongst the banes and tree teacher spirits.

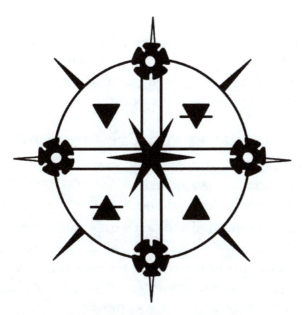

Chapter Six:
The Green Circle

s Witches we traditionally learn to create our temple, our sacred space, through the use of a circle. Sometimes the circle is created through formal ritual casting, other times through dance and movement. This circle form also suits the work of the plant world, as a symbol of the cycles and seasons, as well as the Earth, Sun, and Moon that rule over the green herbs. Yet many of the traditional circle-making procedures are performed in ways that are sterile, or appear to disconnect us from the very forces we are seeking to connect with. Rather than becoming openings between the worlds, including the world of nature, they become barriers to nature.

The Green Circle is a method that is not only in harmony with the Green World, but it also specifically invokes the plants' spiritual aid, just as some circle methods call upon animal totems, angels, elementals or deities. The format below will be familiar to anyone in a modern Witchcraft or Wicca background, yet it will have its own perspective on these fundamentals. This ritual summons forth plant spirit guardians for the four elements, and looks at ultimate divinity through the chlorophyll eyes of the plant world.

Cleansing and Preparation

Traditionally a properly prepared space is cleansed of harmful energies and the energetic debris of modern living. Ideally the Green Circle should be done out of doors, where the natural cycles of sun, wind and rain clear a space that is otherwise unmolested by humanity. You can also cast the Green Circle indoors in an effort to commune with the spirits of the green when you cannot be outdoors, as the eternal garden paradise lies just beneath our perceptions everywhere, including our homes and temples.

In ritual magick, the space is cleansed by earth and water through salt and water being aspersed, or gently sprinkled, in the ritual space. The space is also cleansed by fire and air by being censed with incense burning in a censer with charcoal. For the spirit of the Green Circle, I would suggest using the powers of the Green World in both forms of cleansing.

Grind the following herbs into an incense mixture and burn upon charcoal to clear the space with fire and smoke.

Green Circle Incense
3 Parts Frankincense Resin
2 Parts White Pine Needles
2 Parts Lavender Flowers
1 Part Angelica Root

Once the incense is smoking, walk around the ritual circle area three times widdershins (counterclockwise) and then set the censer on the altar. The incense can be used continuously throughout the ritual unless you prefer another incense that has a specific purpose to it. The smoke can be used to "smudge" yourself and participants to remove any harmful energies prior to the ritual and attune you to the powers of nature.

Floral waters are an excellent way to both cleanse and bless the space. Mix the following herbs and/or oils with either spring or well water. If you want to preserve the mixture for future use, strain out any plant material you may have used and bottle it with thirty to fifty percent of a high grade alcohol.

Cleansing Floral Water
   2 cups of Water
   3-5 drops of Lavender Essential Oil
      (or 1 Teaspoon of Lavender Flowers/Leaves)
   3-5 drops of Orange Essential Oil
      (or 1 Teaspoon of Orange Peel)
   3-5 drops of Rose or Rosewood Oil
      (or 1 Teaspoon of Rose Petals)

Sprinkle drops of the floral water from your fingertips or from an evergreen branch three times around the circle, widdershins. You can also use it to wash your hands and sprinkle upon your own body and the body of participants to be ritually cleansed prior to the working.

The cleansing might have less to do with really removing energy and more to do with centering and balancing the participants in relationship with the space. It clears the connection between person and place.

Casting the Circle

Many practitioners think of casting the circle as erecting a barrier against all forces that would impede upon the magickal working, as medieval magicians would literally draw out a circle upon the floor and never cross it during the ritual. Witches sometimes mark the bounds of the circle in twigs, flowers or herbal powders, or simply stand and dance in the circle. Modern Witches envision the circle ringed with the flames of life force, often in blue, white or violet fire, traced with tip of a blade or wand.

While the same idea of boundary and barrier is found in our modern magick, the circle is really more a process of peeling back the layer of ordinary reality to reveal the magickal otherworld. The circle pulls back the metaphoric curtain, dropping the scales from our eyes to reveal the paradise upon Earth. In this magickal Eden-Avalon-Hesperides, the spirit world clearly intersects with the physical world, and everything is possible. It is also a protective boundary against those forces that cannot exist in this state of perfect in-between-ness.

In this case, the wand is a much better tool to pull back this spiritual curtain and create your space. Most practitioners of British Traditional Wicca use the athame to create sacred space, but the athame can ward off the very forces with whom we seek to commune. Many folk traditions prohibit the use of iron in ritual, as iron is said to be the bane of the faery races, and in general, harmful to most spirit entities. It acts as a magickal lightning rod—discorporating their etheric bodies and banishing them from the area at best, or destroying them at worst. Faeries in particular are, at the very least, the spiritual guardians of, if not the embodiment of, nature. Those seeking to commune with the forces of nature and the plant world ideally should use tools from that world, rather than the realm of the blacksmith's forge. Those who insist on using metals in Green rituals should use faery-friendly metals such as copper, bronze, pewter, silver, and if available, gold.

The wooden wand is an excellent tool for conducting energy. Each wood has different properties, coloring its energy just like a colored glass alters the light that passes through it.

More importantly, the wooden wand helps to align you with the deep wisdom of the tree teachers.

Crafting the Wand

Crafting the wand can be a very profound process of spiritual union with a Tree Teacher. Classically-minded magicians may prefer wands of Hazel or Almond, and some believe that wands from five-petaled flowering trees, such as Apple, make the best wands so as to imitate the five pointed star on the magician's archetypal wand, but the choice must be up to you. Choose the type of wood for your wand based on your knowledge, research, and most importantly, your intuition. Which Tree Teacher wants to work with you? The one your head chooses can be very different from the one your heart may prefer, so when in doubt between the two, follow your heart's call. It will lead you to the Green Wisdom.

Once you find the appropriate tree, commune with it. Make sure that specific tree wants to sacrifice a limb for your wand. Speak with it in meditation. Lean up against it and enter a trance state. When you feel that this is the correct tree and that it is willing to work with you, make an offering to it. Say a blessing and give it your thanks for this work. If you feel the offering is accepted, then proceed.

Lore will tell you not to cut the wand with an iron or steel blade, and though I agree in principle, true silver blades are difficult to come by, and I've found copper and brass don't do such a great job. A silver coin can be sharpened to an edge to make the first cut, but it's hard to cut an entire branch with a coin. I struggle with the choice between the damage I may do to the tree and the potential wand by using inferior blades or simply breaking the branch off, and the affront steel might offer the tree. I often arrive at the conclusion that a steel hacksaw is simply the best, safest, most "humane" tool for the tree. I do bless the hacksaw with silvered water. I'm not sure if this truly sanctifies the steel or somehow "fools" the tree, but it tends to work for me. Make silver water (see the following) and sprinkle it upon the blade before using it. Before you cut, ask the tree to retain some portion of its power and spirit in the wood, even as it is separated from the body of the tree.

Silver Water

Silver water can be created by several different methods, depending on the tradition. For the work of the Green World, I prefer the simple method, though you will find more complex methods in various ceremonial traditions. Some magicians may either use silver chloride to ritually prepare a tincture of silver, or heat a piece of silver jewelry and then submerge it in a safe container, forcing molecules of silver to shed from the jewelry and enter the water. Colloidal silver from a health food store can also be used, and ambitious alchemists will make their own with electrical devices.

The simple method is to put a ritually cleansed piece of silver jewelry, with no stones or other adornments, into a clear glass bowl of spring water and leave it out overnight under the light of the Full Moon. Collect the water before sunrise and bottle it in a dark blue or amber bottle with 50% clear alcohol to preserve it. Sprinkle this water on tools you wish to bless with the power of the Moon and the metal silver.

Carefully strip the bark. Again, I use a pocket knife, but I have hallowed the blade with silver water. Save the bark—you can use it for magick later, either in the formulation of a spirit pot or plant homunculus, or as a powerful ingredient in various potions and incenses. Let the wood dry naturally. Some make a fire of the dead wood and bark of the same tree type, and dry their wand by the fire. I prefer the natural method of letting the wood air dry. When the wood is fully dry, mark the wand with paint or by burning it with a wood burning kit, or simply leave it plain. Oil the wood to preserve it and prevent it from cracking and to consecrate it ritually. An anointing wax formula is given below to both empower and protect a new wand. A good folkloric rule of thumb for wood preservation is to "oil" the wood with such a mixture once a day for a month, then once a month for a year, and then once a year for the rest of your life. This regular anointing creates quite a bond with the instrument, particularly if you ritualize the annual process on a specific day, like your anniversary with the magickal wand. Some bless the wood by anointing it with either blood or sexual fluids. The traditional ritual I learned for wand blessing included passing it through purifying smoke and/or saltwater, and with both hands holding it, mingling your energy with that of the wand, saying the following three times:

I consecrate this wand to catalyze my every thought and deed, by my highest will.
So mote it be.

Wand Anointing Ointment

3 Oz. Linseed Oil
1 Oz Beeswax
4 drops of Frankincense oil
3 drops of Myrrh oil
1 drop of Vitamin E Oil

Gently heat the linseed oil and add the beeswax. Pour this mixture out into a salve container and add the remaining oils as it cools. Frankincense and Myrrh add magickal virtue, and Myrrh helps preserve, along with the Vitamin E oil. Cap the jar but do not tighten it as it cools, and then when the ointment is fully formed, seal the jar and use as needed.

To cast your circle, hold your crafted wand and point it towards magnetic north. Inhale and draw the energy down from the heavens and up from the earth together into your heart. Feel the rose of the heart bloom within you, for that is your key to the garden. As you exhale, project the energy of your heart through your shoulder, down your arm, and into the wand. Feel the fire extend outward from the tip of the wand. Notice the color of this fire. You might find different wands exude different colors and powers.

As the fire reaches the edge of your envisioned circle, start imagining the boundary coming to life. Traditional circles are nine, twelve, or thirteen feet in diameter, but you can create a circle any size you desire. The fire of the circle does not create a solid wall, but out of the fire are formed the spiritual seeds of the garden. The casting of this circle creates a hedge, a grove within the garden. Imagine growing in the boundary-flames a hedge with wild rose, hawthorn, blackthorn and a variety of herbs and wildflowers entwined. The circle is cast three times, moving clockwise or deosil, and when you make your second and third pass, imagine the briar growing stronger and more vibrant. As you cast, recite these words:

We cast this circle to protect us from all forces that may come to do us harm, conjuring the hedge of the wild, with fruits and briars, to guard and sustain us.

We conjure this hedge circle, to allow entry to the spirits and forces that are in harmony with our working and bar the door from all forces that would do us ill, intentional or unintentional, and from all those not in harmony with the First Garden.

We conjure this hedge maze, like the labyrinth, to grant us access to the mysteries in the land below and between, to worship in the Garden Temple where the Divine Mind, Heart and Will are sovereign.

With these words and ritual actions, the circle is cast and you are standing in the First Garden.

Calling the Quarters

Traditional quarter calling involves opening a "gateway" into the elemental realms of earth, fire, air and water. Each of these spirit realms is viewed as being populated by spirits of these individual energies, known as elementals and often viewed in their popular medieval images of gnomes, salamanders, sylphs and undines respectively. Each quarter is usually charged with a guardian that works to mediate and control the flow of these elemental energies, while also protecting the participants and maintaining the integrity of the cast circle in order to contain the energies generated within it. Such guardians include archangels, elemental "kings," deities, and animal totems. In the Green Circle, we call upon plant spirits.

Plant spirit quarter calls can be adapted in any manner you see fit. This particular example uses those banes traditionally associated with Witchcraft —Mandrake, Monkshood, Henbane and Datura. These banes create a particularly intense energy in the circle for exploring the mysteries. The origin of these quarter calls is found in a version of the Green Circle I conducted for a Samhain rite. You could adapt them using only balms, which would be particularly good for general Green Circles and for healing work. You could also do a circle of Tree Teacher spirits. Any combination of balm, bane and tree could also work, as long as you feel it's balanced spiritually and energetically. I might suggest two balms and two banes, with the banes opposing each other and the balms opposing each other. You could also have two trees forming an axis, such as North-South, and a balm and bane on the East-West axis. Experiment, explore and commune with your green allies to see how, where, and when they wish to be called upon, if at all. See Appendix I and II for more ideas regarding quarter calls using balms and trees.

The orientation of the four elements below is based upon the work of the Greek philosopher Empedocles. He was a philosopher, healer and magician, situating the elements in opposition to each other in reference to their qualities of warm/cold and wet/dry. His orientation and philosophies were then adopted by alchemists using Western elemental theory. I personally find this particular theory of elemental orientation more powerful and intense in exploring the mysteries, and associate it with the work of the underworld. I favor this set of orientations over the more popular archangelic associations of air in the east and fire in the south.

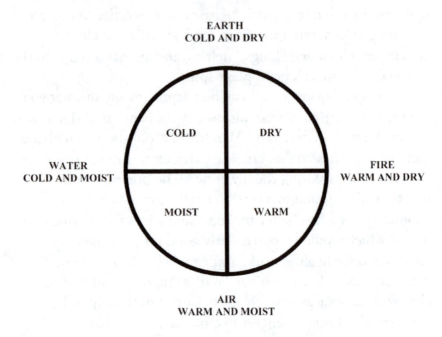

Fig. 11: Alchemical Elemental Orientation

To the North,
We call to the element of Earth in the Great Below,
and we call to the green spirits of Wisdom.
We call the bane Mandrake, root of love, death and wisdom.
Mandragora of the Midnight Scream that brings madness,
Whisper the secrets of the deep earth to us.
Hail and Welcome!

To the East,
We call to the element of Fire in the Great Below,
And we call to the green spirits of Power.
We call to the bane Monkshood, bane of wolves and slayer of monsters,
Aconite of the Hooded Veil, Burning Angel of Death.
Hail and Welcome!

To the South,
We call to the element of Air in the Great Below,
and we call to the green spirits of Knowledge.
We call to the bane of Devil's Eye, Henbane,
      giver of second sight, true sight,
Black Solanaceae summoner of storms
      and winds of whispering knowledge.
Hail and Welcome!

To the West,
We call to the element of Water in the Great Below,
and we call to the green spirits of Love.
We call to the bane of Thorn Apple, the Angel Trumpet,
Datura, open the heart and soul with your venom
      and numb us from overwhelming pain.
Hail and Welcome!

Evocation of the Gods

The evocation of the gods is simply an invitation to the divine and an opening of the way. In our working, we call upon the divine as Goddess and God—Mother and Father of our way. In particular, we ask for the manifestation of the Goddess and God in their aspects most appropriate for the working, so the calls can be modified to suit your needs. I prefer a universe mother figure encompassing all things for my work, and the evocation of the god of the green for my plant workings. The Mother is all of nature, the typical image of Mother Nature, but I acknowledge that nature includes all the burning stars and empty space, gravity and time, while I focus more specifically on the God as the plant life on this planet.

Evocation of the Goddess

To the Great Lady of Earth and Starry Heavens,
  She who is neither black nor white,
  we call for your blessings in this work.
Hail and welcome.

Evocation of the Plant Lord

To the Great Lord of the Green, Two Faces to the Past and the Present,
  we call you.
To the Leaf Faced Lord of Light, granter of balms and medicines,
  we call you.
To the Rot Covered Lord of Dark, giver of banes and forbidden
  wisdom, we call you.
Angelic Lord of the Forest, Devilish God of the Swamps,
  we call you.
Open the way to the Garden. Grant us knowledge of the Plant Fetch.
Show us the ways and wisdom of the Green Blood.
Hail and welcome.

In Pagan theology, we believe that the gods are ever present, immanent in everything, so why would they need to be *invited*, particularly with green magick, since the gods are themselves the land, the plants, the very air and light all around us? The evocation opens a conscious connection between our human consciousness and their non-human consciousness. It bridges the gap between us, and entices us all into communion with each other. The goal of our work is to be in a constant rapport with our gods, but the ritual evocation makes a clear declaration of this intention in the circle and, when the process is too overwhelming for us, devocation offers a clear release of that connection.

If you are working with any plant spirits specifically, call them to the center of the circle as well, now that the Green Man is present to clearly open the way.

Anointing

Anointing is the ritual action of applying sacred oils or waters to participants in the ritual. Sometimes it is done prior to the ritual, as a preparatory blessing to clear unwanted forces and invoke helpful forces beforehand. Other times it is done as a sacramental act within ritual, to attune our flesh and blood to the forces we wish to evoke within the ritual, or invoke within our bodies. Certain topical oils and ointments, through scent or absorption into the skin, can also alter consciousness by altering the body's chemistry. When anointing, you might say these or similar words:

I use this potion/ oil /unguent to bless and consecrate me/you in the mysteries of the green. Blessed be.

If your working isn't to attune to a specific plant or group of plants, this basic blessing oil can be used in the Green Circle.

> ### Green Blessings Oil
> 3 drops Patchouli Essential Oil
> 3 drops Oakmoss Essential Oil
> 2 drops Cedar Essential Oil
> 1/8 Oz Grapeseed Oil

Sacrament

A sacrament is simply any visible ritual that corresponds to an invisible act of divinity. Though many think of it as something unique to the Catholic—or at least Christian—faith, sacraments are present in all religions. One needs to only look at the roots of the Catholic Eucharist to see its Pagan origin, and to find parallels with the Wiccan ritual of Cakes and Wine/ Ale when performed in its true spirit of consecration. All are looking at the ritual meal as embodiments of the divine, to be consumed by the faithful.

In our Green Circle, the act of sacrament is in consuming the plant or plants with which you wish to commune in ritual. By having them ritually evoked in spirit, and then additionally physically ingested, you are best able to commune with the wisdom of the plant. This sacrament can take the form of an herbal tea, tincture, mulled wine, herbal beer, cakes, or in the case of plants that produce fruits, seeds or nuts, simply the natural food itself.

In the context of modern Witchcraft, the Great Rite can be said to constitute the sacrament. Traditionally either a sexual act in fact, or a sexual act in token performed with ritual tools, for the Green Circle the Great Rite is best done with a chalice/ cauldron filled with an herbal potion or wine for the Goddess force, and a wand for the God. Many prefer the ritual athame as the symbol of the God's phallus, but for a green working, wood is far better than metal, for the same reasons as cited above regarding why we cast the circle with a wand rather than a blade. Elementally, the Great Rite enacts the descent of the fire into the sacred waters, creating waters that burn with light. That is said to be the true meaning of the words "Ishi baha," the waters of life and light. The words I use when plunging the wand into the chalice are:

As the lance is to the grail in the mists of time,
The wand is to the chalice in the center of the circle,
The phallus is to the yoni in the world of flesh,
The stamen is to the pistil in the world of sap,
Power is to Love in All Worlds.
May the Rose of the Heart bloom in the Wasteland,
And open the gate to Wisdom.
Ishi Baha!

As a ritual of the green, generally the sacraments are of plant origin, and animal flesh or products are not used, with the possible exception of honey, since it is a perfect blend of the plant and insect world. If the plant matter is baked into a cake or wafer, eggs and dairy can also be an exception, but the main sacramental focus should be plant-based, not animal-based.

Alternately, a huzel style ritual can be used here as the sacrament for those not inclined towards the rituals of Wicca. A Christian magician of the Green World could adapt something similar involving the Eucharist. See Part Three for more discussion of sacraments in the work of the Green Witch.

Working

The working of the circle includes any ritual action in which you wish to partake. This is the true purpose of the circle, and will change with every circle you cast. Your working can be a communion with, or journey to, the plant spirits and divinities for knowledge, wisdom, guidance, healing or power. It can involve simple spellcraft – casting a spell or creating a charm. Ideally, a spell in the Green Circle is one of herbal magick, where you are asking the plant spirits to directly participate in the spell. Any spiritual work, subjective or objective in goal, can be performed in the heart of the circle. Many of the previous exercises can be done inside the context of the Green Circle.

If you experience a visionary journey or use a gateway as part of your working, you might receive a unique magickal name, visual sigil, song or dance for a plant spirit that is intended for your use only when communicating with that plant. Each of these is evocative of that plant spirit's medicine, and can be used as a part of the ritual's working.

The entire working should include a beginning, execution, and any necessary balancing and grounding before the ritual is released.

Devocation of the Gods

In proper ritual procedure, you deconstruct the ritual space much as you created it, working from the inner powers out, and moving backwards, widdershins, to the place you began. As the gods and specific plant spirits were last to be called to the circle, they are the first to be thanked and released from the circle.

We thank the Great Lady of the Starry Cosmos
*   and the Land Beneath us.*
We thank She who stands between the light and dark
*   for Her aid and protection.*
Hail and Farewell.

We thank the Great Lord of the Green,
Looking forward to the future and looking behind to the past.
We thank the Living Leaf Lord of Light, for the wisdom of balms, and
*   we thank the Dying Rot God of Darkness, for the wisdom of banes.*
We thank you for your blessings.
Hail and Farewell.

Release of the Quarters

Like the devocation of the divinities, it is now time to release the quarters, closing the gateway to the four elements while thanking and releasing the plant spirits that held their power. Traditionally I start in the north, as I did for the quarter calls, and then move widdershins.

To the North of the Great Below,
We thank and release the element of Earth
*   and the Green spirits of Wisdom.*
We thank and release the bane of Mandrake, human root of wisdom.
Hail and Farewell!

To the West of the Great Below,
We thank and release the element of Water
    and the Green Spirits of Love.
We thank and release the bane of Thorn Apple, the Angel Trumpet.
    Hail and Farewell!

To the South of the Great Below,
We thank and release the element of Air
    and the Green Spirits of Knowledge.
We thank and release the bane of Henbane, Giver of Second sight.
    Hail and Farewell!

To the East of the Great Below,
We thank and release the element of Fire
    and the Green Spirits of Power.
We thank and release the bane of Monkshood, Burning Angel of Death.
    Hail and Farewell!

Release of the Circle

Release the ritual circle. Point your wand to the north and again move widdershins. Though you cast it three times, it's only necessary to release with one circle. Imagine the powers that gathered to form your hedge casting its seeds to the cosmos. With this imagery, I envision us replanting the sacred garden with these spirit seeds. The more they spread, the more people will awaken to realize that we have never left the garden. We have always been in the sacred paradise and need to start acting like it.

We cast this hedge out, casting seeds for the future, touching the sacred circles of our sisters and brothers here and between the worlds. The hedge is open, but never broken. So mote it be.

Green Circle Ritual

The following is a brief outline of the Green Circle Ritual to assist those learning how to perform it. Adapt it as you see fit.

Cleanse and Prepare the Space and Participants

Cast Circle

We cast this circle to protect us from all forces that may come to do us harm, conjuring the hedge of the wild, with fruits and briars, to guard and sustain us.

We conjure this hedge circle, to allow entry to the spirits and forces that are in harmony with our working and bar the door from all forces that would do us ill, intentional or unintentional, and from all those not in harmony with the First Garden.

We conjure this hedge maze, like the labyrinth, to grant us access to the mysteries in the land below and between, to worship in the Garden Temple where the Divine Mind, Heart and Will are sovereign.

Calling of the Quarters

To the North,
We call to the element of Earth in the Great Below,
and we call to the green spirits of Wisdom.
We call the bane Mandrake, root of love, death and wisdom.
Mandragora of the Midnight Scream that brings madness,
Whisper the secrets of the deep earth to us.
Hail and Welcome!

To the East,
We call to the element of Fire in the Great Below,
And we call to the green spirits of Power.
We call to the bane Monkshood,
*   bane of wolves and slayer of monsters,*
Aconite of the Hooded Veil, Burning Angel of Death.
Hail and Welcome!

To the South,
We call to the element of Air in the Great Below,
and we call to the green spirits of Knowledge.
We call to the bane of Devil's Eye, Henbane,
*   giver of second sight, true sight,*
Black Solanaceae summoner of storms
*   and winds of whispering knowledge.*
Hail and Welcome!

To the West,
We call to the element of Water in the Great Below,
*   and we call to the green spirits of Love.*
We call to the bane of Thorn Apple, the Angel Trumpet,
Datura, open the heart and soul with your venom
*   and numb us from overwhelming pain.*
Hail and Welcome!

Evocation of the Goddess

To the Great Lady of Earth and Starry Heavens,
*   She who is neither black nor white,*
*   we call for your blessings in this work.*
Hail and welcome.

Evocation of the Plant Lord

To the Great Lord of the Green, Two Faces to the Past and the Present,
*   we call you.*
To the Leaf Faced Lord of Light, granter of balms and medicines,
*   we call you.*
To the Rot Covered Lord of Dark, giver of banes and forbidden
*   wisdom, we call you.*
Angelic Lord of the Forest, Devilish God of the Swamps,
*   we call you.*
Open the way to the Garden. Grant us knowledge of the Plant Fetch.
Show us the ways and wisdom of the Green Blood.
Hail and welcome.

Anointing

I use this potion/ oil /unguent to bless and consecrate me/you in the mysteries of the green. Blessed be.

Sacrament

Great Rite:
As the lance is to the grail in the mists of time,
The wand is to the chalice in the center of the circle,
The phallus is to the yoni in the world of flesh,
The stamen is to the pistil in the world of sap,
Power is to Love in All Worlds.
May the Rose of the Heart Bloom in the Wasteland,
And open the gate to Wisdom.
Ishi Baha!

Working

Perform the working of the rite.

Devocation of the Goddess

We thank the Great Lady of the Starry Cosmos
*   and the Land Beneath us.*
We thank She who stands between the light and dark
*   for Her aid and protection.*
Hail and Farewell.

Devocation of the Plant Lord

We thank the Great Lord of the Green,
Looking forward to the future and looking behind to the past.
We thank the Living Leaf Lord of Light, for the wisdom of balms,
*   and we thank the Dying Rot God of Darkness,*
*   for the wisdom of banes.*
We thank you for your blessings.
Hail and Farewell.

Release of the Quarters

To the North of the Great Below,
We thank and release the element of Earth
*   and the Green spirits of Wisdom.*
We thank and release the bane of Mandrake, human root of wisdom.
Hail and Farewell!

To the West of the Great Below,
We thank and release the element of Water
*   and the Green Spirits of Love.*
We thank and release the bane of Thorn Apple, the Angel Trumpet.
Hail and Farewell!

To the South of the Great Below,
We thank and release the element of Air
*   and the Green Spirits of Knowledge.*
We thank and release the bane of Henbane, Giver of Second sight.
Hail and Farewell!

To the East of the Great Below,
We thank and release the element of Fire
*   and the Green Spirits of Power.*
We thank and release the bane of Monkshood, Burning Angel of Death.
Hail and Farewell!

Release the Circle

We cast this hedge out, casting seeds for the future, touching the sacred
circles of our sisters and brothers here and between the worlds. The
hedge is open, but never broken. So mote it be.

Part Three:
The Blood Runs Green

Chapter Seven:
Elixirs of Wisdom

 o deepen your experience of the Green World, to fully live the love, power and wisdom of the plant familiar, you must enter into a symbiotic relationship with the plants. So many plants have a variety of chemicals within them that alter the physiology of animals. Why? Many plants produce foods—fruits and vegetables—with seeds, arguably to help the spread of the seeds and ensure the success of that plant species. But why do so many plants have properties that seem to have no benefit to the plant? Why would so many plants contain medicines to heal animal and human illness that could ultimately end in destroying the individual plant or large portions of it, rather than propagate it?

Those of us with a relationship to the Green World know that the answer to these questions lies in the pattern of creation; we are all weaving and reweaving strands of connection between the realms of mineral, plant and animal, and from the realms of matter and spirit. Plants want to be consumed by animals; they develop their own consciousness through interacting with animals. So we animals, too, develop our consciousness while interacting with plants. Though in many ways, out of the three realms of mineral, plant, and animal, animals are the youngest and need greater incentive to do this work. Humans in particular need that incentive, so food, medicine and magick all function as ways of enticing us into working directly with the plant realm. Forging connections between the three realms strengthens all the realms and aids in the evolution of all the spirits in those realms. We are all here in the garden to learn and grow from each other.

Plants grow out of the Earth, feeding off minerals from the land and the light of the sun. Animals eat the plants, gaining connections to both pure light and to minerals, the bones of the Earth. We are therefore born of both the Earth and the Starry Heavens. Some animals eat both plants and animals, or just other animals, which distances them from the direct chain, but they are still fed by it spiritually and physically. After ingestion, animals physically move mineral and plant matter in the world, giving plants and minerals a measure of freedom and an opportunity to mingle with other energies not found in their original location. Conversely, plants and minerals teach the animals about rooted-ness, growing, and the depths of consciousness by their very presence within the bodies of the animals.

There are those in the human realm that understood this on a deep level, consciously or intuitively. They knew the plant realm has mysteries to reveal and that it can be a powerful ally. But such blessings also come with dangers, as many of the "safe" plants to consume, in the forms of well-known foods, do not unlock the same powers that the more dangerous and unusual plants do. So those humans who sought this knowledge walked the edges of the plant world. They sought out the medicines of the briar hedge and the deep forest. They were the ancestors of the Witch. They knew how to work with the plants to brew the elixirs of wisdom, in the external cauldron of the kitchen, in the laboratory of the alchemist, and in the internal world of spirit and energy within the body of light itself.

Sacraments

Sacraments are discussed as part of the Green Circle, but they require further study as they become very important in the evolution of our consciousness while on the green path. Sacraments are simple acts of sacred communion. Outer visible ritual actions indicate a greater invisible occurrence within the spiritual planes. While most Witches believe that every act is filled with sacredness, the ritual act of ingesting or otherwise metabolizing plant matter is a particularly sacred act of union. It is a physical union between the plant and animal realm, but also a spiritual exchange of knowledge, energy and experience. The Huzel or shared Cakes and Ale are but two examples of this ritual union.

Sacraments of every religion recognize this exchange, though the importance of the plant world is not emphasized in other religions as it is in Witchcraft and shamanism. Sacraments are primarily seen as rituals coming from the Catholic tradition, including rituals that are seen as rites of passage in that community: baptism, communion, penance, confirmation, ordination, marriage, anointing of the sick, and extreme unction. Many if not all of these rituals involve the use of salt and water, oil, wine, and bread. Older versions of these ceremonies took place in a church with incense smoke wafting up to the rafters. These natural objects become interface points for holy experiences, and from the Pagan perspective they are not simply mediums for other heavenly forces, but divine experiences in and of themselves.

Sacraments of the Green World come in many forms, including those ingested, inhaled or applied topically.

Potions

Potions include all manner of liquid-based plant preparations used in magick. Though by the broadest definition potions can include topical oils made from infused or essential oils, the term most often refers to solutions that have a base of water or alcohol, and can often be consumed by the user. Potions include water-based infusions (also known as herbal teas, tisanes or brews), tinctures (alcohol based extracts) and more technical preparations such as alchemical herbal elixirs, also known as spagyric tinctures.

The benefit of any of these potions is in direct digestion and assimilation of the plant matter into the physical body. Many of the herbs used in potions not only possess magickal qualities, but will also stimulate direct physiological actions in the body. Some act as stimulants, while others are sedatives. Both states can be helpful in different forms of trance to experience personal gnosis.

Some herbs simply enhance the natural functioning of the body. Such herbs are traditionally called blood purifiers, but they are truly known as alteratives, as we're not really sure if they do anything to purify the blood itself, yet they work to enhance the functioning of the entire body. Famous Witch Sybil Leek was a well known proponent of all Witches drinking a cup of red clover tea, a classic alterative, every day.

Other plants aid specific functions or systems in the body, helping to enhance the immune system, kill parasites, aid digestion, remove inflammation, or absorb nutritional value. Many herbalists and Witches believe for every state of imbalance and illness in the body, there is at least one plant in nature to address the issue, and more often than not, you can find your cure growing locally.

Beyond what can be measured by traditional science, these ingested plants are also influencing the energetic systems that support our physical health. Various traditional medicine systems name energy centers in the body and subtle pathways that connect these points. Not only do they provide the life energy needed by the organs of our body and regulate the endocrine system within our body, but these energy centers also comprise the mechanism of our subtle senses, psychic ability and magickal talents. Herbs can stimulate and enhance these abilities. From the perspective of plant spirit medicine, each plant spirit has its own specialty, its own area of interface with humanity, and its own influence over various health issues and magickal perceptions.

Water Infusion

To prepare a water-based infusion of an herb or mixture of herb, take 1 tablespoon of the ground dried herb (2 tablespoons of bruised herb if using a fresh herb), charge it for your magickal intentions, and pour one cup (8 oz) of boiling water over it. Depending on the purpose of the infusion, the steeping time will vary. A good average is anywhere from five to fifteen minutes. Some herbs used just to make a pleasurable beverage shouldn't steep too long, as they will become bitter. Many medicinal teas are steeped overnight in a covered container. When the herb is finished steeping, strain the herbal matter out and drink the tea.

Plants that are very woody or consist mostly of hard roots are better prepared as decoctions. Place the mashed woody material in a saucepan and put cold water over it. Cover the pan with the lid and bring the mixture to a boil for at least twenty minutes. Let the mixture cool, strain, and use like a tea, or bottle and refrigerate if making more than one dose.

Dreaming Tea
1 Part Hops
1 Part Scullcap
1/2 Part Valerian
1/8 Part Poppy Seed

Tincture

Obtain an airtight glass container, such as a mason jar, to make your tincture. Fill the container 1/3 full of dry herb, or completely full of fresh herb. Make sure to consecrate the herb to your purposes, to bring out all the virtues and powers of the herb in both magick and medicine. You will be using alcohol as your *menstruum*, i.e. the substance that will extract the plant's medicinal and magickal virtues. I prefer a clear alcohol, like vodka, at least 80 proof. Different types of alcohol will "tint" the mixture based on the plant substance used to make the alcohol. The mixture of water and alcohol in 80 proof vodka will extract quite a bit of the chemicals from the plant, changing the color of the liquid. Fill the container with your chosen alcohol. If the cap of the jar is metal, prevent the metal from coming in contact with the liquid or herb by using plastic wrap or other non-porous lining between the jar's mouth and the lid. Seal and shake vigorously. Let it sit for four to six weeks, shaking regularly. Strain out the herb and bottle the liquid in a dark glass container. Medicinal doses can be one dropper full one to three times a day, depending on the herbs and the ailment, and magickal doses can be just a few drops. A few drops in spring water or wine can be used in the chalice of a ritual to the plant spirits, to attune you to the specific plant of the tincture you are using.

Vibrational Remedies

Vibrational Remedies are also known as Flower Essences or Flower Remedies when made from the flowers of herbs, trees and plants. Though they can potentially be made from the leaf, berry or even the root of the plant, the flower is said to be the most etherically potent part, radiating the life force of the entire plant, and is thereby ideal for imprinting the spiritual pattern of the plant upon water.

While practitioners continue to strive for such remedies to be accepted by modern mainstream health care practitioners, it remains that Vibrational Remedies are quite effective potions to be used in magickal and ritual healing. One of the greatest benefits in using Vibrational Remedies in Green magickal work is the ability to use them in internalizing baneful plant spirits without fear of physical poisoning. While energetically potent, essences can be made of Monkshood, Datura, Belladonna, and all the rest without fear of toxicity, as the potion is highly diluted and the dose is only a few drops.

Try using a few drops of a flower essence in your ritual chalice to attune to a plant spirit for a journey, communication or celebration. Taking an essence over a long period of time, such as three drops three times a day for a Moon cycle, can teach you deeply the wisdom of the plant while it aids in your own spiritual healing process.

Flower Essences can be mixed in combination to yield formulas for specific purposes. The most famous of these mixtures devised by Dr. Bach is now known as Rescue Remedy, a mix of five flowers (Rock Rose, Impatiens, Clematis, Star of Bethlehem, and Cherry Plum) designed to assist with those suffering from shock and trauma. Other mixtures can be crafted for a more magickal purpose in mind.

Flying Flower Essence

4 drops Yarrow Flower Essence
3 drops Monkshood Flower Essence
5 drops Datura Flower Essence

Mix in solution of 1/4 alcohol to 3/4 pure water. Take 3-10 drops to aid you in the practice of spirit flight. This blend is a safe substitute for the more toxic flying ointments in European tradition.

Return Essence

5 drops St. John's Wort Flower Essence
5 drops Rose Flower Essence
2 drops Star of Bethlehem Flower Essence
1 drop of Potato Flower Essence

Mix in solution of 1/4 alcohol to 3/4 pure water. Take 3-10 drops to aid in grounding the spirit back in the body and physical reality after an intense journey.

Wine & Beer

Wine and beer are both considered magickal drinks. They are used in mystery traditions because they are both "spirits" that have risen again through the fermentation process. Like the stages of alchemy, fermentation indicates a resurrection that is akin to spiritual rebirth or initiation in the mystery traditions. That's why wine and beer, along with bread, are used in the sacraments of various religious traditions. Wine is used in the mysteries of Dionysus in the Greek tradition, and "barley water" is used in the Eleusinian Mysteries of Demeter and Persephone. By identifying with something that has been resurrected and transformed, the one who consumes the sacrament also becomes resurrected and transformed.

Beer is one of the oldest forms of fermented drink known to humanity, dating all the way back to Sumeria. It is created from cereal grains, yeast and water, and is often flavored with hops to aid in both taste and preservation. Various additional herbs have been included in beer over its history, such as henbane.

Wine is created from fermented grape juice. In Pagan circles, honey wine, or mead, is a favored drink. Mead is said to be a gift from the gods and plays an important role in Teutonic Paganism and mythology. It is said to inspire men and gods, and heal and alleviate depression. While its basic form is honey, water and yeast, its can be flavored with a variety of fruits, herbs and spices. Many mixtures were first considered medicines rather than drinks, but they tasted good enough to become social and religious drinks.

These drinks are quite potent on their own in magick and can be used as they are. For more novice herbal alchemists, other herbs can be added to the mixture by mulling herbs into the blend. Mulled wines work best in my experience; the wine is gently heated while soaking with herbs, and the herbal qualities, magickal and medicinal, are thus transferred to the wine.

Oracular Wine

1 bottle of White Wine
1 tablespoon of Bay Leaves
1 pinch of Mugwort
1 tablespoon of Honey

Slowly simmer the wine in a pan and add the herbs and honey in it. Keep it simmering for another five minutes and then allow it to cool. Strain the herbs out and drink a glass before performing oracular or divinatory workings.

Planetary Wine

1 bottle of Mead
1 pinch of St. John's Wort
1 pinch of Mugwort
1 pinch of Fennel
1 pinch of Vervain
1 pinch of Coriander
1 pinch of Cinnamon
1 pinch of Horsetail

Like the recipe above, slowly simmer the wine in a pan and add the herbs to it. Allow it to cool. Strain the herbs. Drink this wine to align with the seven planetary powers.

With the advancement of home brewing processes, it can be fairly easy to make your own wine, beer and mead. I'll be sharing instructions on making mead that I learned from following my friend and fellow author Alaric Albertsson's recipe for Hillbilly Mead, found in his book, *Travels Through Middle Earth*. In it he gives much greater detail on mead, its variations and use in Saxon Paganism.

While it is easy to brew mead, it can be difficult to achieve a pure mead with the right flavor. Other flavoring agents can be added to it, creating a wide variety of meads. A cyser is a mead made with apple juice, and is an excellent type of mead for first-time brewers because the flavor of the juice can cover some "off" tastes generated by an inexperienced brewer. Start with this basic recipe, and if you are drawn to brew more "professional" mead, you can get more intricate equipment found in brewing stores and catalogs.

Hillbilly Mead
1 large pot
1 long-handled stirring spoon
2 one-gallon jugs (glass or ceramic is preferable)
2 corks or caps for the jugs
2 balloons
1 needle
2 pounds of honey
1 packet of yeast (Sweet or Dry Mead Yeast is best, or baking yeast)
Water/apple juice
Spices, fruit or herbs (optional)
2 tea bags
2 or more elastic bands

Thoroughly clean all your equipment, and then start by boiling three quarts of water in the pot for ten minutes. If you are brewing a cyser, which I recommend, substitute six cups of your favorite apple juice for the water. Remove the pot from the heat and slowly stir in your two pounds of honey. You don't want to boil the honey, but have the water hot enough to dissolve the honey into the water or water/juice combination. More complex meads will have fruit, herbs or spices added at this point. Don't add more than a pound of fruit. Let the mixture cool until it becomes room temperature. Cover the pot when it cools to keep the mixture sterile. Once it is cool, add your yeast and stir it in. Pour the mixture into your jugs. They should each be about half full, and you will want to have that space when they start fermenting. Drop a tea bag into each jug to add tannins. Tannins help the mead taste "dry" and clean. Without them, it can taste flat and unappealing. Use your needle to put three holes in each balloon and place the opening of the balloon over the mouth of the jugs. They will allow carbon dioxide generated from the fermentation to escape, while keeping bacteria out. You can secure them with elastic bands. Keep the jugs at room temperature and out of direct sunlight. It will take a few weeks for the fermentation to complete. Fermentation is complete when your jugs are transparent and no more bubbles appear on the sides. Once you are sure it is done fermenting, cork the jugs. To improve the mead, you can siphon the mead off into two new clean jugs before corking it in order to separate the mead from the dead yeast cell sediment at the bottom. This improves the taste, particularly if you are not drinking it right away but storing it. The taste of mead can improve and mellow with time.

For a mead involving underworld mysteries, pomegranate seeds are an excellent flavoring, being sacred to Persephone. Blackberries can align your drink with energies of the goddesses and are sacred to Bridget. A spicy and energizing mead will have a small amount of ginger root; orange slices or orange peel are very complimentary with ginger. Citrus works well with mead too; I like lemon- and orange-flavored mead. Fruity mead, with grapes, cranberries or strawberries, can all be delicious and carry the magick of their appropriate fruit. Bitter herbs are usually avoided in meads, but spices such as ginger, cinnamon, nutmeg and clove can all work well.

Alchemical Elixirs and the Vegetable Stone

The creation of an alchemical elixir, also known as a spagyric elixir, is a powerful method of plant magick. Just the act of making such an elixir attunes you to the plant and brings you through the process of purification and rectification. Ingesting the essence you have made can bring profound healing and insight; so much so, that only very small doses are used in comparison to a normal medicinal tincture. Such elixirs are said to be fully "alive."

To make an alchemical elixir, create a tincture according to the standard method outlined above. Make sure to use a high-grade clear alcohol, 190 proof. Many suggest using the grain alcohol brand Everclear or a grape alcohol. Devoted alchemists will often place the tincturing jar or bottle in a "womb-like" clay vessel designed for this purpose, or cover it with silk cloth to keep its vibrations pure, shaking it ever day. Others cover it with tin foil to keep out light and unwanted vibrations. Some place it on a magickal grid made up of symbols from the plant's astrological ruling planet or Zodiac sign. These planetary seals, sigils, kameas (numbered squares) and glyphs are used on such "birthing" talismans. In fact, traditionalists will time every operation by the associated planetary day and hour, starting each operation at the New Moon.

Upon completion, rather than discarding the spent, wet herb—also known as the "marc" in herbalism or the "feces" in alchemy—place it in a heat proof glass baking pan and set it on fire. This process is known as calcination, where the herb is reduced to ash. Upon the first burning it will become black ash. Stir the ash with a nonflammable spoon to make sure it burns entirely. Metallic implements are fine as long as they are not aluminum, though a fireproof glass or ceramic utensil is ideal. Then heat the pan of ash in an oven or camp stove until it turns grey or white. The ultimate goal is white, though it might take almost a day to simply get the ash to turn light gray, which is sufficient for our needs. The additional heat purifies the ash. Bottle and preserve your alcoholic tincture, minus the herb. When the ash is purified, grind it to a fine powder in a mortar and pestle, and then add it back to the tincture. Cover and shake daily to allow the tincture to dissolve and absorb the ash. After a few weeks, strain the mixture through an unbleached paper filter. Discard the undissolved "salt," and you have a new "living" tincture of the plant. Some practitioners keep the salt and alcohol separate, and only add a few grains to a dose just before taking it, considering this a more powerful method. I myself prefer the traditional alchemical elixirs to this delayed approach if one is not attempting to make the Vegetable Stone (see below). Just a few drops on the tongue, or better yet in water or wine, will bring its purified effects to you. It makes an excellent sacrament or medicine, depending on the need. One powerful technique is to make one tincture for each of the seven chakras/planets, working your way up this "ladder to heaven"—Saturn, Jupiter, Mars, Venus, Mercury, Moon, and Sun —until you have experienced each of these powers and brought yourself clarity and insight.

A variation on the alchemical tincture is the plant stone or Vegetable Stone. Alchemists are always seeking the Philosopher's Stone, with its ability to turn lead into gold, though some believe this is a metaphor. Such a stone is also called the Greater Stone. The Vegetable Stone is known as the Lesser Stone, a preliminary working in the operation of the Greater Stone. Alchemists worked in the animal, vegetable and mineral kingdoms, and saw metals as the highest of the high in terms of spiritual allies and ingredients. But the plant stone is also powerful and useful on the quest toward enlightenment.

In the creation of the Vegetable Stone, instead of the gray/ white ash being added back to the tincture, it is brought together in small pile. The tincture is then added to the ash drop by drop. Ideally the ash should be as purified (i.e. as white) as possible. If the conditions are right, the mixture of alchemical salt from the ashes and the tincture will form a waxy substance that can be shaped into a ball or pellet, like a stone. The stone is usually fragile, and should be kept in a safe place. I usually place a single stone in small, clean wide mouth jar like the kind usually used for creams and ointments. The container is small enough that I can carry it on my person. It acts as a talisman for the plant's powers, and is said to grow "wise" the longer you keep it. Simply carrying it on your person confers its power to you. Meditating with it in your hands, even holding the jar that contains it, will allow it to radiate its vibration into your own aura. As the ultimate sacrament, it can be dissolved in water or wine in ritual, and its power, love and wisdom consumed much like a powdered philter (see below). Some dip the stone in water to bless it, without dissolving it. The Vegetable Stone is hard work, both manually and spiritually, and success on the first try is not typical. Aborted stones that don't quite form can always be converted into the more simple alchemical elixirs.

Powders

Powders are simply a "dry" potion, made from ground ingredients without a liquid base of water and/or alcohol. Powders have long been used in magick, and can even be found in more modern folks traditions such as Hoodoo. Dry potions are also sometimes known as philters. Philters can technically refer to dry or wet potions, and often a few grains or pinches of a dry philter can be added to a drink to create a wet potion. Philters were designed to be powerful and concentrated, and to be used in secret, slipped into the drink of an unsuspecting target. Modern Witches tend to refer to any dry mixture as a philter. When they are finely ground, they might also be referred to as a magickal dust.

Some magickal powders are simply ground herbs, woods and resins, with oils added to bind the mixture. Other powders use a mineral base, such as talc, salt or sulfur. Herbs are then added to this base. Others achieve a similar effect with an organic base, such as cornmeal, cornstarch, eggshells or sawdust. Ash and even dirt, particularly dirt from a sacred place or even a graveyard, can be used in a magickal powder.

The methods of using a powder are varied, depending on the ingredients and purpose of the powder. When nontoxic and edible, they can be put into food or drink, or a few grains can be placed directly on the tongue. They can be scattered in the area where you desire their effect. In particular they are good for creating boundaries and sacred space with a particular purpose, most often protection. Many folk magick powders are scattered across a threshold, so people pass through them and are thus affected by the mixture. They can be placed into bowls and left out where you want them to have an effect. They can also be smoked in pipes, again depending on their content and toxicity, or used as incense.

Incense

Incense is probably one of the most popular uses of magickal powders. While most people are familiar with incense in the form of a cone or stick, usually only magickal practitioners are familiar with granular incense. Known as "loose" incense because it is not bound, it is traditionally burned on charcoal. Unlike commercial incense in sticks or cones, loose incense must be sprinkled on charcoal to continuously keep the smoke wafting. Witches use a flame proof container for this charcoal. Easy to light "self igniting" charcoal can be purchased at most occult shops in the shape of small thick discs. The incense burner, sometimes known as thurible or brazier, should be of a heat resistant material, such as brass or iron, and be lined with sand to diffuse the heat. Many ceremonial-oriented practitioners use a brazier similar to those used by the Catholic

Church—a brass vessel hanging from chains that can be swung to diffuse the smoke in the ritual space. I like using a small iron cauldron.

The virtues of incense are many. On a chemical level, the smell of the smoke can actually alter body chemistry. As a form of aromatherapy, our body responds to scent, and some plant substances, when burned, can induce a powerful trance experience. On a magickal level, it is believed that when a substance is burned, particularly a plant, wood or resin, it releases its spiritual vibration and effect into the area where the smoke reaches. So incense works on two levels to aid in our communication with the spirit world.

To formulate your own incense, any herb that can be burned is a potential ingredient, but to make a pleasing incense, tradition has shown that a mixture of resins, woods, herbs and oils are best. Resins and woods make up the base of most incenses. Resins burn longest and smell the best. They comprise the classic incense ingredients in both the old and new worlds, used in ancient temples and even today in many modern churches. Many woods also give a pleasing scent when burning and can be quite magickal in effect. Some use a light wood and color it with food coloring or vegetable dye to add color magick to the mix. While roots are woody and burn more like bark or wood, the stems, leaves and flowers of a plant burn quickly and when burning smell different from the plant in its fresh or dried state. Don't expect burning rose petals to release the scent of rose, though when mixed with other ingredients, they can be both pleasant and effective in magick. Natural essential oils also aid in the aesthetics of the desired scent, and help to bind the incense together. Some recipes call for wine, mead or honey in small amounts to also help bind the incense; when using these ingredients, make sure all the parts mix thoroughly, as otherwise the heavier bits may settle at the bottom of your jar. Ideally incense should sit in an airtight container for at least a month to let it "mellow" and to allow all the scents to mix thoroughly.

> **Trance Incense**
> 1 Part Bark from your Teacher Tree
> 1 Part Myrrh
> 1 Part American Mandrake (May Apple)
> 1 Part Mugwort
> 1 Part Wormwood
> 1/2 Part Nutmeg
> 1/8 Part Datura Seeds
> 3 Parts Red Wine (To Bind)

Oils and Unguents

Oils and unguents are types of "potions" that are not usually ingested but are rather used topically. They are not made in a water or alcohol base. Alchemically, some practitioners relate the quality of oil to the earth elemental realm rather than water, even though oils flow like water. Mineral oil is the best example of a liquid carrying an "earthy" magickal charge. Oils and unguents are used in the traditions of magick and medicine in both the East and the West. In America, the occult traditions of Neopaganism have blended with the African Diasporic tradition of New Orleans Voodoo and the American folk craft of Hoodoo to create some interesting combinations.

Magickal oils are generally liquids that are a blend of a true plant oil, used as a base, and the volatile scented chemicals extracted from plants that are referred to as essential oils. Essential oils are extracted from plant material using distillation, expression or solvent extraction. They carry the scent, taste, medicinal qualities and magickal qualities of the plant, though the extraction method can chemically change the properties of the oil from its natural state. The mixture of base oil and essential oils creates a viscous perfume-like mixture that can be used to anoint the body and ritual tools, added to bath water, sniffed, diffused through the room, burned, or in certain cases, used to flavor food. Use of these oils affects the vibration of the user or the environment where they are used. It infuses vibrations with the combination of the plant spirits in its formula, and many plant spirit energies work synergistically together for greater effect in this way than they would on their own.

Medicinally oriented oil makers will mix 1/8 of an ounce of base oil, such as grape seed, apricot kernel, almond or jojoba (a natural plant wax), with five to ten drops of an essential oil. More occult-oriented oil crafters usually mix a dram, or twenty drops of an oil, using ten drops base oil and ten drops essential oils.

Uplifting Oil
3 drops Lavender
3 drops Melissa (Lemon Balm)
2 drops Sweet Orange
1 drop Peppermint
1/8 oz Base Oil
Mix the essential oils with the base oil drop by drop. Sniff and wear when you feel like life is "heavy" and you need to be lifted up from any responsibility or light depression.

Unguent is a fancy name for an ointment or salve, though technically an unguent is said to be more oily, while an ointment is more waxy. Essentially, unguents are a mixture of wax and oil used topically on the body. The plant oil can be infused with plant substances, mixed with melted wax (or in some cases, petroleum jelly) and scented with essential oils.

The most classic use of an ointment in Witchcraft is the medieval flying ointment. Flying ointments are concoctions of potentially deadly herbs that help induce shamanic out-of-body experiences through poisoning the body. Safer, but arguably less effective, modern recipes are followed by many Witches today who dare not use what are believed to be more traditional formulas. Other ointments are used for healing, protection and blessing.

Traditional Flying Ointment Ingredients
Parsley
Aconite
Poplar Leaves
Water Parsnip
Sweet Flag
Cinquefoil
Deadly Nightshade
Henbane
Datura
Hemlock
Soot
Bat's Blood

Historic flying ointments usually contain some of the listed ingredients. This list is reproduced here for historical purposes only to assist the reader in understanding herbal formulations in the context of the history of Witchcraft. Understanding of entheogens, toxic or otherwise, is expanded upon in the following sections.

Many traditional formulas also contain sensational elements modern Witches believe were part of the Inquisitors' colorful imagination, such as baby's fat. Animal fat was probably used. Animal ingredients in general may or may not have been a part of the ingredients, as some believe these ingredient names were codes for herbs in a cipher we no longer know.

> **_Modern Flying Ointment_**
>   1 Oz Beeswax (measured by weight, not volume)
>   3 Oz of Olive Oil
>   Myrrh
>   Mugwort
>   Wormwood
>   Parsley
>   Vervain
>   Sweet Flag
>   Cinquefoil
>   Lemon Balm
>   Yarrow
>   Datura Leaves
>   Datura Seeds
>   5 drops Mugwort Essential Oil
>   Vitamin E Oil
>
> Heat the oil gently and put a pinch of each of the listed herbs in it. Let it simmer for at least forty minutes if not an hour or two on low heat to extract the herbal qualities from the plant material. Break up the beeswax and melt it into the oil. Pour the oil into a container and add one to five drops of vitamin E oil. Add the Mugwort essential oil and put the cap on the container without sealing it, letting it cool down while covered. It will cool to an ointment that can be used to help induce "flight." Traditionally it is applied to the most sensitive and absorbent skin on the body – sex organs, anus, beneath the arm pits, palms of the hands and soles of the feet.

Food

Herbal allies can flavor food and be baked into a variety of sacramental cakes. Like wine, beer and mead, leavened products like bread and cake are particularly favored because they have "risen" again in the baking process, helping to confer the connection to immortality on the consumer. In modern Wicca, the sacramental meal is known as Cakes and Ale or Cakes and Wine, and covers a wide range of fresh to store-bought sabbat and esbat cakes. Ideally, one makes cakes to fit specific ritual purposes and astrological alignments by choosing herbs and spices that compliment the energies to be evoked. Making your own cakes for the offering of shared Cakes and Ale or the Huzel is an ideal way to deepen your connection to the magick in these rites.

Sabbat Cakes
> 1 1/2 cups flour
> 1/4 cup cornmeal
> 1 tablespoon baking powder
> 1/2 teaspoon salt
> 1/2 cup plain yogurt
> 2 eggs, beaten
> 1/4 cup sugar
> 1/4 cup maple syrup
> 1/4 cup canola oil
> 2 teaspoons vanilla extract

Preheat oven to 400 degrees. Coat an 8-by-8-inch pan with nonstick cooking spray or butter. Mix all ingredients together in a large bowl until blended. Pour into pan and bake 25 to 30 minutes, until a knife inserted into the center comes out clean. Let cool and slice into squares.

You can mix in additional ingredients for flavor and magickal properties. Add 1 1/2 cups of cranberries, raspberries, blackberries, blueberries, or strawberries (fresh or frozen). Add two teaspoons of freshly grated lemon or orange zest for flavor and lunar or solar qualities, respectively. For a spice cake, add 1 teaspoon ground cinnamon, 1 teaspoon ground ginger, or 1/2 teaspoon ground nutmeg, or a mixture thereof.

Entheogenic Awakening

Entheogen is a relatively new term used to refer to substances formally classified as hallucinogens or psychedelics. Entheogen means "to generate/create/release the god within" and places these substances in the context of a spiritual experience. Hallucinogen implies that the experience is a hallucination, something not real. Psychedelic means to make the "psyche" or mind/soul, depending on the cultural context, visible, but can also imply a level of unreality. Entheogen places the experience squarely in the religious context, specifically within the paradigm of shamanic or pantheistic theology.

By using the term entheogen, we are separating the substance from secular, recreational use, though many entheogens are taken recreationally without a religious or ceremonial context. Many entheogens might also be taken for medical reasons as well, outside of the context of religion, but in the most ancient cultures, there was little separation between the areas of religion, medication, and recreation, so our current divisions are fairly arbitrary. In a historical and geographical survey, we find mention of entheogenic use all over the world, and even potentially in mainstream religions like Judaism, Christianity, and Islam. More overt and familiar references are found in the Pagan religions of the Middle East, Mediterranean, India, Siberia and the Americas. Entheogens could be at the heart of Mystery Traditions found all over the world. Plant gnosis plays a key role in the traditions of initiation into the priesthood for our ancient ancestors, and that role can be reclaimed in the modern era.

Entheogenic sacraments are part of the time-honored tradition of religious intoxication. While most think of intoxication as primarily drunkenness, referring to the imbibing of alcohol, its true meaning is to "take in a substance that is debilitating, harmful or infectious," a substance that will stupefy or excite. By their nature, such substances are considered toxic and poisonous to humans because of their actions upon the brain and central nervous system that alter perception, actions, mood and awareness. Yet as we know via our relationship to the baneful plants, what constitutes a toxin is a matter of dose and use. Many substances classified as toxic can be keys to new awareness and power when used appropriately. They can quite literally awaken the god within, granting awareness of the higher self, as well as becoming a gateway to commune with non-human intelligences that can grant healing, wisdom and power.

Many different substances are considered entheogens. Most are classified as illegal in the United States due to their psychoactive effects. Some are fairly harmless or benign. Modern Witches on the green path should do their best to educate themselves on the major entheogenic families, particularly those included here. This overview is not intended as a directive for illegal behavior or a clear manual on the safe and effective use of entheogens. Each of us must engage in the necessary intellectual research and spiritual practice to determine which experiences and substances are right for us in our own spiritual evolution and initiation. These teachings simply open the door to further discussion and insight.

Alcohol – Alcohol is probably the best known of the intoxicants. While the term *alcohol* can refer to a range of substances, alcohol meant for consumption is technically ethanol, a colorless volatile liquid that is derived from the fermentation of sugars. Technically considered a depressant in terms of effect upon the body, it also possesses qualities of a relaxant, euphoric and aphrodisiac nature, and many consider it to be artistically or religiously inspiring. The use of alcohol in food, medicine, celebrations, recreation and religion goes back to the ancient world and continues to this day. While specific alcohols are used in regional traditions where particular forms of this intoxicant are more readily available, the most commonly used form of alcohol in Witchcraft is wine, specifically red wine, to represent the blood of the Goddess. In fact, many traditions of the Craft prohibit "hard" or distilled alcohol, and only allow wine, mead, and some forms of beer that are used to emulate the "barley water" of the ancients. The classic guideline states that a single glass can help open the gates during ritual and journey work, while a whole bottle leaves one with little control or discipline for magickal work. Some seership traditions use a shot of distilled alcohol to actually shut down the second sight and give the seer a rest, while African diasporic traditions use distilled alcohol, particularly rum, as an offering to feed the spirits and aid in their manifestation, though the rum can also be grounding when consumed by participants after a possession.

Artemisia – The Artemisia genus of plants has long been associated with magick, shamanism, Witchcraft and healing, with varieties found all over the world, ranging from common mugwort to the sagebrush used in Native American smudging rituals. Named for the Greek goddess Artemis, known as Diana to the Romans, the Artemisias are sacred to the Moon, for she is a Moon goddess and Artemisias are generally known to promote physic ability. Common mugwort, or *Artemisia vulgaris*, is used in tea, incense and essential oil to promote psychic ability and lucid dreams. The most entheogenic of the Artemisia family is Wormwood, *Artemisia absinthium*. It has been both treasured and feared as a major ingredient in the potent drink absinthe. Known for possessing a higher content of thujone, a psychoactive chemical found in artemesias, absinthe is said to distort time and space, facilitate the creative process, and ease contact with spiritual entities. Absinthe has been called the "Green Fairy" because reportedly poets and artists drinking it would have visions of green fairies. Modern research disputes the reputation and effect of thujone, indicating that it has no hallucinogenic properties and that absinthe is no more potent than other alcohols. Magickal practitioners who use absinthe in ritual do notice a potent effect.

THC – THC, or Tetrahydrocannabinol, is the psychoactive element found in the cannabis sativa plant and related species popularly known as marijuana. The leaves or resin can be smoked or the oils extracted to be used in food, medicine or drink. The function of THC in marijuana preparations defies conventional classifications. Chemically, it is considered to be psychoactive and entheogenic due to the presence of THC, but the hemp plant, when consumed, also exhibits the same traits as a depressant, stimulant and antipsychotic drug. Practitioners of a wide variety of spiritual disciplines believe it induces trance and alters consciousness to permit communication with other realms of existence. It has a history dating back to the Stone Age and has been used in religious rites throughout Asia and Europe, including the rites of Dionysus in Greece. It has even been used in the history of Judaism, Christianity and Islam. Some British Traditional Wicca books of shadow contain instructions for the use of "hemp" in incense and ointments, warning the Witch not to use "too much."

Belladonna Alkaloids – Chemicals found in the belladonna family of plants, also known as the Solanum botanical family, are the traditional psychoactive ingredients in European flying ointments. They contain the alkaloids scopolamine and hyoscyamine, and the drug atropine is derived from them. The most psychoactive members of this group containing these alkaloids are also the most deadly, and include plants such as Deadly Nightshade, Henbane, Mandrake and Datura. The less toxic and non-psychoactive relatives of these plants include the potato, tomato, pepper and eggplant, and tobacco, though tobacco straddles the line in terms of its danger level. This group of chemicals is known to produce a dream-like stupor, a seeming "delirium" of otherworldly visions, vertigo, and amnesia, and can also act as a sedative. Most of the plant spirits in this group have an underworld, dangerous, sexual and feminine quality to them. They signify some of the key spiritual components in European Witchcraft, which illustrate the different qualities Witchcraft engenders compared to other forms of indigenous shamanism that use natural entheogens.

D-Lysergic Acid Amide – This chemical is the psychoactive component found in Morning Glory seeds and is a natural relative to the synthetic LSD popularized by Timothy Leary. In the spiritual practices of Mexico, D-Lysergic Acid Amide plays a role in combination with other psychoactive plants, primarily the species *Rivea corymbosa*, though North American practitioners have experimented with other species, particularly *Ipomoea violacea*, or Heavenly Blue Morning Glories. Traditionally the seeds are infused in a very purgative tea. Commercially obtained seeds are treated with a chemical to prevent recreational use, so practitioners must grow their own, and an effective dose is often considered to be comprised of hundreds of seeds. Other plants also contain similar chemicals, such as Hawaiian Baby Woodrose (*Argyreia nervosa*) and Sleepy Grass (*Stipa robusta*), but there is very little, if any, traditional lore related to these plants. LSD itself was synthesized from the Ergot fungus (*Calviceps purpurea*) which grows in ryegrass, and is associated with both the Greek Eleusinian Mysteries and the European witchcraft trials. In the former it was a holy sacrament, and in the latter a toxin that unwittingly released paranoia and hysteria that led to "evidence" regarding the presence of the Devil.

Mescaline – The North American peyote cactus (*Laphophora williamsii*) contains the alkaloid mescaline. Unless you are a recognized and official member of the Native American Church, it is illegal to use peyote in the United States. The San Pedro cactus (*Trichocereus pachanoi*) also contains mescaline, but in a much lower dose. Both plants are known to cause vomiting when eaten.

DMT – While DMT, or Dimethyltryptamine, is a chemical that is naturally produced in the human brain, most entheogenic discussions of DMT usually involve the South American sacramental brew known as Ayahuasca. Found primarily among the traditions of the Quechua, its name means "Vine of the Soul" or "Vine of the Dead." While popularly believed to be one herb, Ayahuasca refers to a mixture of plants. Each shaman has his or her own particular recipe, but most Ayahuasca formulas require two particular plants, so as to have two specific chemicals within it. The *Banisteriopsis caapi* vine contains a beta-carboline chemical, such as harmine or harmaline. The *Psychotria viridis* bush contains tryptamine alkaloids, such as *N-dimethyltryptaimine* or DMT. Harmine alkaloids act as an MAO inhibitor, which is necessary for DMT to work effectively. Without both, the brew is not psychoactive. When western scientists ask native practitioners how they learned to combine two unrelated plants that do not necessarily grow near each other, they respond that the plant spirits told them how to make it. The plant spirits also instructed them in a variety of dietary restrictions and social taboos, along with the Ayahuasca songs and rituals. It is a very powerful and healing mix, and is not recommended at all for recreation, as it's said to "straighten" the bends in your soul, forcing you to face your fears in the spirit world to find harmony. Chemically it is also very purgative, particularly if you do not follow the dietary restrictions. It is quite dangerous to combine with other forms of entheogens or street drugs. Modern practitioners are currently experimenting with other forms of DMT and other combinations of plants that contain these two types of chemicals to make new effective psychoactive brews.

Psilocybin Mushrooms – Psilocybin mushrooms and related species are the popular "magic mushrooms" of the 1960's drug culture. The psychoactive alkaloids psilocybin and psilocin are considered relatively "safe" in the form of this mushroom, and while every psychoactive substance has its inherent danger, compared to many of the more toxic plants of the Witchcraft traditions, psilocybin has been enjoyed in ritual and recreation with a fair amount of safety, though the effects can sometimes be disconcerting and I feel are best experienced in a ritual context.

Fly Agaric Mushrooms – The red capped mushroom, decorated in white spots, is a familiar element in European faery lore, Witchcraft and shamanism. The fly Agaric, or *Amanita muscaria*, is native to the Northern Hemisphere and great debate exists as to its use in modern Witchcraft and Wicca. Some say Gerald Gardner had no knowledge of it, and cite this as proof of his ignorance of the native Witchcraft tradition. Others, including Doreen Valiente, say that of course he knew its use, and obviously he didn't talk about it in public with people he didn't know as he wanted to discourage those seeking drug-induced thrills from involving themselves in the Craft, or to prevent governmental investigation into Wicca. If the early initiates of Gardnerian Wicca had this training, few retain it today, or simply follow Gardner's lead in not talking about it at all. Depending on the variety of the fly agaric and its location, season and growing conditions, it can be a powerful psychoactive sacrament, but can also potentially be a poison and should always be used with care and educated supervision.

Diviner's Mint – Diviner's Mint, or *Salvia divinorum,* is a minor psychedelic used in Mexico in healing and divination ceremonies. During ritual use, it is said to produce powerful visions, and in the Mazatec Indian traditions one must master this mint before moving on to morning glory seeds, and then master the morning glory before moving onto psilocybin mushrooms. The elusive catalyst in the plant is very unstable and the plant is best used fresh. I must admit that the use of this plant as an incense employed by traditionally trained Mayan shamans had little effect on me, though the tincture was more effective.

For those seeking a more in-depth understanding of the use of entheogens, I highly recommend the work of Dale Pendell, Terrence McKenna and Jim DeKorne. Connection with a living teacher or mentor experienced in these arts can be quite helpful in assuring the effective use of these plants in a ceremonial context. Those who are already familiar with a specific plant spirit can more safely initiate you into the mysteries of that plant.

Formulary in the Heart of the Earth

The deepest wisdom of ages both past and future is said to be held within the consciousness of Mother Earth. Some traditions view this wisdom more celestially as residing in the Akashic records, which are held in some invisible ethers that cannot be pointed to, while other more chthonic traditions believe this wisdom is locked with the body of the planet. In such traditions the wisdom of the ages is found within the planet, or within the underworld light found by descending into the planet. I've heard such repositories of wisdom referred to as the Laboratory or Workshop of the Holy Spirit, representing a grand alchemical workplace for those in the pseudo-Christian Hermetic traditions. Others call the up-swell of such wisdom through the Earth vortices the Fountains of Hecate. One teacher of mine who was firmly established in the Green World rather than in a strictly Pagan or Christian view, referred to it as the Formulary in the Heart of the Earth.

The Formulary is like a green Akashic Records, holding the medicine wisdom of ages past, and can be used to devise new potions and tinctures, as well as reclaim lost techniques. My teacher believed it stretched back across time, into the mythic lands of Mu, Lemuria and Atlantis – times when our knowledge of the plant world was both more spiritual and yet still developing, as the etheric patterns of the plants were just taking form, and those entities that would be considered "human," i.e. the dominant race on the planet, which to us might be more akin to an elder faery or titan race, took part in shaping and co-creating these plant patterns. Their knowledge of the healing virtues and spirits was more intimate and detailed than ours today. In many ways, we've lost touch with the plant spirits and how they work together. The Formulary in the Heart of the Earth is one way to regain such knowledge.

Recorded within the Formulary are not only the formulas, recipes and techniques of all our ancestors for the arts of potion making and herbal healing, but also an understanding of the plants' wisdom and patterns, and the knowledge of how the plants work together synergistically. We can use visionary techniques to access this grand formulary, and return with seemingly new information that is in reality elder wisdom tailored to our current age.

Since being introduced to this concept, I've used this resource to gain information on many formulas, and to add to my knowledge about traditional potions. It has been particularly helpful to me in making combinations of flower essences, and in understanding alchemical patterns to spagyric tinctures.

Journey to the Formulary in the Heart of the Earth

If at all possible, do this journey outside, whether by day or
night. It can be done in a temple space, but a living connection
to the land is best. If you must do it indoors, have a bowl or pot
of sacred soil from a special place with you to form that
connection. Make sure you have a paper and pen with you, or
an easy-to-use recording device, to assist you in remembering
any information or formulas you retrieve.

If you desire, cast the Green Circle as a sacred space around
you. An offering can be made to the land around you, or to the
bowl of sacred soil, to later be disposed of directly back to the
land.

Lie down for a shamanic style journey, but lie facedown to
facilitate entry into the underworld realm. You can use the
following position, based upon the records of a seventeenth
century German traveler, as an ecstatic body position to
facilitate this journey. It is believed to be a position used by
Northern tradition shamans to facilitate journeys to the
underworld.

Fig. 12: Underworld Journey Position

Chapter Seven: Elixirs of Wisdom

Lie face down with arms outstretched. The right arm is extended further. The head is turned to the right, and the ankles are crossed, right over left. Traditionally a drum is strapped to your back and an assistant beats it, though I've never done that part personally.

Through self-inducted trance, induced via drumming or quiet focus, project your awareness downward through the land. Go through the living land into the core of the planet, to the space that is the gateway between the depths of the Earth and the beginning of the underworld. Here you find the Heart of the Earth. Enter the laboratory of the Holy Spirit, where Hecate's Fountains and the Telluric currents rise and envelop the Earth.

There in the depths you will find green knowledge. There is a record of all the medicinal, magickal and spiritual workings of plants, animals and minerals. This record contains all that was, all that is and all that potentially will be. Every formula. Every cure. Every potion, incense and ointment. Seek out the formulas that are correct and good for you at this time. What need do you have? The Formulary in the Heart of the World responds to need. Communicate your need and have confidence in the knowledge there *is* a cure for your issue. Allow the formulary to fill you with green knowledge on how to find, mix or access your herbal cure.

The Formulary in your vision may take the shape of a laboratory, a wizard's chamber, an herbalist's hut, a vast library, or a space-age computer system. There might be a guardian or guide present for you to commune with, or who may challenge your right to this information. The key to success is a clear, honest and open heart. The Earth powers will respond to it and aid you if your intention is true.

When done, affirm that you will remember all, and return the way you came, giving thanks to all powers in the Heart of the Earth. Record your information. Release your sacred space.

Ultimately the formulas and recipes you devise in alliance with the deep wisdom of Earth and the plant spirits will yield elixirs of wisdom that will assist you on your own path of evolution and initiation.

Chapter Eight:
Crafting the Herbal Homunculus

he origins of familiar spirits are many. We've discussed how such entities can be allies discovered through psychic work and spirit journey, how they can be "given" to us by a higher authority such as a deity, and how they can even be a part of one's own soul structure. Yet little has been said or written about the art of crafting your own familiar.

Often when this topic is discussed, it is taught in an almost sterile and safe form. Named the artificial elemental, spiritual construct, servitor spirit and/or semi-permanent thoughtform, each of these names, while accurate, fails to point to the gate of deeper magick and mystery. So without a marker, few people find this gate and fewer still walk through it. The idea of the artificial familiar, while more complex than a simple candle spell or charm, is still portrayed as relatively safe. It's described in terms of creating an etheric "widget," a mechanical box that will do what you say the way you say it. While this is certainly true on one level, it's not the whole truth. Few warnings are given about how such elementals can get "loose" and become harmful, potentially feeding off their maker. Yet, if it is a spiritual construct, look to the real world for your parallels. When was the last time your toaster, television or phone lost control and started to feed off you? No, there is something more going on with these "constructs." There is something deeper, more magickal and primal here, for those who want to see it.

In the traditions of alchemy there are also magickal constructs. Alchemical texts speak of the homunculus, the artificial human created in the laboratory. Meaning "little human," the term homunculus referred to life created in the laboratory. At first, texts viewed such "men" as personifications of the alchemical metals and elements and associated them with the principle of the ouroborus, but later in the history of alchemy this creation of life, thus becoming akin to "God" with the power to create, was one of the goals of the alchemists, along with the Philosopher's Stone and the Elixir of Life. It's possible this homunculus teaching went on in some measure to influence Mary Shelly in her fictional work, *Frankenstein*.

Many of the homunculus teachings were associated with sperm, perhaps arising from the more scientifically minded male mystics seeking to create life in the womb of the laboratory in order to become more like the divine, and lacking wombs in their own bodies. One method for creating a homunculus involved making a small hole in the egg of a black hen, removing a bean sized portion of egg white, and replacing it with the alchemist's own semen. The hole was then covered by virgin parchment and buried in manure, usually horse dung, during the first day of a lunar cycle in the spring. At the end of the cycle, a little man would emerge from the egg in the manure, and go to work as aid and protector to its creator, feeding on lavender seeds and earthworms. Other variations of this formula exist, including the conception of the homunculus in a flask. I don't know anyone who has successfully undertaken these operations personally, though alchemical philosophers have reported success.

While it sounds like something more akin to modern science-fiction, or perhaps closer to scientific fact at this point in our technology, with laboratory embryos and genetic engineering, the existence of homunculi was a popular belief among the best and brightest of the occult science communities from the Greeks to the Renaissance not just the realm of mere superstition. Perhaps they were talking about something real, rather than a mere fantasy, as assumed by popular science and mainstream society today. Or perhaps the homunculus was more akin to our artificial elemental or servitor spirit, but made from a more complex ritual technology; etheric and not physical at all, but couched in the veiled symbolism of alchemy.

One historical manifestation of the homunculus common to both the alchemist and the Witch is found in the root of the mandrake. True mandrake, *Mandragora officinalis,* is a plant with a root that looks like a man. Surrounded by much folklore, mystery and even superstition, Mandrake is a powerful plant magickally and herbally, and some believe the "apple" or fruit from the plant was the true "apple of knowledge" from the Biblical tale of Genesis, a psychotropic that gave insight into the true nature of reality. Many in medieval Europe believed it to be a gallows herb, growing from the sperm ejaculated from the convulsing hanged man going through death spasms. Folklore tells us that Mandrake root screams when dug up, and that its scream is deadly to humans, so a variety of rituals and prohibitions were performed to harvest it, usually requiring the process to be done in the midnight hour or just before dawn.

One interesting approach included tying the plant top to a black dog and then placing raw meat just out of the dog's reach. As the dog struggled for the meat, it uprooted the plant. It's unclear whether this piece of folklore implies that dogs are immune to the scream or that the Witch or magician is simply willing to accept the moral repercussions of the dog's death in order to obtain this powerful plant. Once obtained, the root fetish would then be animated through rituals of washing, fumigating and "feeding" with milk, honey and sometimes the owner's blood. The root was said to come alive like the alchemist's homunculus and do the bidding of its owner, usually in protecting the owner, her family and home, as well as in granting immortality, riches and power. It was often believed that Witches possessed this manakin, and that it acted like a familiar spirit, doing the Witch's bidding and teaching them the secrets of healing and hexing. The fetishes would be kept out on the mantle in some cases, or hidden beneath the bed.

What all these rather outlandish tales, mingled with magick and superstition, have in common is the creation of a spirit vessel, and the act of either conjuring a familiar spirit from nature to inhabit that vessel, awakening the spirit already inherent in the materials of the vessel to a new nature, or the crafting of a new spirit all together, and working with it like a traditional familiar. The act of creation is a spiritual mystery, an initiatory ritual, and plant familiars, crafted as a type of homunculus, offer us the opportunity to go deeper into the mysteries of life and creation, beyond the simple servitor spell constructs. As they come from nature, they hold the mysteries of nature, and possess the power to assist you in personal transformation.

The Body of the Green Homunculus

The homunculus can be crafted from a variety of materials, some more complex than others. The vessel for a homunculus spirit can be large or small, though the large vessels tend to carry more energy and are potentially more viable as spiritual teachers, and the smaller ones tend to be more portable, easily hidden and carried within your pockets or bag, to be used for specific acts of localized magick.

Charm Bags

The simplest container for a plant spirit is a small bag containing the dry herb. The bag may be a color that matches the herb's elemental or planetary correspondences. Ideally the dry herb should not be cut and sifted herb from a commercial supplier, but should contain all parts of the plant – roots, stems, leaves, flowers, fruits/seeds. That way all the powers and virtues, all the intelligence of the plant, will be accessible in this simple vessel. If possible, you should grow the plant yourself, harvest it in alignment with astrological timing, and dry it yourself.

Root Fetishes

Root fetishes draw us closer to the true spirit of the homunculus, the little herbal man. Roots are used in all forms of magick, and both European and African-American traditions view roots not only as complete charms, but also as possessing a spiritual presence to be communed with in order to manifest one's desires. European Witchcraft traditions are more familiar with the mandrake root, also known as the *manakin* or *alraun*. The term *alraun* was also used to indicate a German magician or Witch, as well as their root charm. The mandrake was so prized that imitations where carved out of the roots of ash and rowan trees, or from white briony, also known as English mandrake or false mandrake. Though there is a high demand for its use in magick, sources are scarce, leading modern American Witches to use chopped may apple, also known as American mandrake, as a substitute in spells and incense. While these plants can have similar properties superficially, for the purpose of creating homunculi and familiars, they are not at all the same spirit as Mandrake.

Traditionally one had to care for the manakin; dressing it in fine white linen with a golden girdle, and washing and bathing it on Friday. Perhaps this was a cultural day of bathing, or perhaps the mandrake, due to its planetary associations with Venus and Saturn, would be bathed on or near those days, Friday being the day of Venus, and Saturday for Saturn. One could not get rid of a mandrake by throwing it away, as it would come back, and could only be sold at a price higher than what you paid for it. I'm not sure what you would charge if your harvested it yourself. Perhaps those who had the knowledge to properly harvest mandrake roots were not quick to give them up.

A similar concept is found in American folk magick systems such as Hoodoo, New Orleans Voodoo and Southern Conjure, which are influenced by African traditions. A root shaped like a man is not used, but a variety of roots are made into charms in these systems. One of the most popular being High John the Conqueror Root. Though there are several different roots that have been named High John the Conqueror, the most popular is *Ipomoea jalapa* root. Its uses are varied, and generally its magick is considered male, as it resembles testicles. The Iroquois Indians called it "man root" or "man in the earth," giving it some similarity to the mandrake. Those who use High John root will "dress" it, i.e. anoint it with oil, and then wrap it in colored cloth or carry it in a colored bag. Sometimes this is part of a larger charm, and other times it's carried on its own. Conjure magicians will talk to the root, telling it what they want it to do, as it can be used for gaining money, success in gambling, virility, mastery and leadership. While High John does have similar lore to the mandrake, its use in American magick, from native cultures to more modern folk magick, is well documented. I know a British ceremonial magician transplanted to the United States who keeps her High John on the mantle of the family room, asking it to bring her and her family whatever resources they need, and this bit of American folk magick has worked better for her than the traditions of Qabalah and British Traditional Wicca while living in America. A variety of other roots are used in Hoodoo and Conjure, each with specific functions and dressing, to be used alone or in a more complex charm.

American Witches also experiment with root fetishes, using plants that are both powerful in magickal virtue and easily grown. Similar root fetishes are made, dressed, spoken to and used in magick, from simple wish fulfillment to asking the roots to act as true familiars and teachers, opening the ways to deeper magick. I have personally experimented with the roots of Mugwort, Angelica, Solomon's Seal, Parsley, Comfrey and Datura. Datura specifically has been an amazing teacher for me in dreams and visions. Mugwort has acted as a miniature "broom" to aid in my shamanic journeying. Comfrey protects our home. Angelica and Solomon's Seal have aided me in the study of Qabalistic magick, while Parsley has been my tutor in underworld teachings.

Fruit

Like the root, the fruit of a plant can be used in magick to craft a simple charm, or even a homunculus vessel. The fruit must be able to be preserved, either in a liquid (see the Familiar Bottle below) or dried. I prefer to dry the fruit, either whole or in part. Some fruits, such as apples, are more conducive to this work than others, such as the tomato. Berries can be dried and strung with a needle and thread to create a talisman that can contain the plant spirit. Rowan berries and acorns make familiar Witch jewelry that can also double as plant familiar vessels. I've had mixed success pressing and drying an American Mandrake fruit for a homunculus vessel. It worked for a time, but eventually succumbed to rot.

The Familiar Bottle

One of the most powerful homunculus familiar techniques I've performed involves making a bottle home for the plant spirit. I learned this technique primarily from writings on the traditions of South American Ayahuasca shamans, and applied them to my own European Witchcraft. In the end, I think it embodies a fairly universal technique mythologized in the Genie/Djinn in a bottle found in popular Middle Eastern stories. Drawing upon shamans' lore, I've found two manifestations of this technique. Both require a sealable bottle to be used as the vessel, or body, of the familiar, at least in the physical world. I like stylish clear glass bottles and hunt craft stores for new bottles, antique stores for older ones, and even find emptied liquor and wine bottles appropriate in some cases. I find it interesting that some of the Ayahuasca shamans prefer plastic bottles with screw caps. We in the west tend to think of plastic as being non-conducive to magick and spiritual evolution, but they see it as a great boon that the bottle will not break while traveling through the jungle, on boats or up mountains. So use what works best for you and your own practice.

The first manifestation of this familiar bottle is as a "home" for one plant specifically. You place into the bottle as much of the plant, magickally harvested with the permission of the plant itself, into the bottle. Ideally you want roots, stalk, leaf, flowers and, if applicable, fruit. All parts don't have to be put in at once, as flower and fruit will obviously not occur at the same time on the same plant. Take your initial harvest and put it in the bottle. Fill the bottle with a high grade alcohol and seal it. When it is the time and season to add another component, do so.

The second form is more challenging, but also potentially more rewarding. Rather than a bottle home as a touchstone for one specific plant spirit, this bottle is an amalgam of all your primary plant allies. Into a larger bottle, place a mixture of fresh plants from all your allies and fill the bottle with high proof alcohol. As times goes by, and as you are moved, add to it with other plants, or other parts of plants from the allies already in the bottle. The bottle eventually takes on a personality and presence that is more than any one plant, and becomes a tutor and interface for the entirety of the Green World.

In each of these cases, when necessary, a small amount of the bottle's liquid can be used in ritual, usually to anoint or empower you or a ritual tool. You don't want to do this too often, however, as the liquid contains the virtue, the magickal medicine, extracted from the plant matter that carries its intelligence within it. You don't want to end up draining your crafted familiars.

Tree Teacher Pot

Drawing from the public traditions of the Cultus Sabatti, as presented in the work of Daniel Schulke, I've found deep connections in keeping a tree spirit "pot." My first experience with such spirit pots came not from the world of herbal Witchcraft, but from the African Diasporic traditions of Voodou, Santeria, and Ifa. Practitioners of these religions keep various pots as a ritual focus for a particular spirit entity such as a lwa, orisha, or ancestor. Each spirit had a specific type of pot, from terra cotta to hand carved wood. Those spirits a western magician would associate with Mars may require a cast iron cauldron. Spirits with "finer" tastes may require a ceramic or china pot as a vessel. Stones, herbs and ritual tools are placed inside, and offerings may be made into the pot. This is such an effective technique of spirit communion that it has made its way into some branches of the Anderson Feri line of Witchcraft and other branches of Wicca and Witchcraft. The power is balanced by responsibility, as the pots must be cared for. Priests and priestesses dedicated to that spirit will teach new initiates how to care for and "feed" the spirit pot. Due to the high level of care and responsibility required, many modern Witchcraft practitioners don't use this technique. Once you start one, it's a large responsibility to maintain it. Such service is not always easy for the modern practitioner who is not raised in such traditions.

The Tree Teacher Pot is similar, but perhaps less intense than a pot established for a lwa or orisha. Ideally the Tree Teacher Pot will be made of wood, and made from the wood of the same type of tree you wish to establish or deepen a relationship with. I've found that particular point difficult to manage however, and have ended up getting a "pot" in the form of a thick paper-like box made from an unspecified wood from a craft store. Decorate your pot in any way you feel would be appropriate for the tree. If the tree is one of the Ogham trees, using its Ogham character would be appropriate. The pot is then filled with bits from the tree, gradually added over time – including fallen and harvested leaves, branches, bark, seeds, wood and even ash from the burned wood. As you add to it, you create a talisman to help evoke the power and presence of the tree teacher in your life, even when you are not physically present with the tree itself. The tree spirit can then better act as a guide and tutor to you. My own first Tree Teacher Pot started with shavings of bark from a new wand. Every time I meditated with the tree in its physical presence, I asked if anything needed to be added to the pot. I would sometimes be told to take something, often something fallen to the ground near me, until I had aspects of the tree from all four seasons in the pot. A small portion of wood, leaf or seed mixture from the Tree Teacher Pot can be added to potions and incense when making something that needs extra power, love and wisdom from your plant ally, but such uses should be done sparingly, not in every concoction you make. Again, you don't want to drain your vessel of material or energy.

Chapter Eight: Crafting the Herbal Homunculus

To evoke the power of the Tree Teacher Pot, take off the lid and inhale the smell of the wood. Speak words from your heart and mind to the tree spirit, asking for its presence. Commune with the spirit ritually, and when done, cap the pot again, thanking the spirit for its presence. Store the pot in a place of honor and significance among your magick tools. You can even create a specific "green" altar for just your Tree Teacher or all your plant spirits and homunculi.

The Living Plant

In modern Witchcraft, one of the few traditional teachers sharing instruction and knowledge regarding the plant familiar is author Raven Grimassi. In both *The Witch's Familiar* and *The Book of Ways Volume I and II* books, Raven gives instructions on developing a plant familiar from a living, growing plant. This is somewhere between our ideas of the plant familiar spirit and the homunculus. It is not simply a plant totem figure, as it focuses on growing a literal, embodied, individual plant. Yet, the material vessel is living, not harvested or preserved in any way, so its body is not really a "tool" in the traditional sense. I've chosen to include it here in the homunculus section, as its magick is more akin to working with a specific plant form than a journey to work with the overarching intelligence of a plant species.

In his texts, Raven outlines several methods for working with the plant familiar. In essence, they can be summarized as containing the vital life force, what Raven refers to as the *numen*, of the plant. Choose an appropriate plant, or a location where you will plant a seed for your chosen plant species. On the morning of the full Moon, create a ring of eight quartz stones around the spot where you will place the plant or seed, like the eight-spoked Wheel of the Year. Align the quarter stones with the north, east, south and west. This ring will contain the numen and help build the presence of the plant spiritually. In the center of the ring, six inches deep, place another quartz stone. This will help provide the plant with extra direct energy. Plant the seed or living plant you've prepared for this space above the central stone. If the plant is already where you want it, dig around and beneath it to place the power stone under its roots. I personally prefer smooth river quartz stones rather than quartz points for this operation.

If you desire "backup" plants in case the primary center plant does not survive, wait until the morning of the new Moon. Remove the four stones in the cross quarter positions (northeast, southeast, southwest, northwest) and place a seed (or seedling) of the same type as the primary plant in these spots. They are "back up" plants, should the primary plant not survive. Take the quarter stones in the north, east, south and west and bury them six inches deep to charge the roots of all five plants. If you plan on using "backup" plants, make sure your original circle has enough room for these five plants to grow comfortably.

Fig. 13: Plant Familiar Circle

Chapter Eight: Crafting the Herbal Homunculus

Bond with the plant by taking good care of it – watering, fertilizing and protecting it from all damage. You might water it with a quart of water mixed with three drops of your own blood. Speak with the plant. Mentally communicate with it in words and pictures. Envision what you want to do with the plant familiar. With your index fingers and thumbs, form a triangle around the stem of the plant, and send forth personal power to "feed" both the plant and the crystal beneath it. The last step in conjuring this plant familiar is to bond with it fully by sitting in the north (facing south) while facing the plant. Stare at the plant and allow yourself to go into trance, blurring the image of the plant. The plant will send you its own familiar spirit image. It might look like an animal, insect or some other, perhaps mythic, creature. To summon it in magickal workings, imagine it in its natural setting, envisioning it in your mind's eye. Then see it take on its spirit form and call it to you.

Raven also includes some other variations on this technique and methods for extra empowerment, including drawing down full moon energy to psychically charge the plant and the stones with energy as well as watering the plant with Moon Water. To make Moon Water, leave a jar (ideally green) out where the moonlight will directly touch the jar on the night before the full moon. Collect it before dawn. Use this water on the night of the full moon in a lunar attunement ritual for the plant. *The Book of Ways* details a moon sigil that can be drawn around the primary plant in cornmeal, using extra crystals and the water used to feed the plant, increasing both the chemical and magickal potency of the plant.

This technique is ideal for long term familiars when using houseplants or when living in an area with a temperate climate. In shorter, harsher climates, it can create a temporary or at least seasonal familiar spirit or the plant can be brought in during the winter.

These are simply some of the forms of the herbal homunculus that I'm familiar with. There no telling what an enterprising Witch might create as a talismanic vessel for green consciousness.

Purpose of the Homunculus

The purpose of the homunculus is two-fold, like most magick we undertake. Much of our magick can be divided into the realms of thaumaturgy and theurgy, or "low" folk magick and divine "high" magick. While these are very charged terms that most practitioners of the Craft do not care to use, they do demonstrate a very clear division between magick with a practical application and magick that focuses on the mysteries of initiation, divinity and consciousness expansion. I, like many other Witches, believe that the two are not so different from each other, and each type of magick, practical or religious, leads us to the same place. The regular use of theurgy makes practical changes in day to day life that at first might not be apparent, but are present nonetheless, while practical folk magick leads us into the exploration of desire and personal will, to ultimately find our own divine will and true purpose.

The crafting of the homunculus is a blend of high and low forms of magick. Like the crafting of more complex thoughtforms and servitor spirits, there is a very real and practical application to the homunculus in terms of how it can aid you in your life and in your magick. But the deeper purpose of the homunculus is in awakening our own divine nature.

In many traditions, not just Biblical traditions, we are said to be made in the image of the divine. While some assume this means the divine has a quality of "humanness" to it, ranging from a humanoid figure beyond creation to beings possessing emotions and thoughts similar to human beings, magicians know that this philosophy actually refers to something else. It refers to our creative power. Unlike many other creatures, we are blessed with imagination, magick, desire, will, love and power. We can create in a manner that is similar to the divine. We have had to sacrifice our sense of automatic "oneness" with all things in order to create in this way, and our potential to create develops our awareness beyond the instinctual, thereby separating us from most of nature. But like the alchemists of old who would work through the stages of dissolution, separation and coagulation, we have the opportunity to regain that oneness while still retaining the power to create and do magick while walking the path to enlightenment. Thereby we become more like the Goddess or God, and awaken to our inherent divinity.

The application of the magickal will is our first step on this path—realizing we are creative beings spiritually, as well as scientifically, artistically and culturally. Through that spiritual creation we become aware of the potential for oneness again, for all things are connected. If they weren't, then our magick would not work. We learn this philosophy from the Hermeticists and the Principle of Mentalism, which states that we are all thoughts within the Divine Mind. Beyond this knowledge, we embody its principles through the application of our magickal will in our ritual workings. If we are all part of the Divine Mind, any action we take affects the whole.

Each act of creation then takes us deeper upon the path. More complex operations, such as the creation of a spirit, or the co-creation of a spirit-man, a homunculus, with the green intelligences of nature, brings us closer to our divinity, and to unlocking the mysteries of nature herself. While this work might smack of the hubris of modern day scientists, geneticists and medical researchers, or ghosts of Mary Shelley's *Frankenstein*, it is done in the spirit of the ancient alchemists, in *union* with divinity, and listening to nature as well as speaking the desires of our will. Only through a partnership with nature can we truly and safely unlock the mysteries of nature and our own soul. Is it dangerous? Yes, but most things in magick are even when we don't realize it. So much of life is dangerous. The chance to awaken, empower and realize the godself is worth the risk.

Working with the Homunculus

How does one work with a homunculus from the green realm? I think the answer depends on the Witch, their own style of magick and spirit communication, but generally, a homunculus acts like any other familiar, plant or animal. There is no right or wrong way to work with it. Through regular interaction, it will reveal its own nature to you and you will evolve your magickal traditions together. Here are some simple yet effective ideas to start you on the path.

Ritual and Spellcraft – Your homunculus can assist you in any magickal ritual, from celebration and mystery to specific spellcraft. Awaken it through ritual evocation. Hold the form of the familiar and summon it as you would a spirit. Call to it. Having it present, physically and spiritually, during rituals that are appropriate to its nature, works well to improve the ritual. Like a more traditional familiar, a homunculus lends energy and power to the rite. If the plant is in alignment with the working, its natural virtue will permeate your circle. Even if it's not specifically attuned to the ritual, it can still lend power via its attunement to you. In specific acts of spellcraft, you can ask the spirit of the plant homunculus to actually perform the spell for you, to manifest or banish whatever you require. Its spirit will go forth like an artificial elemental, and manifest what is desired. While they work with a bit more wisdom and higher intelligence from the Green World than the typical artificial elemental, their point of view is still very different from our human point of view, so be clear and specific in your instructions.

Consecration – Your plant familiar can lend power in consecrating, or charging, potions, oils, incense, crystals, candles, amulets and talismans. Summon forth the spirit in your magick working and ask it to enter the tool to be empowered. Tell both the tool and the plant familiar what you want the device to do upon completion. Envision the familiar entering into the liquid or charm and then envision the results you desire from the magickal instrument. Call it back out when the tool is fully charged.

Healing – Plants are naturally attuned to the powers of healing through their medicinal virtues. Thus, the empowered familiar is able to do all that the herb can do and more. Mandrakes in particular were well known for the healing powers. One would soak the root in water, and the water would then be used in a variety of ways, including anointing women in labor to ease childbirth, or sprinkled on animals for healing. It could also be soaked in milk and then the milk would be drunk for healing. One may wonder if any of the medicinal or psychoactive properties of the mandrake may be extracted into room temperature water or milk, though the process is more akin to creating a vibrational remedy such as a flower essence. Perhaps the chemical was not in the water/milk and therefore creating an herbal remedy, but the spiritual essence was present instead to effect healing. Some display their mandrake root in a jar of alcohol, and use this liquid in magick and anointing when Mandrake is needed. Psychically you can ask your plant familiar spirit to enter your body, or the body of the recipient of your healing magick, and ask the spirit to heal from the inside. You might envision the familiar devouring or expelling the illness from the person, or constructing healthy new tissues and restoring balance to the entire body. This healing is similar to the modern alternative health practice of Plant Spirit Medicine or Plant Spirit Healing, or the attunements of the previous chapters, but in this case it is specific to your homunculus plant spirit, rather than just an archetypal plant spirit. Ideally the spirit you summon will be in alignment with healing in general, such as a balm, or even better, a remedy for the specific illness at hand.

Protection – The herbal homunculus, like an animal familiar, is said to protect the home or temple from all harm. Witches who were open about their practices would place the mandrake upon the mantle for all to see, presumable so that visitors would, on some level, fear it and never cross, steal from or harm the Witch. Those who were more hidden in their practices placed the mandrake beneath the bed, yet it was still an effective guardian to the home, preventing unwanted forces from entering. If the alraun was soaked in water or alcohol, the liquid used to heal could also be used to protect the home, aspersed around the threshold or the borders of the property.

Sending Forth – The spirit of the plant homunculus can be sent forth, and due to its unique link to you, this sending can work toward a variety of purposes. The homunculus can act like an extra set of "eyes" in terms of remote viewing or astral travel. Yet rather than requiring your constant focus, you can send it out and recall it when needed, absorbing the information then. Such familiars can act as "spies"—telling you the things you want and need to know without being physically, or even psychically, present yourself. It can go forth to perform remote spellcraft, distance healing and protection of loved ones. Anything it can do while present with you it can theoretically do when sent forth into the world.

Communication – The plant spirit homunculus can also communicate with others when it is sent forth, projecting messages in words or pictures into the minds of others who are receptive to them. Adepts might receive a specific message and know who and where it came from, though most people will generally receive a vague sense of the message or purpose. Theoretically the homunculus can also be sent forth to influence the minds and emotions of others through this green telepathy. Certain plants influence people in ways that are in alignment with their nature. Fiery plants won't necessarily calm someone down, and water or lunar plants won't stoke someone's energy. The appropriate plant must be used for the appropriate intention. It is quite effective when influencing others through dreams. The ethics of such work is dubious at best, though I've found it quite effective to use the homunculus familiar to influence my own dreams, reprogramming my own attitudes and perceptions around difficult topics.

Instruction – A deeper relationship with the homunculus can open a gateway into the mysteries. The plant spirit itself will instruct the Witch on not only its use, but the spiritual powers of the plant world. Hold the fetish or charm during meditation, or keep it on your nightstand or beneath your pillow to evoke dreams of the plant teacher. It can instruct you in how it has been used in the past, how it can be used in the present and how it will be used in the future. It will connect you to the ancestors of blood and spirit who used it before you, forging a new link in the tradition where older direct links have been lost.

Assistance – As the homunculus consists of an intelligence from the green realm beyond what you have imbued it with, it will operate on its own, in what is perceived as its and your own best interest. Any of the effects above can be performed spontaneously by the spirit as it assists you in the manner it sees as most fitting. This is only a problem if the assistance is unwanted or occurs in a manner that is contrary with your wishes. This is why a strong relationship with the spirit ally is required for this working, and clear communication and boundaries are necessary.

Creating and Empowering the Homunculus

Creation of the plant homunculus is not a simple formula suitable for all practitioners. This chapter has illustrated a wide range of manifestations of the homunculus. If only specific one size fit all and all instructions worked, such as the traditional egg, sperm and horse manure technique, it might be easier. But I've found that each plant, or amalgam of plants, has its own way, and a good Witch must learn to listen to the plants and understand what they want in order to effectively manifest this spirit helper. Each homunculus will be different.

Two of my most important plant familiar charms were directly inspired by the plants themselves, and spurred my investigation into this method of magickal development. I was gifted with the root of a Datura plant from a friend and psychedelic mage who grows a variety of substances. As the Datura was withering, it told him to give the root to me. Though he knew of my Witchcraft practices, he did not know about my special relationship with Datura. He told me that I would know what to do with it, as the root is not specifically used in entheogenic preparations like the leaves and seeds. I meditated with the root, and evidently I held it too tightly in meditation, as it broke into three pieces. I meditated again with it, sad this time that I had broken it. Datura then communicated to me in a wave of clairsentience that I should wrap each part with a different color – white, red and black. I should then braid cord of these three colors and tie the three roots together. I should anoint it with the essential oil from my balm plant familiar, Lemon Balm, and then anoint it with my semen and sleep with it under my pillow. I did as instructed, and as a result I had amazing dreams where Datura came to me in humanoid/faery form, a woman with silver white hair, and explained many of the mysteries of Datura to me, including how to safely prepare it for myself, and what mysteries such rituals could teach me. This experience greatly deepened my relationship with Datura and my own understanding of the Underworld. Later when I spoke to friends who were part of a Traditional Craft group, they shared with me a teaching on working with roots where you are suppose to "lay with it as if it were your wife," a euphemism for exactly what I had done. Every so often, we (Datura and I) repeat this practice to deepen our connection. While we think of many of our Witchcraft traditions as "lost" to the persecutions of the past and the march of "progress" this experience shows me how anyone with sincere intent, practice and purpose can regain and advance any lost information through direct spirit contact.

My second example involved Pokeweed (*Phytolacca americana*), also known as Pokeroot or Pokeberry. Though a bane and a purgative, its root is sometimes used as a medicine if harvested at the correct time. The spiritual power of this plant is its ability to aid us when we get stuck, to help us get to the next level of spiritual insight and power. It helps us breakthrough to the next level by purging all that might block us, consciously and unconsciously, new and old. Pokeweed's stock is hollow, and represents the power to journey in life and in the spirit world. As a flower essence, it's a great remedy for those who feel they have lost personal power. It helps us get out from under the control of anyone else, particularly a mother, wife or sister, and it also aids in male impotence. I have always had a love/hate relationship with pokeweed, as once you get it into the garden, it's hard to get it out; the berries are messy (though they can be made into a lovely "invisible ink" for spell crafting), and birds tend to eat the berries and then leave a mess on your porch, car and doorstep.

At a time in my life when I was stuck, but probably didn't realize it, I began to obsess about the pokeweed in my garden, seeing it everywhere. In meditation, I got a clear message to harvest it by the light of the full moon and put it in a decorated bottle, with vodka to preserve it. This mixture wasn't to be a potion or tincture, but a magickal charm. Pokeweed told me to take the stalk, berries and leaves from a specific plant, easily found not too far off a road I know well. It was the end of fall, and the plant was almost dying off, but I got the dark berries, stalk and leaves and followed my instructions. The alcohol turned a light purple. I thought I was done. In meditation with it, however, I was clearly told by the plant that I was not. The charm needed to be "whole" and have all its parts present – root, flowers, green berries – everything. There was no way I would be able to discretely dig up the root of the large plant by the side of the road under the moonlight where I first made my harvest. While dreaming with it by my nightstand, it told me where to go to find a smaller version, still in flower, and to dig up the baby plant root and flower, and put these in the bottle as well. I was also told to go at dawn. It turned out to be the day and hour of Saturn, the ruling planet of Pokeweed, though I didn't realize it at the time. I thought it was to avoid detection, but it was to make sure to have parts collected both in the daylight and at night. I thought it wouldn't be possible to find it so late in the season, but I found the plants exactly where I was told, dug up the roots with my hands (it had specified no metal) and collected the flowers and green berries. Into the charm went all the parts, and the liquid turned a black purple. Unlike with the Datura, none of my own bodily fluids or parts needed to be included.

I meditated with this Pokeweed charm for days, and was told to open the cork but to not touch the liquid; just to let the "Spirit of Poke" out to do its work and then ask it back into the bottle and close it again. I must admit to feeling little to nothing at the time, and did not receive any direct messages, but I performed these meditations with the Pokeweed bottle charm for the prescribed time – eight days. I was then told to put it on my altar and leave it alone. Though I didn't at first subscribe the changes in my life, my practice, my job and my temple to Pokeweed, it was later revealed how it had acted as a catalyst for personal power, uncovering healing issues in my life to be addressed and getting several things moving that I felt were stuck or on hold. It was almost too much change all at once, but it was ultimately beneficial. I was given no specific instructions to feed or care for it, and only on occasion have I used it with other people and clients who are also stuck, and ask them to meditate with it during a session. After a year, I was instructed by the Poke spirit to create a second bottle familiar, and give it away to a person who would be made clear to me. I did, and this person had some amazing Poke inspired meditations and dreams.

My experiences with Datura and Pokeweed are two powerful, yet distinctly different examples of communion with the plants in crafting the homunculus. I've found that in such magick there are generally four points to consider:

Body – The homunculus can be "housed" in several different vessels, depending on its nature. Most common are the charm bag, root, fruit, bottle, pot and living plant. I'm sure there are other options available, but those are the ones I have experience crafting. Which one is most appropriate for the herb(s) involved? What materials should be used, if any, in the construction of the body? Any specific colors or symbols? Any ritual preparations to purify the body of the familiar?

Harvesting – How should you obtain the plant material for the familiar? Will it be freshly harvested or dried? Can it be store bought or must it be grown or wildcrafted? Are there any prohibitions or instructions for harvest, such as no metal tools? You might be asked to wear a specifically colored piece of clothing, or to be alone, or with a specific person. When and where should the plant be harvested? Does the phase of the Moon, day, time of day and hour matter? Is an offering necessary?

Awakening – What must be done to awaken the spirit of the homunculus? Will it be a conduit for a specific single plant, and called by that plant's name, or will be bear its own individualized name, like a constructed elemental? Will it have a sigil? Will it have instructions on how, when or why it should be dismantled? Does it require a special "spark" to bring it to life? Such actions are usually elemental – passing the homunculus over a flame or dousing a lit match inside it, censing it in specific incense, or adding drops of special water, alcohol or oil, or adding a sacred stone or crystal. Does a specific invocation or word of power need to be uttered? Should the awakening occur in the magick circle, or some other form of sacred space? Where and when should it be awakened?

Care & Feeding – What must you do to care for and sustain the familiar in this environment? Does it need to be cleansed regularly? Does it need to be talked to regularly? Does it need to be approached in any specific manner? Some require you to fast for a few hours, refrain from sex or visit at a particular time of day. Does it need to be fed, and if so, with what – water, sexual fluids, a drop of blood, incense, oil, sacred herb or grain? Some might not require much care at all, depending on the nature of the plant. Often plants that require care in gardens require more care in this homunculus form, while wild plants with little or no maintenance require less attention.

In meditation, ask the plant spirit, and your own individual spirit teachers and guides, these questions. Work out the details and design your own plant homunculus ritual of awakening and empowerment.

Parting with the Homunculus

Unlike some other totemic relationships with the animal and plant world that seem to come and go over time as needed for both parties spiritual development, the work of homunculi and manakins are an ongoing responsibility. Mandrake lore alone suggests that there is a heavy price for trying to casually discard such an entity and teaches us that we must do so with respect and honor. If not, there is a chance the homunculus will turn on its "creator-owner," just as the ceremonial magician's artificial elementals and spirit constructs can, and feed off their creator.

Just as in the creation of the familiar, I don't think there is one ritual that fits all occasions for parting from it. Each relationship is specific and personal, and just like ending of a friendship, or saying good bye as your journeys take you in different places, you must communicate with the plant your intentions and work together to determine what is best for you both. These familiars can be given away when done with respect and knowledge that the new caretaker will truly care for them. But usually they are released back into nature, into the overall intelligence of their plant species, the higher devic aspect of the plant. With inner guidance and advice from the spirits, you should design a parting ritual that involves the following:

Gratitude – Thank the homunculus specifically for all its aid in your time together. Acknowledge the development you have shared together.

Release – Specifically release the homunculus from service, and release yourself from further obligation to it.

Opening – Open the way to its higher intelligence by invoking the deva of its species. Ask the higher guides of the plant world to take this spirit back into their collective community, to enrich their collective experience and aid it on its next journey of evolution.

Destruction – Ritually destroy the "body" of the homunculus, so it has no earthly vessel to return to or feel attached to in the physical world. Fire is the preferred method of such destruction, as it purifies and prevents any remnant from being a vessel, much like cremation in human funerary rites. If you are using a living plant, it is not always necessary to destroy it, but you must destroy the container of its life force.

Remove the stones you buried and if you have "backup" plants, separate them into different parts of the garden.

A ritual that includes these elements should be enough to safely release the homunculus in an honorable way.

Chapter Nine:
Green Gnosis &
Plant Spirit Initiation

hile many of us come from lineage initiations where the power and name of the Witch is conferred from one individual to another, creating a holy chain stretching through time, one must ask, much like beloved High Priestess Doreen Valiente, "Who initiated the first Witch?" I think the answer could only be the gods and spirits themselves. But which gods confer what initiations?

Each "family" of spirits can confer a different type of initiation, opening a different type of gnosis. Animals confer the mysteries of the hunt, of shapeshifting and of living in harmony with nature. The fey folk confer the mysteries of the deep earth and of the ancestors. The angelic races confer initiatory wisdom of the heavens. But I believe a special type of wisdom is reserved for the teacher and initiators of the green realm.

I call initiation from the plant world "green gnosis." While Gnosticism is commonly thought of as the mystical side of

Christianity, the term predates Christianity. The word *gnosis* is Greek, and is defined as "knowledge"; not the knowledge of books and teacher, but rather the knowledge one must experience directly. Green gnosis is the direct experience of the plant world.

Green gnosis can take many forms, from the seemingly benign and peaceful to more disturbing ordeals. This initiation can simply confer informational gnosis, a secret knowledge of the plant world, and the relationship such secret knowledge can foster with the plant spirits. Those who know the true names and shapes of the spirit world work their magick infinitely better than those stumbling around in the dark for the proper keys. The gnostic experience might be conferred sexually, with a representative from the plant realm, not unlike the sexual initiations of some lines of British Traditional Wicca, reminiscent of the ancient temples of the Middle East where it is said that the secret name of the Goddess was whispered into the ear of the initiate at orgasm. On the furthest end of the spectrum green gnosis can be an ordeal, an experience where one is broken down and built back up again; a trial of wisdom, love, wits, and even power. This is similar to the classic stories of shamans being devoured by demons and gods only to find themselves resurrected with something "new" in the body, as a sign of their newfound power in the spirit world. In this case, the red blood of flesh is often replaced with the green sap of the plant spirits, or a seed, flower or fruit is placed within the energy body, radiating a particular "medicine" and energy for others to see and feel if they know how to look for this "green" Witch's mark.

The initiatory process, while always "green," can also take the form of the three major phases of "work" in the alchemy tradition. The first phase, the black phase, is the most confrontational. It is the phase of destruction and separation. Psychologically one would say the black phase is about facing the shadow, all repressed aspects of self, and all fears of the Green World. The white phase is the reconstitution of the self, union with a greater sense of purity. While many think of the color white as the ultimate color in terms of spirituality, in alchemy, the color red, sometimes preceded by yellow, is actually the last stage of the alchemical work. Red is the indicator of divine power, beyond the confines of black and white. It is the symbol of the Elixir of Life and the Philosopher's Stone, and the coagulation of all purified elements into a harmonious whole. Magickal initiations outside the strict traditions of alchemy may also follow this pattern of destruction, regeneration and empowerment.

While green gnosis can happen spontaneously, and perhaps such events are best because they are orchestrated by the spirits themselves, usually it occurs because a daring Witch actively seeks out the experience. Rituals in nature can trigger a gnostic experience with the plant spirits. Anything that tunes you to the plant world when your intention for such initiation is clearly within your heart has the potential to trigger gnosis. Vigils are appropriate; for instance, spending an extended time out in nature. Some traditions suggest sleeping in nature, either in daylight or at night, with a pillow of stone and a blanket of flowers and leaves. Then the Green World will reveal itself to you. Others perform an extended vision quest-like rite somewhere in nature. Entheogens are a natural part of such gnosis-seeking, and as mentioned before, should be approached with caution. The sacramental drink, psychoactive or not, is a powerful trigger of green gnosis when combined with intense ritual work.

Gnosis can be triggered by many things and historically those who have been touched by the realms of nature, the fey, and the angels have not always sought the gifts and responsibilities such initiations can produce. Think wisely before walking this path.

The Green Tutor

The Goddess of the Green has always been known as the teacher of Witches and herbalists. The Witches of Rome, the Venefica, are followers of Venus in her aspect as the Goddess of the cultivated garden and blooming flower.

Among the Irish Celts, one humble mistress of all wild craft is the goddess Airmid. As one of the Tuatha De Dannan and daughter to the physician god Diancecht, Airmid tried to improve on her father's work with her brother, the surgeon Miach. King Nuada had lost his hand, and Diancecht provided him with a silver one, but Miach and Airmid went a set further and regenerated his hand completely. In a rage, Diancecht killed his son, leaving Airmid to grieve. She placed stones around his grave, and soon after flowers grew up from the land where he was buried; three hundred and sixty five herbs grew from Miach's grave in the appropriate spot on the body, signifying their individual use. She gathered them up according to their use in her cloak, but when Diancecht found out, he scattered the herbs to the wind, letting them grow wild and denying the information to any other generation. Only Airmid remembers the proper use of these herbs and she will teach those who call to her.

Nature herself is the greatest tutor of them all. As Venus-Aphrodite, as Airmid, as Mother Earth or the Witch Queen, Nature will show you if you have but the eyes to see and the ears to hear. But to speed this process along, the Spirit of Nature, of the Goddess as teacher, can help you make connections and see the power of the herbal allies.

Evocation of the Tutoring Goddess

Go out into nature in your cloak or special blanket. Lay it out upon the land. Commune with the Goddess of the Land and ask her spirit and knowledge to enter the cloak. Place it around yourself again and ask for knowledge, the true green gnosis, to enter you. Ask to know the medicine and spirit of the plants around you and in your life.

Goddess of the Green Ways,
Keeper of Charms, Worts and Banes,
Aphrodite-Airmid, Venus Morning Star,
Open the Green Gates of Knowledge.
Let the grimoire of nature be etched upon my soul,
And awaken the Mysteries all around me.
Let me speak the language of the trees, the flowers,
*   of the birds and beasts.*
Grant me this knowledge in your service and trust,
Now unto the end of time.
Blessed be.

Let the voice of the Goddess whisper to you and affirm to yourself that you will remember what she says. When done, thank her and return to your home. Use that cloak or blanket whenever you need more information on herbs and their use, and her voice will return to you.

The Green Devil

While any initiatory path should ideally confer upon the initiate all three color stages of the alchemical work, some tend to focus on one specific stage. A rite I've come to call The Ritual of the Green Devil most certainly focuses on the more confrontational black stage of the work.

The Green Devil is the dark side of nature, and more specifically, the dark side of the Green Man. Many Pagans divide the God of Witches into two sides, like the sides of the coin, one being bright with golds and greens and the other dark with blacks and reds. Thus we have the classic images of the Sun God and Green Man on one side, for what is the Green Man but the Sun captured in the foliage on Earth, and the Horned God, Hunter and Lord of the Dead, on the other. Yet each side has its own inner division. The Dark God can be loving and gentle and the Light God can be cruel and burning. Thus the embodiment of the Green Man has sides both light and dark. Nature is vibrant, green and growing, but it can also be destructive. In the forest also exists the rot, the decay that destroys. I call this aspect of the Green Man, the Green Devil. Actually, such terminology is not my creation. I personally try to distance myself from Christian mythos, yet this is the name he gave me. His whole message is to absorb that which you seek to be separate from, let it rot and become one with you, and evidently for me this includes much of the Christian mythos.

My first experience with the Green Devil was spontaneous and unexpected, and came about through simple meditation and pathworking. In that first connection, I received a very clear message to take an entheogenic sacrament of psilocybin mushrooms in order to make further contact with this aspect of the God. Though I don't shy away from many of the more toxic, and frankly dangerous, herbal allies, a part of me was afraid. I had never taken magic mushrooms recreationally, feeling that they were a powerful force for true magick and should not be abused. Much of the Green Devil's work is with what we call "the shadow," the repressed part of the psyche and all the thoughts, feelings, words and actions associated with it. So for some reason I came up with all sorts of excuses not to do this ritual until the psychic pressure built up and I could do nothing *but* perform the ritual I was asked to do. On a tiny island-like outcropping in a local stream within my favorite forest, with my Witch's "medicine" bag in one hand and a blackthorn walking stick in the other, I took my mushroom sacrament with honey and met with the Green Devil.

The whole experience washed over in several waves. First the aura of the plants, trees and stones became more pronounced. Then the Devil came. It was as if I was inside him. He was the forest, right along with the brighter Green Man. I was in his body, yet his body was within the vessel of the Anima Mundi, Mother Earth. The duality of the Green Man and the Green Devil became apparent. The patterns of life and decay merged into each other became clear. Sitting cross-legged with my blackthorn stick thrust to the ground between my legs as a support, as some might use the broom to enhance a shamanic journey, I noticed that my left eye saw the patterns of rot and decay while my right eye saw the patterns of life. When I moved the stick to the right, the decay grew. When I moved the stick to the left, the patterns of life grew. They were concurrent, but I saw two different things at the same time, demonstrating that life is with death and death is with life. The Devil took the center of my vision, where life and death merged, and showed me a bit of how to use both patterns to manifest, banish and heal through the process of both growth and decay. One interesting aspect of the Green Devil was that his body was not only composed of rotting wood, decaying plants, and fungi, but there were also a variety of insects—termites, ants, flies, mosquitoes, spiders and black butterflies—present spiritually and physically.

The Green Devil took many forms over the course of the ritual—the forest itself, a praying mantis-like creature in the center of the web, and a snake with wolf head made entirely out of evergreens and ferns—but a continuing theme in all his forms was the relationship between temptation and sin. I was offered anything I wanted, and then asked if I was willing to let go of certain things, to let them flow or let them rot, in order to make space for what I said I wanted. I was willing, and so made my bargain with the Green Devil. I was also questioned quite extensively on the seven "deadly sins" of Christianity, and had many things, both pleasant and unpleasant, pointed out to me. Many issues came up, and some of these even offered resolution and peace. Other spirits visited, including the spirits or ghosts of "dead" trees from the forest that was there before and was now long gone; and through the contemplation of the short life cycle of the insects, I saw the pattern of cycles of life and death —all the little apocalypses or Ragnaroks we all experience personally every day—yet life, like the life of the Green Gods, goes onward. By the end of the experience, I was given the bare bones of the Green Devil ritual and the herbal "keys" to move through the Seven Gates of his realm.

The final revelation was the fact that there was little difference between the "good" Green Man and the "bad" Green Devil. Two different sides of the same god, but of the same nature. It is our shadow, our "sin," our issues that separate us from nature and make divides such as "good" and "bad," as nature is both and neither of these things.

The Ritual of the Green Devil

The concept behind the Ritual of the Green Devil (what some who study with me have affectionately called the Ritual del Diablo Verde), is to return to the veritable paradise, the primordial Eden. Though we are most familiar with the Christianized imagery of Eden, we find similar concepts of the garden in the Egyptian myths of the Zep Tepi, the Greek Island of Hesperides, the eastern Shambhala and even the Theosophical images of Atlantis and Lemuria. These are all places and times when humanity was more in tune with all of the natural world, and all of the spirit world, and lived as one with them. I simply call this realm the Garden of the Gods, and propose that we already live there, we simply don't realize it. In our post-Christian era, it is often the concept of sin that separates us from this realization. The devil, the diabolos, is the force that literally acts as adversary, as the accuser that crosses our path to the garden, seemingly blocking entry. This is closely related to our concept of the Dweller on the Threshold, the guardian that first appears as an adversary, but later becomes a gatekeeper. The key to working with both of these forces is the shadow. Self knowledge, and all knowledge that is denied or repressed, gives us access to the psychic forces that allow us entry into greater worlds of power, wisdom and love, where we are one with the gods and all of nature.

This ritual takes us through seven gates to "hell" much like the story of Inanna in Sumerian myth, or many British Traditional Wicca initiations, as well as the fifth degree initiation in the Temple of Witchcraft tradition. Unlike Goddess-focused traditions that challenge initiates at each gate to give up a tool, gift or symbol of worldly authority, the Ritual of the Green Devil uses herbal "keys," baneful herbs, to trigger issues surrounding the seven deadly sins in Christian theology and their corresponding "virtues." Rather than whole-heartedly label either side of the equation as wholly good or bad, the reconciliation of both is attempted, just as the Green Devil ultimately teaches us that he is none other than the Green Man in shadow. There is no difference. There is only one.

If you have never done any "shadow work," meaning you've never examined the repressed parts of yourself, I highly discourage you from starting with this ritual. This is a more advanced form of shadow work best done by those who already have some measure of self-awareness. For a simple but meaningful look at shadow work, I suggest my textbook, *The Temple of Shamanic Witchcraft*.

Prepare for the ritual by placing the following on your altar:

Purifying Incense
Herbal Wash
Casting Powder
Broom
Earth Oil
Anointing Stone
Air Incense
Incense Burner and Charcoal
Wood for Fire Offering
Cauldron for Fire Offering

Herbal Tea for Water Offering
Horn or Chalice for Water Offering
Bowl
Flower Essence(s)
Alcohol Libation
Small Stones in Bowl or Bag
Monkshood Flower Essence (Crown)
Oil (Brow)
Incense (Throat)
Potion (Heart)
Fire Offering (Solar Plexus)
Sacrament (Belly)
Ointment (Root)

Whether you are performing the ritual alone or in a small group, start by smudging all participants with a cleansing incense. This ritual brings up all sorts of issues as it is, so we want to be clear of any extraneous energies from the day or our environment. It should be performed outdoors in the evening, but it can be adapted for a temple working indoors. I prefer to process to the ritual area to establish the right mindset, and would suggest using an herbal wash on the hands and feet, in order to attune to the Green Devil.

Cleansing Herbal Wash
1 Part Mugwort
1 Part Lavender
1 Part Lemon Peel
4 Part Sea Salt

Steep the above herbs and salt in hot water and let it cool and bottle. Use it fresh as a hand and foot wash before entering the circle.

If necessary, you can even sweep the space of unwanted energies with a besom or broom.

After the space is cleansed, the Green Circle is cast, but rather than a wand, an herbal powder is used to mark the boundary. Much like the medieval magicians of the past, who marked their circles in salt or chalk, we mark a large, but strict boundary with herbal powder. Traditionally, circles are marked with a nine, eleven or thirteen foot diameter.

Casting Powder
Cornmeal
Tobacco
Wormwood
Yarrow
Angelica Root

The four elements are also called through the power of herbs.

Earth Anointing Oil
1/8 Oz of Mineral Oil
5 drops of Patchouli Oil
3 drops of Vetiver
1 Pinch of Comfrey Root

Start by anointing a quartz crystal or other stone with Earth Oil and recite the invocation to the North:

To the North, I call upon the Earth of the Heavens, Hells
and Land Around us.
I call upon the Starry Bull Taurus.
I call upon the Devouring Worm and the Slithering Snake.
I call upon the deep rooted plants of the element of Earth.

Hail and Welcome.

To call in the power of the East, light a small cauldron in the east filled with sacred woods. Oak, pine, hazel, birch and ash would all be appropriate. Avoid willow wood, as it is aligned too strongly with the element of water.

To the East, I call upon the Fire of the Heavens, Hells
*   and Land Around us.*
I call upon the Starry Lion Leo.
I call upon the blood sucking Mosquito and the hunting Wolf.
I call upon the flowering and thorned plants of the element of Fire.
Hail and Welcome.

To call in the power of the South, light an herbal incense.

Air Incense
    1 Tablespoon of Benzoin
    1 Part Lavender
    1/2 Part Vervain
    1/2 Part Peppermint
    3 drops of Lavender essential oil
    1 drop of Peppermint essential oil

To the South, I call upon the Air of the Heavens, Hells
*   and Land Around us.*
I call upon the Starry Water Bearer Aquarius.
I call upon the buzzing Fly and the Wise Crow.
I call upon the broad leafed plants of the element of Air.
Hail and Welcome.

To call in the power of the West, pour a libation of herbal tea out at the western edge of the circle. Willow bark, spearmint or jasmine tea would all be appropriate.

To the West I call upon the Water of the Heavens, Hells
    and Land Around us.
I call upon the starry Scorpio.
I call upon the poisonous Scorpion and the trusting Frog.
I call upon the flowing sap of plants of the element of Water.
Hail and Welcome.

(If you need to simplify the ritual, you can omit the earth oil, cauldron fire, air incense and water tea libation.)

To call the center, prepare a bowl of water in the center of the circle, and place flower essences into the bowl. Use any essences that you feel appropriate to the work, though rose would be an excellent choice. This is also a good time for all participants to call in their own personal guides, guardians, gods and ancestors, silently or out loud, depending on the style and size of the ritual.

To the Center I call upon the Spirits of the Heavens, Hells and Land Around us.
To the allies in all three realms: angels, fey, animals and ancestors,
All who come in Perfect Love and Perfect Trust.
Hail and Welcome.

To call the gods and remaining spirits, take the remaining casting powder and draw this sigil in the ground to the best of your ability. You can even have the sigil prepared in advance, and activate it with a simple libation of alcohol or essences upon it now.

Fig. 14: Sigil of the Green Devil

We call to the Green Devil,
Master of Rot and Decay.
We call to the Green Devil,
Embodiment of the Grave.
Withering Death and Decomposition,
All that hides from the light.
We call to the Green Devil,
Twin of the God of Life.
We call to the Rotting God,
Master of the Forest Blight.
We call upon the Greater Mother, Mother Earth as the One Land
    Around and Within Us.
Open the gates to all your gardens.
    Let us pass safely through all your wards.
Blessed be.

One of the manifestations of disconnection in our current society is the separation between the body and the spirit. We don't think of things like eating, drinking, sex and dancing as sacred, as do most tribal cultures. Our modern western religious ceremonies are stoic, not ecstatic. Thus, one of the ways that we are able to get back in touch with embodied ecstasy is through dance. This can be free form dance, with or without music, to get back into touch with the body and the life pulse. If you are dancing without music, try to hear the music of the world around you: the song of the plants, trees and even the music of the spheres, the heavens above.

When working in a large group, I prefer the triple ring circle dance. Start with a small circle of people in the center holding hands right over left, facing outward from the center, and have them dance in a grapevine step widdershins, or counterclockwise. A larger group comes in from the boundary of the circle holding hands right over left, and dances deosil, or clockwise, around the circle, facing the first group. Those who are unable or unwilling to dance will remain stationary and hold the edge of the circle. These three rings represent the three worlds: the underworld, middle world and the heavens, from the inner ring to the outer, respectively. They also represent the three "wheels" of the cosmic loom: the wheel of fate, the wheel of adjustment and the wheel of judgment or the Aeon, i.e. the loom of the cosmic cycle.

Grapevine Step

To dance the grapevine, simply take the foot furthest from the direction you are heading and swing it in front of the stationary foot and leg, so that your legs are crossed while standing for a moment. Then the stationary leg is swung in the direction of the dance to bring the legs together, uncrossed. This motion is then repeated, now with the foot that is furthest away swung *behind* the stationary leg. So if you are moving clockwise, facing inward, your right leg would swing over the left, bringing the feet together crossed. Then your left foot would swing out to uncross the legs. Your right foot would then swing behind the left bringing your feet together crossed, and your left foot would then swing out to uncross the legs, all the while moving your body to your left, clockwise, in a circular motion.

You can also synchronize your dance with a mantra. This mantra came to me during a healing session while working with a client to evoke the Green Devil and reconcile various aspects of the shadow:

Verde Anoos Morte Vivicum
Verde Anoos Morte Vivicum
Verde Anoos Morte Vivicum

It is akin to the classic "barbarous words of power"—words both real and nonsensical from various languages strung together to induce trance. Once the group is chanting this barbarous mantra of power, build to a frenzy until you are all ready to journey.

Once the dance has built up to a crescendo, release your hands and collapse, moving back to your positions within the circle, and use the energy generated by the dance to help propel you through the seven gates of hell.

A container full of stones will be passed at this point. Take one and keep it near you during the ritual. This will help you reconnect and reconsecrate your relationship with Nature and Humanity.

Chart 1 – Seven Hells

Chakra	Planet	Sin	Virtue	Balance
1 Crown	Sun	Pride	Humility	Esteem
2 Brow	Moon	Sloth	Diligence	Satisfaction
3 Throat	Mercury	Envy	Kindness	Aspiration
4 Heart	Venus	Greed	Charity	Benevolence
5 Solar Plexus	Mars	Wrath	Patience	Righteousness
6 Belly	Jupiter	Gluttony	Temperance	Moderation
7 Root	Saturn	Lust	Chastity	Taboo

Tool	Plant Keys
1 Flower Essence	Aconite, Morning Glory, Lotus
2 Oil	Datura, Poppy, Hemp, Wild Lettuce
3 Incense	Belladonna, Lobelia, Valerian
4 Potion	Foxglove, Rose, Mushrooms, Lady's Mantle
5 Fire Offering	Wormwood, Tobacco, Nettle
6 Sacrament	Hemlock, Pennyroyal, Henbane, Wine
7 Ointment	Mandrake, Yew

Insect	Animal
1 Beetle, Butterfly, Bee	Crow, Raven
2 Moth	Bat, Owl
3 Fly, Flea	Ferret
4 Ant	Wolf
5 Mosquito	Hare
6 Termites, Grubs	Toad
7 Worms, Centipede	Snake

By glancing at this chart, you will realize that most of the plants used fall within the "bane" category, and would be somewhat harmful to use without expert supervision. For those who would err on the side of caution, most of these plants can be found in homeopathic form, and can therefore be consumed safely in this form. I highly suggest working with these banes in flower essence and homeopathic form.

Chart 2 – Homeopathic Remedies

Plant	Homeopathic Name	Homeopathic Uses
Aconite (Monkshood)	*Aconitum Napellus*	Fear, shock, anxiety, anguish, influenza and fevers
Datura	*Stramonium*	Restlessness, delusions, terror, hyperactive sexuality, poor eyesight
Atropa belladonna	*Belladonna*	Unpleasant heightened awareness, tantrums, high fevers with redness & delirium
Foxglove	*Digitalis*	Heart conditions, angina, fear of moving, fear of death
Wormwood	*Absinthium*	Spasms, vertigo, nervousness, sleeplessness, hallucinations
Tobacco	*Tabacum*	Forgetful, discontented, upset stomach, collapse, sea sickness
Hemlock	*Conium Maculatum*	Paralysis, suppressed sexuality, withdrawing, exhaustion, no interest in life
Henbane	*Hyoscyamus Niger*	Twitching, nervous disorders, coughs, sensitive skin, obsessive behavior, jealousy, shamefulshameless
Mandrake	*Mandragora Officinarium*	Numbness, poor concentration, headache, paradox of drowsiness and excitement
Yew	*Taxus Baccata*	Feeling of emptiness or hunger, puffy and pale, night sweats, nausea

The leader of the ritual will be guiding the visionary portion of the rite, and the assisting priestesses/priests will be administering the preparations, so no one will have to worry about dealing with bottles while maintaining a trance state. For larger rituals, I suggest that those who call the four elements act as attending and assisting priests and priestesses. If a full four individuals are available to do so, then each is responsible for administering potions to one quarter of the circle of participants. Those with medical issues or lack of access to these plants or to safe substitutions can simply use the invocation of the plant spirit at each gate. The energy and consciousness of the plants are the true keys.

The following gate evocations are written with the primary plant spirit ally envisioned for the gate, even though the formulas might call for other plants to be included. You can rewrite the material if you use another plant as the primary ally, or you can theoretically do this ritual with no plant substances themselves, and simply evoke the power of the plant spirits. The ritual leader should read the evocations and, with the assistance of the plant spirits, open the gates. For larger group rituals, the ritual leader can also read the pathworking through the gates.

First Gate

The key to the first gate is a flower essence, ideally Aconite (Monkshood) or Morning Glory. Even if you have concerns about toxicity levels, flower essences are one of the safest ways to work with these plants. The ritual assistants should circle behind the participants, who are facing toward the center of the altar, and place one drop of flower essence on the head of each participant, on the crown chakra.

By the guardian of the First Gate, the Gate of the Crown,
*   the Sun and the light of day,*
We all upon Aconite, the fiery light of Monkshood,
*   Illuminator of True Purpose and Power.*
Bane of Monsters,
We call upon you.
Hail and Welcome.

Bring yourself to the edge of the World Tree. Envision the tree burning with an otherworldly flame of red, blue and gold. In this shimmering light, the tree takes its form, and only then can you enter it. The tree may bear fruit this time, when all other visits have shown it barren of fruit or nut. Notice what kind of fruit it is. Slip through the veil of your mind and stand before the great tree, the teacher of all wisdom and folly. Look deep within the roots for an opening, and step towards the first gate, descending downward. Leave the light of the Sun, Moon and Stars behind, and go into the darkness of the land.

Though you are in the depths, you are surrounded in a strange, luminous white glow, like the glow of the elder faery races from the myths of old, who were dazzling white like the dawn, and spectral in form. They were the Phantom Queens and Kings, the Ladies and Lords of the Otherworld. Enveloped in this light, you begin to feel like them as well. Feel your magick and your strength. Feel your power. All your successes and victories come to mind. Begin to relive all that you have done that has received praise, attention and blessing. Believe yourself to be invincible and utterly correct in what you do. Spirits of the past and present will challenge you.

For you are walking the path of Pride. (Pause)

Pride in moderation is self-esteem. Pride in excess leads to arrogant destruction. Pride's shadow is Humility. To be humble is a virtue, yet too much humility leaves us crippled, unable to enjoy the world around us or accomplish our Will. Can you find the balance point between Pride and Humility? Can you find the place within yourself where the two become one? Can you find the place where both are true? This paradox will reveal the key. Find the place of true esteem.

Second Gate

The key to the second gate is usually an anointing oil placed gently upon the brow to open the third eye to greater inner vision.

> **Second Gate Oil**
>   Olive Oil
>   Datura Seeds, ground
>   Hemp Leaf
>   Mugwort Leaf
>   Mugwort Essential Oil

The assistant anoints the participants' brow with a gentle dab, or the sign of a cross and a circle.

By the guardian of the Second Gate, the Gate of Vision,
*   the Moon and the night sky,*
We call upon Datura, the silvery light of the Devil's Weed,
*   opener of the Living and Dead.*
Thorned Apple Moon Flower,
We call upon you.
Hail and Welcome.

Now that you've passed through the gate of the Sun, of Pride and Humility, we descend further, spiraling deeper. We descend into the depths of the Earth and the underworld, through the path of the Moon. The white light of the first gate turns silvery, almost a pale lavender. Everything seems to slow down. The dynamic sense of Pride you felt, which is now in balance, leaves you. Things feel a bit heavy, a bit slow, a bit more like a daydream, as you walk the descending path to the underworld. You feel unrushed, even lazy. You wonder why you are here, why you are walking, and whether you have to go any further. You don't want to take any action at all. You seem to move forward only in slow motion, in tiny increments. You think about all the things you should do, all the things you could do, and you don't want to do anything. You just want to rest. You just want to sleep. But will you? Spirits of the past and present will challenge you.

For you are walking the path of Sloth. (Pause)

The light of the Moon spurs you on and opens a door of knowledge within you. You realize that you are being trapped. Rest is critical to our well being, but too much makes us lazy and indifferent. Work is essential to fulfilling our purpose in life, our Will, yet to pursue work only drives us to the point of breaking. Can you find the point of balance between Sloth and Diligence? Can you find the harmony where the two become one, and your work is your joy and your joy is your work, each rejuvenating each other? Can you find the place where both are true? The paradox will reveal the key. Find the place of restful satisfaction.

Third Gate

The herbal key to the third gate is incense smoke.

> ### Third Gate Incense
> Belladonna Leaves
> Datura Seeds
> Lobelia
> Bay Leaves
> Mugwort

The assistants will slowly walk around the circle, wafting the smoke around the participants.

By the guardian of the Third Gate, the Gate of Voice, the Messenger and quicksilver,
We call upon Belladonna, dark eyed beauty, opener to the night side of Eden.
Deadly Nightshade, Darkstar Door,
We call upon you.
Hail and Welcome.

You've passed through the gate of the Moon, of Sloth and Diligence, and now you descend further. The glow becomes a dull metallic quicksilver, reflecting your thoughts, and ideas in the space around you. Memories, ideas and plans come to you. In the images you begin to see all the people you know, and you start to think about who has what and how much. Who is doing better than you? Who has the things you want? Who has the life you want? Who would you want to be, if you could just take over their life? The feelings of envy grow stronger within you. Spirits of the past and present will challenge you.

For you are walking the path of Envy. (Pause)

Recognition of others' accomplishments, and to wish for things, is healthy. Using these feelings for inspiration is powerful. But letting our envy poison us and our relationships is the source of our undoing. Kindness is the cure—but too much kindness, too much cheering on of others, distracts us from your own goals. Can you find that point of balance between Envy and Kindness, where you can recognize what you want, and still be happy for another who already has it? Can you find the point of inspiration that draws from both? Can you find the place where both are true? The paradox will reveal the key.

Find the place of aspiration.

Fourth Gate

To open the fourth gate, the herbal ally is a potion.

Fourth Gate Potion
   Foxglove Flower Essence
   Rose Hips
   Yarrow Flowers
   Rose Water

The assistant priest/esses can either pour a bit into small cups, or, if participants bring their own chalice, pour a bit into the chalice.

By the guardian of the Fourth Gate, the Gate of the Heart,
*   the morning and evening star,*
We call upon Foxglove, faery cup, the Holy Grail of the Green.
Digitalis,
We call upon you.
Hail and Welcome.

You've passed through the Mercurial gate, and now the path takes on an emerald tone. The dark is illuminated strangely by green. Within the canopy of green around you, like a primordial forest, you see all the things you want, all the material things you wish to possess. You think about all you are lacking, all you wish to purchase, all you wish to own and control. You think about money; no matter how much you have, there is always a need for more. Think of what else you could do or get if you had more money than you do. As you walk, you are filled with a strange desire to gather up all of these things within you. You feel the overwhelming feeling of material desire and want. Spirits of the past and present will challenge you.

For you are walking the path of Greed. (Pause)

Desire leads us to Will and is therefore not wrong. Overwhelming desire, however, distracts us from what we truly want by allowing us to falsely fill some void or gap, and give us the illusion of control. Charity is the shadow of greed, the act of giving away all we can to those less fortune than us. Irresponsible charity, however, leaves us bankrupt, and unable to take care of ourselves, much less help others. Can you find the point between Greed and Charity where you can have what you want because it truly serves you, and yet give away what you don't need when it no longer serves you? Can you find the point where the two become one? Can you find the place where both are true? The paradox will reveal the key. Find the place of benevolence.

Fifth Gate

The fifth gate's key is comprised of simple fire offerings of Wormwood and/or Tobacco into a campfire, cauldron fire or onto charcoal. It can be passed around like an incense if placed upon charcoal.

By the guardian of the Fifth Gate, the Gate of Power,
*   the red star and the inner fires,*
We call upon Wormwood, summoner of Spirits
*   and destroyer of parasites.*
Artemesia Absinthium, Guardian of the Green Faery,
We call upon you.
Hail and Welcome.

The journey has taken you through the gate of Venus and now you walk the path of Mars. The green light turns red, like the green knight transforming into the red knight in the Celtic mythos. The red light on the path empowers you. It energizes you. It brings vitality and power. You feel the power coursing in your blood as you grow stronger. After a while, the red light even begins to agitate you. You become upset. You start thinking about all the things that upset you, that anger you – all the people, all the situations, all the past angers, all the future fights. Your anger begins to build and build. You feel it in your blood. You feel it as a palpable energy. You feel vengeful, wanting to strike out at all those who have done you harm. Spirits of the past and present will challenge you.

For you are walking the path of Wrath. (Pause)

Anger is a natural defense. It is our reaction to blocked energy, when we feel out of control or unable to express our true will. The shadow of blind action is patience, yet too much patience prevents us from acting, and often shields us from our very real and needed emotions under the guise of being "spiritual." Can you find the balance point between Anger and Patience, where you can respond with your will to the situation, rather than blindly react? Can you find the place where both are true? The paradox will reveal the key. Find the place of righteous action.

Sixth Gate

The key to open the sixth gate is a sacrament. I like to use a pellet of homeopathic Henbane, called *Hyoscyamus*, but a sacramental cake can also be baked with the homeopathic remedy placed within it.

By the guardian of the Sixth Gate, the Gate of Womb and Tomb,
*   of storm kings and riches,*
We call upon Henbane, caller of lightening and storms,
*   opener of eyes and ears.*
Jupiter's bean,
We call upon you.
Hail and Welcome.

Walking through the gates of Mars, you now walk the path of the Belly, of Jupiter. The red light turns shades of both orange and blue, complimentary colors. The journey has been long and you feel yourself losing stamina. You need to re-fuel. You become hungry. Even though you've already consumed sacramental food and drink, it has not been enough. You hunger. You hunger not just for food, but your soul also hungers. You want something to fill you. You think of all the hungers that have gone unfed within you, and your desire to satiate them all, but no matter how much you have, you are never satisfied. Spirits of the past and present will challenge you.

For you are walking the path of Gluttony. (Pause)

Gluttony is a natural desire to be filled, to be satiated, to not hunger. Yet we live in a world where we constantly consume. To be spiritual we are told to restrict ourselves, yet this goes against our nature as being creatures of the world. All creatures seek to fill themselves, to feed themselves. Temperance is not denial, but rather the skill to temper the point between want and need, to enjoy consciously rather than consume volumes unconsciously. Can you find this point of true satisfaction? Can you find the place where both are true? The paradox will reveal the key. Find the place of moderation.

Seventh Gate

The final gate uses an ointment to open the way.

Seventh Gate Ointment
  Oil
  Beeswax
  Mandrake
  Damiana
  Mugwort
  Wormwood
  Datura
  Rose

While this ointment should ideally be placed on the perineum point, near the genitals, the attending priest/esses can put a little in each participants outstretched hands, and the individual can determine where best to put it. Other options include the soles of the feet, or between the legs on the inner thigh.

By the guardian of the Seventh Gate, the Gate of the World Unseen and Seen, of sex and death and madness,
We call upon Mandrake, the Root of Wisdom, the Apple of Immortality, and the Dead Man's Seed.

Mandragora Alraun,
We call upon you.
Hail and Welcome.

Now you enter to the deepest levels, walking the path of the Root, or Saturn, where the light turns dark crimson, almost black. You are walking the path of the Root, the lowest point before you meet the Green Devil. You feel yourself to be, after the path of Gluttony, slightly more substantial. You feel your energy in your body. You feel the sensation of your skin. You feel the craving of the flesh grow within you. You feel the desire to touch and be touched, to feel pleasure. Spirits of the past and present will challenge you.

For you are walking the path of Lust. (Pause)

Lust goes down to our DNA. Our desire to experience pleasure is hardwired in our reproductive system, but it goes beyond reproduction, ensuring survival not only to our race, but to the soul and the spirit as well. Lust generates an energy that helps us reach the darkest corners of the self and the brightest heights of heaven. Yet such power leads to obsession, to misuse. It's so powerful that it can generate powerful bonds between people, and destroy us when all parties do not use these bonds consciously and clearly. Religion, such as Catholicism, tells us that chastity is the cure, and to only use sex for procreation, yet this is a perversion of our own inner calling, meant to prevent us from finding the heavens and depths ourselves. Moderation is key. Consciousness, clarity and communication are keys. Can you find the point between abandoning all to lust all the time and locking yourself up in the house of flesh? Can you flow with the currents of sexual energy and express them as they are meant to be expressed? Can you find the place where both are true, the sacred and that which seems profane? The paradox will reveal the key. Find the place of taboo.

At the deepest point of the seven hells you will encounter the Green Devil himself. No one can tell you what to expect, as it will be different for everyone. Commune with the Green Devil, in words, pictures, feelings, or however he relates to you. Ask to see the Emerald Heart of the Earth, the supposed emerald that fell from the crown of Lucifer, another devil figure. In its redemptive phase, this emerald, in whole or part, was used in the crafting of the Arthurian Holy Grail. Thus, it has been redeemed.

The experience should synthesize all the vice and virtues of the seven gates, and hopefully result in the reception and understanding of the complete image of the Green Man, both life and death, both living and dying, not a romanticized and sterilized view of an all benevolent, safe and clear God of Nature.

Return quickly through the seven gates, reflecting on each of the virtue and vices, and the synthesis you have experienced of each. As you ascend, you notice flowers blooming in your wake. You are like newly born Aphrodite, rising from the foamy depths and rejuvenating the land with every step. You find that a green light follows you from the underworld. When you leave the ritual, you will find your presence, your energy, rejuvenates not only the land, but humanity's relationship with the land, with the body, and with the material world, starting with yourself.

Take the stone that has been with you this entire time and consecrate it. Bless this stone with the powers beyond virtue and vice now found within you. Bless it with the words:

I am at peace with my own True Nature, and I am at peace with all.

When the ritual is done, place this stone someplace special, so it may radiate out the connection between the human realm and all of nature and supernature. It can be outdoors, indoors or anyplace in between. But make sure it is out and open, not lost in a bag or drawer somewhere. If you are in a group setting, I encourage you to pass around and trade the stones with each other, declaring your peace with your own True Nature and all of creation as you do. This exchange represents the weaving of the web, as all our work is dependent upon our sisters and brothers in the work. Feel the light of the underworld radiate out from it.

Devoke the deities gathered as the ritual is brought to its conclusion:

We thank the Green Devil, the Green Teacher, the Green Master.
We thank you for showing us your truth.
Neither this nor that, you stand between life and death,
At one with your twin, not separate.
For if there is to be life, there must be death.
And if there is to be death, there must be life.
Stay if you will, go if you must.
We thank you for all
Hail and Farewell.
We thank the Great Earth Mother,
    the One Land Around and Within Us.
You whom give your body to make our own bodies.
We thank you for this journey.
We thank you for this wisdom.
We thank you for this life.
Blessed be.

To completely release the center pour out the bowl of flower essences upon the land. You can also pour them out on the remnants of the Green Devil's sigil.

To the center, I thank and release the Spirits of the Heavens, Hells and
    Land Around us.
May there always be peace between us. Hail and Farewell.

Release the quarters, moving widdershins and starting in the north.

Chapter Nine: Green Gnosis & Plant Spirit Initiation

To the North, I thank and release the element of Earth in the Heavens,
Hells and Land Around us. I thank and release the stars of Taurus,
the Worm and the Snake.
I thank the deep rooted plants of Earth.
I thank you all.
Hail and Farewell.

Face the west.

To the West, I thank and release the element of Water in the Heavens,
Hells and Land Around us. I thank and release the stars of Scorpio,
the Scorpion and the Frog.
I thank the sap flowing plants of Water.
I thank you all.
Hail and Farewell.

Face the south.

To the South, I thank and release the element of Air in the Heavens,
Hells and Land Around us. I thank and release the stars of
Aquarius, the Fly and the Crow.
I thank the broad leafed plants of Air.
I thank you all.
Hail and Farewell.

Face the east.

To the East, I thank and release the element of Fire in the Heavens, Hells
and Land Around us. I thank and release the stars of Leo, the
Mosquito and the Wolf.
I thank the flowering and thorned plants of Fire.
I thank you all.
Hail and Farewell.

Release the circle by ritually breaking the boundary of the
casting powder with your broom.

I release this circle in the land. As these herbs rot and join the One Land,
may the deep wisdom gained here be accessible to all of Nature.
May there always be peace between us. Blessed be.

The entire ritual experience will be different for everyone.
Those raised in traditional forms of Christianity, particularly
Catholicism or Fundamentalism, might react strongly to the
format and imagery. For some, it is confrontational, yet within
that confrontation is an element of surprise. The fiery "hell"
tree does not burn. Nature reveals her secrets to those who
have the eyes and ears to learn. For others, it has been
described as surprisingly gentle from the start, like the process
of leaves and brush rotting way at the floor of the forest,
revealing what is truly there. The ritual itself can be described
oneiric, dream–like, due to the use of plant entheogens, and
particularly due to the use of so many herbs taken in so many
forms. Not only does the ritual itself seem wispy and dream-
like, like a dream of the Witch's Sabbat in the underworld, but
your dreams afterwards might be blissfully magickal or more
nightmarish and confrontational, completing the work of the
Green Devil. I advise you to have a notebook at hand when you
slumber for the next few days.

Crafting the Green Devil's Vessel

You can craft a vessel for the spirit of the Green Devil in order
for him to be present in these rites much like you'd create an
herbal homunculus via the bottle method. I was lucky in that I
acquired a skull shaped bottle gifted to me by friends. I filled it
with herbs, mostly banes, and chanted the magickal words of
the Green Devil: *Verde Anoos Morte Vivicum.*

My own Green Devil Bottle was filled with the following
herbs, freshly picked:

Wormwood
Mugwort
Datura (*Stramonium* and *Inoxia*)
Black Nightshade
Enchanter's Nightshade
Monkshood
Silver King Artemisia
May Apple
Comfrey
Hellebore
Rue
Magic Mushroom

To the mix I added Hyssop Essential Oil, as one of its properties is purification from guilt. This acted as an important counter balance for the banes. It's ideal to make this vessel on the Dark Moon—though I made mine on the Full Moon, and then covered it for fourteen days and dedicated it to the Green Devil on the dark Moon.

Sexual Congress with the Green

One aspect of plant magick, or even magick in general, that is rarely talked about in the open is the experience of sexual and spiritual congress. The Medieval trial lore on witches, the same source ripe with information about the Witch's familiar, is also filled with lore regarding the *succubus* and *incubus*.

Incubi and *succubi* (plural of incubus and succubus) are said to be malevolent spirits that come to men and women in their dreams. They would then lie with these mortals for the purpose of spiritual congress, having "unnatural" intercourse with them to the eventual detriment of the humans, at least according to many religious sources. Incubi and succubi are described as vampiric in nature, stealing both vitality and life force. They are also said to be involved in the conception of children, with the succubi stealing a man's sperm, or the incubi impregnating a human woman, both resulting in unnatural children susceptible to deformity, illness, and evil. In variations of the demonological lore, some incubi and succubi are exclusively heterosexual, while others claim that they're bisexual and can change gender at will, manifesting as the human desires them. For example, they may collect sperm from a human man as a succubus and then change form into an incubus to use this spiritually "tainted" sperm to impregnate a human woman. Some famous figures in mythology are said to be fathered by incubi, including the Christianized version of the story of Merlin, who was born of woman and no man. Such children are known as *cambions* and have great power due to their dual nature.

Modern psychologists speculate that the mythos of the succubi/incubi stemmed from religious guilt over erotic dreams and men's nocturnal emissions, and provided an explanation for both sleep paralysis and pregnancy out of wedlock. The concept of something evil seducing one into the pleasure not normally allowed to them by those who felt it was wrong to experience and enjoy such things, provided them with the opportunity to have the experience but ultimately take no responsibility for it, though such confessions usually led to other problems, such as clergy believing such people were bewitched. Some even speculate that the mythos acted as a coping mechanism to help people deal with issues of rape and sexual abuse, particularly when the clergy themselves were the perpetrators. Devout parishioners couldn't face that fact, so the myth of sexual demons was created.

Mythically the root of these spirits is most directly found within the Hebrew figure Lilith and her demonic children, the *Lilim*. In esoteric Judaism, Lilith was the first wife of Adam who was cast out of the garden for not sexually submitting to him. Once beyond the garden she mated with demons and fallen

Chapter Nine: Green Gnosis & Plant Spirit Initiation

angels and mothered a race of demons, the Lilim, to plague the sons of Adam by causing babies to be still born or suffer cot death, as well as by seducing men in their dreams like the succubi. In turn, Lilith herself probably originates in the Sumerian Lilitu, a class of demons associated with storms and then later with the night and sexual dreams.

While it is easy to think of this lore as strictly associated with the Middle Eastern roots of Judaism and Christianity, and thus the latter's legacy of sexual repression, there exists similarities and cognates with succubi and incubi in other cultures as well, including Greece, Germany, Brazil and Africa. Perhaps this is not a mechanism to explain sexual guilt or crime, but a spiritual phenomenon. If you go into surviving tribal shamanic traditions, you will find the concept of the shaman's spirit lover, or spirit wife, as a primary inner world tutelary spirit and initiator. You find a similar concept in the Celtic faery traditions of a Faery Lover, Faery Bride and every Faery Queen/King mating. In fact, in the more Pagan version of the birth of Merlin, his father is no demon or devil, but an elder faery being. Some ceremonial lore ascribes the same origin to Jesus of Nazareth, another wise magician born of an earthly mother and no human father. In classic mythology we have the Greek gods parenting a wide range of semi divine offspring, the demigods.

Sexual union of this nature, i.e. the transmission of such energy between incarnate and discarnate entities, was both initiatory and sacramental, benefiting both entities in their spiritual evolution and development. Only in a dark age, where such knowledge is lost, would potentially holy contact with the spirit world be interpreted as demonic.

But while such spiritual sexual alchemy is intriguing, what does it have to do with the plant familiar? At first glance, nothing. They appear to be two unrelated phenomena. Yet modern interpretations of the lore in the non-Wiccan

Traditional Craft movement links the animal familiar-fetch to the faery lover or fetch-mate. What is known as the double, or doppelganger, moves from an animal identity to a humanoid identity, usually of the opposite sex.

Still, this has little to do with plant magick until one realizes that the link to the faery lover is a link to the land and to the spirits of nature. Today, faeries are often mistaken in modern lore for the spirits of plants and trees. While they are not plant spirits per se, they are the guardian spirits of nature, the wisdom and power beneath and behind the land itself, supporting the individual nature spirits of the plants, trees, grasses, flowers, rocks and water.

As we are exploring the possibility of the plant spirit as a familiar or totem—and ultimately the pursuit of green initiation, to mix its nature with our own soul, making it part of our fetch self joined to our soul complex—it is only natural that the plant familiar follow the same patterns of other spirit familiars, including the metamorphosis in relationship from impish helper, guide and protector, to lover, teacher and mate. In fact, some would see this step as a key point in finding union with the Green World, beyond ordeal or direct gnosis—a mixing and mingling of the spiritual energies that results in crafting a new being within you to be reborn through plant initiation.

When you truly contemplate it, it's easy to see the plant world is filled with sexuality, even more so than the animal world. There is a wide variety of sexualities and orientations in the plant world, much more diverse than our animal world. Plants can be male, female, bisexual, androgynous, unisexual and self-propagating. As plants are immobile, unlike animals, their sexual congress must involve many others, and their mating, reproduction, and survival is crucial to the survival of the animal races and indeed the entire planet. Plants involve wind, water, insects and animals in their reproductive cycle. We find their flowers the most seductive to us, using them for decoration, medicine, religion, romance, art and magick. Flowers are the peak of the plants power, but are also the sexual organs of the plant.

Even beyond physical reproduction in the Green World, spiritually the process of photosynthesis, while producing energy for the plant, is really an embodiment of the Witch's Great Rite, the union of the heavens and earth, sunlight and matter, God and Goddess. The plant world is filled with sex and the magickal power of sex, so it makes sense that in some cases they would reach out to humanity on a sexual level.

Many of the plant spirits associated with Witchcraft, particularly from the five-petaled *Solanum* family, are highly sexualized and feminine. While influenced by the powers of Saturn and Pluto as poisons, these plants have a strong Venusian undercurrent, in relationship to the dark Venus Witch goddess. To those of us on the green path, they appear as beautiful women, particularly Belladonna, whose name means Beautiful Lady, and her sister, Datura. Mandrake and Tobacco have particularly strong, virile male resonances. Henbane, often thought of as feminine due to the "hen" aspect of the name, is also associated with storm and lusty masculine Jupiterian figures, including Thor. More so than any other family of potentially sacred entheogenic plants, these Witch banes have both danger and sexuality associated with them. When coupled with the sexual repressive consciousness of the Christian European dark ages, the mix is ripe for misunderstanding and demonization.

While even today the concept of sexual union with the spirit world seems far-fetched, such threads are interwoven throughout our mystical traditions, as either literal truth or allegory. Alchemy is filled with images of the Divine Marriage of inner king and queen of Sun and Moon, or of Heaven and Earth, resulting in the initiate becoming a spiritual hermaphrodite, both male and female. Hermetic Qabalah frames the initiate as the Princess of Malkuth, of the world, who unites in matrimony with the Prince of Tiphereth, of the Sun, who is the Holy Guardian Angel. Even modern psychology has distilled these ideas into the somewhat sterile *anima* and *animus*. Many ordained in various Christian orders are said to be "married" to the Church, for example Catholic nuns becoming "brides of Christ." So the concept of fetch-mates, faery lovers and flower brides isn't completely out of context in the Western spiritual traditions.

When you have sufficiently developed your relationship with the plant spirits, if appropriate, they might come to you via the experience of direct sexual congress. Such contact can occur in meditative vision, or, much like the incubi and succubi, through dreams. Sexual congress with the plant world can also be ritually invoked if you feel you are sufficiently advanced and prepared for the experience. Sometimes the union is through an individual plant spirit with a distinct plant species, and other times it is a union with a goddess or god of the green realm, representing a wide range of plant intelligences in the ritual.

Evocation of the Plant Lover

Ritual Evocation of the Plant Lover for spiritual and sexual congress is not a set formula. Any written ritual should only be an invitation, an enticement, or seduction. Anything else would be akin to a summoning and trapping, which is more appropriate to a ritual of the Goetia than to the wooing of a loving familiar ally.

If you are seeking the companionship of a specific plant, use oils, incense and sacraments appropriate to that plant. While generally I find the plant realm generous about the use of their body in preparations, you might find burning your potential lover as incense the most appropriate method to unite with the plant self. The idea of breathing in the very body of the plant's love is quite seductive and erotic. Scent is one of the major triggers of consciousness.

I've found this ritual is best performed as an oneiric rite, meaning an evocation prior to dreaming. Sleep invites the opportunity for the spirit to visit you while you dream, but does not force a manifestation in the ritual circle. If possible, perform the ritual in the bedroom and arrange to sleep alone that evening if you have a spouse or partner. Establish an altar as a shrine for the plant lover. Light candles that will either be doused before bed, or kept in a safe, fire-proof container. Burn incense and anoint yourself with appropriate oils during the ritual. If a potted plant is available, bring it into the bedroom. If not, perhaps the ritual could be done outdoors, slumbering beneath the plant ally. A talisman placed under your pillow, such as a root charm or herbal bag as mentioned in the previous chapter, would be quite appropriate.

When you are prepared, create the Green Circle. Invite the spirit of the plant into your space and life as a lover and teacher. Each plant must be wooed differently. I've found poetry and song to be quite effective. Write your own poetry. This poetic evocation is an example of something I've used for the Datura plant.

Lady Datura of the White Trumpets,
Whose flowers glow like the Moon,
Grant us the Voice of the Spirits,
Lead me to the heavens not the tomb.
I seek the Lady who knows the light from the dark.
I seek the Lady who calls out to me clear.
I seek the Lady who brings pleasure and madness.
I seek your companionship with love and respect, yet not fear.
You have flowers so lovely and fragile,
You have the apples of danger and pain,
You have the seeds of the mysteries,
They fall from you like the rain.

They call you the Devil's Weed,
But they don't know.
They call you Thorn Apple and Witch's Thimble,
For that is how you grow.
They pull you up and cast you out,
Yet your beauty charms and beguiles
Without any doubt.
For the mysteries of the spirit lay within your flesh.
Lady Datura of the White Trumpets,
Whose flowers glow in the night,
Allow me the pleasure of your company,
Open me up to your light.

Some feel the stimulation of sexual energies as an appropriate way to attract the plant and forge a link with your energy, yet the stimulation should not result in climax, but rather remain in a ritualized state of "betweenness" that will aid your dreaming vision. When you feel you have charmed the plant spirit with your invitation, slumber near the living plant or with its token near you. Keep a notebook by your side, and when you awaken, record your experience and insights about the plant lover. Some will use sexual fluids, either from the nocturnal state, or generated upon waking, to anoint the plant, ground or charm, in order to forge a deeper link.

When done, say your farewells for now and release the circle in the normal manner.

The Herba Alba

The *Herba Alba,* the "White Herb," is both a mythic and real plant used in alchemy and magick. In alchemy, it is the mythic white herb, the five-petaled flower pointing upward, as the top point indicates spirit ruling the four terrestrial elements. In the mythic paradise where Nature Herself is the greatest alchemist, the black fertile soil is transformed into the white blossom, indicative of the black phase of alchemy transforming to a purified white. Though seen by some as an aspect of the Philosopher's Stone or Elixir of Immortality, an alchemical Holy Grail, the Herba Alba is not the final phase. One must be transformed ultimately into the power of the red phase, but it is quite a momentous step to reach. Perhaps there is an *Herba Ruber*, or perhaps the true red stage is found through an action or rite that the initiate performs with the white herb.

In more traditional herbalism and botany, Herba Alba usually refers to *Artemisia herba alba*, or White Wormwood. It is also known as the Rose of Jericho. Like most plants in the *Artemisia* genus, including Common Mugwort, Sagebrush and Tarragon, White Wormwood possesses a long history of magickal and medicinal lore. Its smoke can be used to prevent the influence of harmful spirits and malevolent magickal practitioners, much like sage. Some believe the smoke's effect is similar to that of Cannabis. Medicinally it's used for colds, coughs, indigestion, and most notably, to kill parasites within the body. White Wormwood is similar to the species of Wormwood used in the drink absinthe.

Wormwood is mentioned several times in the Bible, but none more prominent than in the Book of Revelations, chapter eight, as the name of a star at the end of the world that turns the waters bitter and poisonous.

And the seven angels which had the seven trumpets prepared themselves to sound.

The first angel sounded, and there followed hail and fire mingled with blood, and they were cast upon the earth: and the third part of trees was burnt up, and all green grass was burnt up.

And the second angel sounded, and as it were a great mountain burning with fire was cast into the sea: and the third part of the sea became blood;

And the third part of the creatures which were in the sea, and had life, died; and the third part of the ships were destroyed.

And the third angel sounded, and there fell a great star from heaven, burning as it were a lamp, and it fell upon the third part of the rivers, and upon the fountains of waters;

And the name of the star is called Wormwood: and the third part of the waters became wormwood; and many men died of the waters, because they were made bitter.

And the fourth angel sounded, and the third part of the sun was smitten, and the third part of the moon, and the third part of the stars; so as the third part of them was darkened, and the day shone not for a third part of it, and the night likewise.

And I beheld, and heard an angel flying through the midst of heaven, saying with a loud voice, Woe, woe, woe, to the inhabiters of the earth by reason of the other voices of the trumpet of the three angels, which are yet to sound!

– Revelations 8: Verses 6 -13 (King James Version)

Some think of Wormwood here as synonymous to the Christian Anti-Christ at the end of the world as depicted in Revelations. Others think of the book of Revelations as a mystic text, an allegory for an initiatory process, and not the end of the physical world. Each of these challenges, including the star Wormwood, is an initiatory experience towards experiencing the Gnostic light of heaven.

A Christian legend tells us that Wormwood sprang up from the depression in the ground left by the Serpent as it exited the Garden of Eden after the Fall. Some use this story to illustrate the malevolent nature of Wormwood as evidenced by its relationship to the Serpent...at least those who see the Serpent as the villain of the story do. For those who see the Serpent as the champion of free choice and the seeking of knowledge, then the herb it leaves in its wake, Wormwood, would also champion the causes of free choice and the quest for knowledge. For many Gnostic Christians, the Serpent is the hero of the story, echoing times when the serpent image was a symbol of creativity, knowledge, wisdom and power in Pagan cultures.

Wormwood, as part of the *Artemisia* family of plants, is also associated with the Greek huntress and moon goddess Artemis, known to the Romans as Diana. Both forms of this goddess are associated with light, mysteries and Witchcraft. What is Witchcraft but the quest for the mysteries and secret knowledge? Artemis is the goddess of the wild woods, where the secrets of nature are kept. Only those who venture forth will discover their secrets.

Another two plants that share the folk name Rose of Jericho with the Herba Alba, but are in fact totally different species are *Anastatica hierochuntica* and *Selaginella lepidophylla*. Both are known as the plant of resurrection, it is unusual for the fact that it can dry up like tumbleweed in a dormant state, but be resurrected with water. This cycle of drying and rebirth can be done many times with one plant. Both plants are associated with the opening and closing of the Virgin Mary's Womb and the resurrection of Jesus.

The city of Jericho is an interesting name for any of these plants, as it is located in the lowest permanently inhabitable site on Earth, far below sea level. Jericho is one of the oldest continuously inhabited cities in the world, currently part of the Palestinian territories. It is known for its many springs and is also associated with ancient Moon worship. It is referenced in the Bible as the City of Palm Trees. Thus, in its desert region, Jericho is associated with life and rebirth.

For our purposes, the magickal spirit of Herba Alba is more like the alchemist's spiritual version, though these other actual plants, through ritual use, can guide us on the quest for mastery over the elements and purity of spirit. But it is the ultimate ideal of the Herba Alba that we are seeking. The Herba Alba is the mysterious spiritual ingredient in all sacred brews. It is the secret ingredient of the greal of Ceridwen's cauldron of inspiration. It is found in the Soma and Ambrosia of the gods. It's the porridge of the Dagda, the kykeon of Demeter and the hazelnut of the Celtic bards. It is the mysterious herb found under the water in the quest of Gilgamesh, the rose-like thorn that blooms beneath the sea, granting health, vitality and immortality to the user. It's the miraculous secret of the first Noah, of Utnapishtum, who advises Gilgamesh. It restores us to the gods.

According to some Hindu teachings, humans are like "seven leafed plants," referencing the seven chakras, not just as a system of energy anatomy, but as the process of "growing" consciousness through seven steps. Only then do we bloom with the flower of the crown, the white flower dazzling with the light of a thousand suns. Some would describe this initiation process as "pollination" from higher divine forces, so we can truly bear fruit. We have been touched by a force beyond us, but to be spiritually pollinated, we must first bloom. Our work, our effort, virtue, and magick all leads us to this blooming, but without a connection to a greater source of spiritual awareness, it is only one step. The blooming of the Herba Alba is the preparatory work for this process. It is the mid-point, the white flower. When we are spiritually pollinated, we can grow the apple fruit of the red phase. In many ways, the apple tree of the Biblical garden is a great allegory for the stages of alchemy – dark soil, white flower and red fruit, with the potential for another tree in its seed.

Ritual Well of the Herba Alba

To prepare for this ritual, you will need a large, clear, glass or crystal bowl to be your "Well of Light," the nexus point for the starlight of the Herba Alba. A bowl made of a clear natural substance is better than an iron cauldron in this case. A true copper, silver or gold vessel would do, but most of us have an easier time finding glass vessels. Acquire some clear spring or well water; it is best if you can obtain it from a spring or well directly yourself, or from a location sacred to you and your traditions. Obtain several powerful herbs, ideally fresh, and among them should be some *Artemisias*, such as wormwood or mugwort. If you can obtain a resurrection plant in the form of a Rose of Jericho, all the better, though it's not native for most of us, and I always prefer to use native plants whenever possible. The Rose of Jericho is used in some forms of Hoodoo and New Orleans Voodoo, so it is possible to obtain from specialty shops and/or mail order. The bowl needs to reflect light, so the ritual is best performed on a sunny day or a moonlit night. If done indoors, a single candle is needed to catch the light upon the water. This ritual can be facilitated with a small sacrament of wormwood in any of its forms, but this is not necessary for success.

Cast the Green Circle and do this ritual as the body of the work. Fill the bowl with water, and then add your green allies to the mix. Speak these or similar words:

I call to you O Herba Alba,
White Herb of Light within all the Green World.
I call upon the Watcher, the Atman of Nature,
O Bornless Essence of the Green, Eternal and Beyond,
Yet Within and Without.
Illuminate me with your light O Rose Eternal,
Offer me the secrets of the resurrection and the light.
May my own green grow black, white and then red with power.
Illuminate me on the path,
So I may climb to the starry heavens and beyond.
So mote it be.

Stir the mixture counterclockwise, in the direction of the stars, and gaze into the water. Let the water settle. Hold the bowl within your lap as you sit on the ground, or place it on a small altar where you can gaze down into it.

Feel it connect to the ground around you. Feel it draw in the light of the green. Feel this "well" connect to the depths below. Feel it draw up the light of the "stars," the stones and metals, within the Earth. Feel the power build up in the bowl. Feel it reach up like a fountain, like a geyser, and feel it reach up to the starry heavens, past the Moon and Sun, touching the Northern Stars. Feel their light also being drawn down into the Well of the Herba Alba.

Gaze into the brilliant light of the Herba Alba well. Feel your consciousness, and even your body, being drawn into it. Become one with the light of the well. Feel your consciousness cycling over and over again, through the Green of the Middle World, through the dark light of the Underworld depths and up to the starry heavens and back down again. Become one with the eternal light that cycles endlessly through life. You may receive your own insights and mysteries.

When the experience is complete, thank the spirits who have aided you. Feel the cycle of the well slow down and stop, leaving you with charged waters and nothing more. You can ritually baptize yourself with the waters of the well at this time, healing and empowering you to never forget the experience. I prefer the motion of the "Goblin Cross" pentacle, anointing the brow, left breast, right shoulder, left shoulder and right breast, returning to the brow. The baptism of the green and white is its own form of sacrament in itself, preparing you for an even deeper gnosis. Meditate, journey and commune as desired. Conclude and release the green circle as you normally would.

Vigil of the Verdant Grave

Of all the rituals of green gnosis, the vigil is the most important. It some ways it is the most basic, and in others the most complex and powerful. I've saved it for last, as many of the experiences outlined in the rest of the chapter can occur outside the context of their rituals, and be a part of the simple vigil without specifically evoking them, so they are discussed as a preparation. Anything can truly happen in the vigil. Within it you may move through all three alchemical phases of black, white and red, or through death, resurrection and holy empowerment.

The vigil is best performed between liminal times of the day. Liminal times are morning, noon, twilight and midnight. Keeping vigil from sunrise to sunset for example would be a powerful window into the Green World, and gives us a specific understanding of the plant spirits when they are most active on the terrestrial plane. Gnosis at such time can give information about the medicinal properties of plants and how to heal. Vigils for the deeper mysteries would be from sunset to midnight, or even better, from sunset to dawn, as the astral forms of the plants rise up and expand to fill the forest with a collective consciousness unmatched by the daylight hours. Some believe that is why plants picked at night are ripe for magick, while plants picked during the day are ripe for medicine.

The Full Moon is best for most magick, though the dark of the Moon has its allure as well. When the Moon is in "green" signs such as Taurus or Virgo, or the nourishing sign of Cancer, the work is best, though the signs of Scorpio and Pisces also open powerful doors into the mysteries.

The most powerful of vigil rites occurs at night, when you seek to become one with the green through the initiation of death and resurrection. Carlos Castaneda speaks of this rite, not for the same purposes, but rather to overcome death and make it an ally. An initiate into Toltec wisdom will dig his own grave, and lay it for the evening to become one with the Earth and to conquer the fear of death. You will find similar rites with a green slant to them in the initiations of both Mediterranean and Scottish Witches, who add the element of "embalming" with vines, grape or ivy respectively. I'm sure other traditions use plants native to their area.

When returning from such a vigil, it is good to speak with a trusted and respected person of wisdom who is attuned to the Green World. Like the vision quests of Native traditions, it is easy to become self-deluded or egotistical in such work, and having a grounded wisdom-keeper with which to share your experiences, and who can help interpret them, is quite useful. In the end the interpretation is up to you, but different views on your experience can open your own perspective on the magick. Such a person can also watch over you from a small distance, making sure you are safe from any unexpected animals. If feasible, you can also have a small campfire nearby, for both spiritual and practical reasons.

Grave Vigil

Start the process by walking in nature often, if you don't already, and find a suitable place that is "between," yet undisturbed. Once you have a site in mind, do a simple meditation and offering there, to commune with the spirits of the land and the green in that place. Do they accept you? Are they willing to host your vigil? If not, move on, but when you find the right spot for you, it will be clear. Ask for an omen.

Prepare the spot by making your own grave. There are many ways to do this, and while Castaneda's six foot deep grave would be ideal, there are multiple reasons why we might choose another way. First would be leaving the land relatively undisturbed. Yet marking the grave is a powerful method and should not be lightly dismissed. I would suggest marking a human/coffin sized boundary, of stones, of flowers, twigs and branches. This is the place from which you will not move. I also suggest placing a larger stone at the head, the literal headstone, which can be used as a head rest or decorated like a gravestone. You can mark the stone with your name and a motto or epitaph. If it was truly your headstone, what would you want it to say? Again, if you want to leave the land undisturbed, I suggest a nontoxic water color or vegetable dye as your medium to mark the stone. It will wash away with the rain, leaving no trace of your presence.

To both help induce trance, and to prevent the need to move from the vigil space due to bodily functions, I suggest performing a fast if you have the necessary constitutional strength to handle it. Hard fasts shouldn't be taken by the very old, the very young, or the sick. You can start with a juice and soup fast, or begin with light food on the first preparatory day, move to all liquids the second day and then water-only the third day. Quit the intake of all liquids a few hours before the ritual and make sure to relieve yourself. In some South American traditions, one might fast upon the plant teacher itself. To attune to a specific plant ally, assuming it is not toxic, one would drink an herbal tea of the plant during the fast, and such a tea would be the only food allowed on the last day. Such South American style fasts allow some light foods, but specifically avoid salt, citrus, red meat and bottom feeder fish and crustaceans. Usually such plant fasts would also be combined with ayahuasca rituals.

Enter the ritual space and perform an appropriate evocation of the plant spirits. Use ceremony and ritual to open the way between your human world of flesh and blood perceptions and the communion of the Green World.

I call upon the Goddess of the Land.
I call upon the Goddess of the Green.
I call upon the Goddess of the Grave.
I come in the spirit of the old ways.
I come with love in my heart.
I come with the fire of the heavens in my hands.
Open your earthen flesh to me.
Open your embrace.
Open your Mysteries.
I call upon the Green Man of the Wood.
I call upon the Green Man of the Forest Floor.

I call to the God of Growth and the God of Rot.
Open the Gate Between Worlds.
Open the Gate Between Flesh and Blood to Sap and Pollen.
Lady and Lord of the Land Between,
I seek the spirit of the Green.
I seek to be touched by the Green.
I seek to be transformed by the touch of the Green Gods
     of Balm and Bane and Tree.
I seek initiation into the Ways of the Herbs
     that heal and hex and resurrect.
Guide me.
Protect me.
Bless me.
May I return with blood that runs green
     with wisdom, healing, love and power.
Now until the end of all time.
So mote it be.

Create sacred space in whatever way you see fit, knowing that your grave boundary acts much like a circle between the worlds, for the "open grave" is truly between the worlds. Perform your vigil in the night, surrounded by nature. Hold fast to your intention, be it for generalized wisdom and initiation, or a specific ability or experience. Hold intention, but allow the green wisdom to guide you in ways you might not suspect. Feel the presence of supernature, as it is the living life force that animates all things. Commune. Be open to your vision, hearing and feelings. Be open to initiation. Be initiated into the ways of the green.

Return upon the end of your vigil, either when the experience is well and truly ended, or when the time period allotted is done. Say thank you and give your blessings as you deem appropriate. Ground yourself. Break your fast with something gentle and light you have already prepared and have nearby. Return to civilization and discuss the experience with a trusted friend or mentor who will help you gain perspective.

Conclusion:
The New Seeds

hough the Call of the Green is not the only way one comes to the path of the Witch, it was the strongest call for me. My green lovers seduced me to the path with promises of healing, wisdom and power. And while they have given it, they have asked for a lot in return. The Call of the Green is not an easy thing. As lovers, they are quite demanding. And beyond lovers, they become family, a loving but fractious lot of personalities that make up the collective wisdom of the green. They each have their own wisdom, their own way of going about things, and they need their kin of flesh and blood to plant their new seeds in far and distant lands. And through our touch, the new seeds are planted in the soil of the soul, where they can grow deep and strong in the next generation.

As witches we are growing away from the model of using plants and tools of all sorts, back to an animistic wisdom, where everything is a potential partner, an ally, a familiar spirit, not a tool. The deeper we work with our plant spirits, the more our view is changed. The line between me and "not me" is blurred. Everything becomes "like me" and we all become part of the garden. The spiritual work of our evolution with the aid of the plant world not only helps us, but helps them. As we work, we spread the seeds and reawaken to the first Garden of the Gods.

Appendix I:
Balm Quarter Calls

Call

To the North,
We call to the element of Earth in the Great Below,
and we call to the green spirits of Wisdom.
We call the spirit of Comfrey,
    deep root of wisdom past, present and future.
Symphytum, Protector of travelers, granting us safe return home.
 Hail and Welcome.

To the East,
We call to the element of Fire in the Great Below,
And we call to the green spirits of Power.
We call to the spirit of St. John's Wort,
    bringer of heavenly light.
Hypericum, dispeller of nightmares and trauma.
Hail and Welcome.

To the South,
We call to the element of Air in the Great Below,
and we call to the green spirits of Knowledge.
We call to the spirit of Angelica, summoner of angelic races.
Angelica, protector from ills and misfortune,
    guiding message in the dark.
Hail and Welcome.

To the West,
We call to the element of Water in the Great Below,
and we call to the green spirits of Love.
We call to the spirit of Mugwort, gateway to dreams.
Artemisia vulgaris, awaken the Witch's eye and see all that is unseen.
Hail and Welcome.

Release

To the North of the Great Below,
We thank and release the element of Earth
*   and the Green spirits of Wisdom.*
We thank and release the spirit of Comfrey, root of memory and home.
Hail and Farewell.

To the West of the Great Below,
We thank and release the element of Water
*   and the Green Spirits of Love.*
We thank and release the spirit of Mugwort, dream gateway
Hail and Farewell.

To the South of the Great Below,
We thank and release the element of Air
*   and the Green Spirits of Knowledge.*
We thank and release the spirit of Angelica, summoner of Angels.
Hail and Farewell.

To the East of the Great Below,
We thank and release the element of Fire
*   and the Green Spirits of Power.*
We thank and release spirit of St. John's Wort, bearer of light.
Hail and Farewell.

Appendix II:
Tree Quarter Calls

Call

To the North,
We call to the element of Earth in the Great Between,
and we call to the green spirits of Wisdom.
We call the tree spirit of Oak, master of Druidic wisdom,
Duir, Protector and gateway to the realm of the Green Spirits
Hail and Welcome.

To the East,
We call to the element of Fire in the Great Between,
and we call to the green spirits of Power.
We call to the tree spirit of Hawthorne, tree of faery fire,
Huath, holy tree of the Tor and fire of the blood.
Hail and Welcome.

To the South,
We call to the element of Air in the Great Between,
and we call to the green spirits of Knowledge.
We call to the tree spirit of Hazel, keeper of wisdom and knowledge,
Coll, keeper of secrets and tree of magicians.
Hail and Welcome.

To the West,
We call to the element of Water in the Great Between.
and we call to the green spirits of Love.
We call to the spirit of Willow, great healer of body and spirit.
Saille reveal your watery mysteries, open the door to the dark.
Hail and Welcome.

Release

To the North of the Great Between,
We thank and release the element of Earth
*   and the Green spirits of Wisdom.*
We thank and release the tree spirit of Oak, Duir to the Wise.
Hail and Farewell.

To the West of the Great Between,
We thank and release the element of Water
*   and the Green Spirits of Love.*
We thank and release the tree spirit of Willow, Saille to the Wise.
Hail and Farewell.

To the South of the Great Between,
We thank and release the element of Air
*   and the Green Spirits of Knowledge.*
We thank and release the tree spirit of Hazel, Coll to the Wise.
Hail and Farewell.

To the East of the Great Between,
We thank and release the element of Fire
*   and the Green Spirits of Power.*
We thank and release the tree spirit of Hawthorn, Huath to the Wise.
Hail and Farewell.

Bibliography

Artisson, Robin. *The Witching way of the Hollow Hill: The Gramarye of the Folk Who Dwell Below the Mound.* Owlblink Bookcrafting Company, USA: 2006.

Beyerl, Paul. *A Compendium of Herbal Magick.* Phoenix Publishing, Inc. Custer, Washington, 1998.

Beyerl, Paul. *The Master Book of Herbalism.* Phoenix Publishing Inc, Custer, Washington, 1984.

Cowan, Eliot. *Plant Spirit Medicine.* Blue Water Publishing. NC: 1995.

Crowther, Patricia. *Witchcraft In Yorkshire.* Harvest Shadows Publications. Southborough, MA: 1973, 2008.

Cunningham, Scott. *Cunningham's Encyclopedia of Magical Herbs.* Llewellyn Publications, St. Paul, Minnesota, 1985.

DeKorne, Jim. *Psychedelic Shamanism: The Cultivation, Preparation and Shamanic Use of Psychotropic Plants.* Loompanics Unlimited. Port Towsend, WA: 1994.

Divakaruni, Chitra Banerjee. *The Mistress of Spices.* Anchor Books. New York, NY: 1997.

Donaldson, Thomas, A. "The Role of the 'Familiar' in English Witch Trials". December, 1995. *http://www.hulford.co.uk/familiar.htm:* April 2009.

Duke, James A. with Peggy-Ann K. Duke and Judith L. duCellie. *Duke's Handbook of Medicinal Plants of the Bible.* CRC Press. Boca Roton, FL: 2007.

Ginzburg, Carlo. *The Night Battles: Witchcraft and Agrarian Cults in the Sixteenth and Seventeenth Centuries.* Translated by John and

Anne Tedeschi. John Hopkins University Press. Baltimore, MD: 1992.

Grimassi, Raven. *The Book of Ways, Volume I and II*. Old Ways Press. Valley Center, CA: 2004.

Grimassi, Raven. *Encyclopedia of Wicca & Witchcraft*. St. Paul, MN: Llewellyn Publications, 2000.

Grimassi, Raven. *The Witch's Craft*. Llewellyn Publications: St. Paul, MN, 2002.

Grimassi, Raven. *The Witch's Familiar: Spiritual Partnership for Successful Magic*. Llewellyn Worldwide, St. Paul, MN: 2003.

Grimm, Jacob. *Tuetonic Mythology*, 4 Vols. Tr by James Stallybrass. Dover, London, UK: 1966.

Guiley, Rosemary Ellen. *The Encyclopedia of Witches & Witchcraft*, Checkmark Books, New York, New York, 1999.

Gundarsson, Kveldulf. *Elves, Wight, and Trolls: Studies Toward the Practice of Germanic Heathenry: Vol I*. IUniverse, Lincoln, NE: 2007.

Gwyn. *Light from the Shadows: A Mythos of Modern Traditional Witchcraft*. Capall Bann, Milverton, Somerset, UK: 1999.

Heaven, Ross and Howard G. Charing. *Plant Spirit Shamanism*. Destiny Books, Rochester, VT; 2006.

Heaven, Ross. *Plant Spirit Wisdom*. O Books, Hampshire, UK: 2008.

Heaven, Ross. *The Sin Eaters Last Confession*. Llewellyn Publications, Woodbury, MN: 2008.

Jackon, Nigel Aldcroft. *Call of the Horned Piper.* Capall Bann, Milverton, Somerset, UK: 2001.

Jackon, Nigel. *Masks of Misrule.* Capall Bann, Milverton, Somerset, UK: 1996.

Johns, June. *King of the Witches.* Coward-McCann Inc., New York, NY: 1969.

Katz , Richard and Patricia Kaminski. "The Twelve Windows of Plant Perception". *http://www.flowersociety.org/twelve.htm:* May 2010.

Montgomery, Pam. *Plant Spirit Healing.* Bear & Company. Rochester, VT: 2008.

Penczak, Christopher. *The Temple of Shamanic Witchcraft.* Llewellyn Worldwide. St. Paul, MN: 2005.

Pendell, Dale. *PharmakøGnosis.* Mercury House, San Francisco, CA: 2005.

Pendell, Dale. *PharmakøDynamis.* Mercury House, San Francisco, CA: 2002.

Pendell, Dale. *PharmakøPoia.* Mercury House, San Francisco, CA: 1994

Potts, Thomas. *The Wonderfull Discoverie of Witches in the Couvtie of Lancaster* (London: W. Stansby, 1612); reprint cited from *The Trial of the Lancaster Witches,* G.B. Harrison ed. Barnes & Noble, New York, NY: 1971.

Shulke, Daniel A. *Ars Philtron.* Xoanon Publishing. Cheshire, England: 2001.

Shulke, Daniel A. *Viridarium Umbris.* Xoanon Publishing. Cheshire, England: 2005

Valiente, Doreen. *An ABC of Witchcraft Past and Present.* St. Martin's Press, Inc. New York, New York, 1973

Wauters, Ambika. *The Homeopathy Bible.* Sterling Publishing Co. Inc, New York, NY: 2007.

Wikipedia. *http://en.wikipedia.org/wiki/Incubus:* May 11, 2009.

Wikipedia. *http://en.wikipedia.org/wiki/Succubus:* May 11, 2009.

Wikipedia. *http://en.wikipedia.org/wiki/Lilith:* May 11, 2009.

Wilson Peter Lamborn with Christopher Bamford and Kevin Townley. *Green Hermeticism: Alchemy and Ecology.* Lindisfarene Books Great Barrington, MA, 2007

Wright, Machaelle Small. *MAP: Medical Assistance Program of the Great White Brotherhood.* Perelandra, Ltd. Warrenton, VA: 2006.

Yronwode, Catherine. *Hoodoo Herb and Root Magic.* Lucky Mojo Curio Company: Forestville, CA, 2002.

Index

About the Author

Christopher Penczak is an award winning author, teacher and healing practitioner. As an advocate for the timeless perennial wisdom of the ages, he is rooted firmly in the traditions of modern witchcraft and Earth based religions, but draws from a wide range of spiritual traditions including shamanism, alchemy, herbalism, Theosophy and Hermetic Qabalah to forge his own magickal traditions. His many books include *Magick of Reiki, Spirit Allies, The Mystic Foundation* and *The Inner Temple of Witchcraft*. He is the co-founder of the Temple of Witchcraft tradition and not for profit religious organization to advance the spiritual traditions of witchcraft, as well as the co-founder of Copper Cauldron Publishing, a company dedicated to producing books, recordings and tools for magickal inspiration and evolution. He has been a faculty member of the North Eastern Institute of Whole Health and a founding member of The Gifts of Grace, an interfaith foundation dedicated to acts of community service, both based in New Hampshire. He maintains a teaching and healing practice in New England, but travels extensively lecturing. More information can be found at *www.christopherpenczak.com* and *www.templeofwitchcraft.org*.

The Temple of Witchcraft
MYSTERY SCHOOL AND SEMINARY

Witchcraft is a tradition of experience, and the best way to experience the path of the Witch is to actively train in its magickal and spiritual lessons. The Temple of Witchcraft provides a complete system of training and tradition, with four degrees found in the Mystery School for personal and magickal development and a fifth degree in the Seminary for the training of High Priestesses and High Priests interested in serving the gods, spirits, and community as ministers. Teachings are divided by degree into the Oracular, Fertility, Ecstatic, Gnostic, and Resurrection Mysteries. Training emphasizes the ability to look within, awaken your own gifts and abilities, and perform both lesser and greater magicks for your own evolution and the betterment of the world around you. The Temple of Witchcraft offers both in-person and online courses with direct teaching and mentorship. Classes use the *Temple of Witchcraft* series of books and CD Companions as primary texts, supplemented monthly with information from the Temple's Book of Shadows, MP3 recordings of lectures and meditations from our founders, social support through group discussion with classmates, and direct individual feedback from a mentor.

For more information and current schedules, please visit: *www.templeofwitchcraft.org.*

CPSIA information can be obtained
at www.ICGtesting.com
Printed in the USA
FFHW010648110219
50480117-55719FF